VOL. 11

Quicknotes

SIMPLIFIED BIBLE COMMENTARY SERIES

galatians
THRU philemon

PUTTING FAITH INTO PRACTICE

CONTRIBUTING EDITORS:
Dr. Robert Rayburn
J. Hampton Keathley, ThM
Dr. Stephen Leston
Jeffrey Miller, ThM

CONSULTING EDITOR:
Dr. Mark Strauss

Produced with the assistance of Christopher D. Hudson & Associates. Contributing writers include Carol Smith and Stan Campbell.

Published by Barbour Publishing, Inc., P.O. Box 719, Uhrichsville, Ohio 44683, www.barbourbooks.com

Our mission is to publish and distribute inspirational products offering exceptional value and biblical encouragement to the masses.

 Member of the
Evangelical Christian
Publishers Association

Printed in the United States of America.

TABLE OF CONTENTS

GALATIANS

INTRODUCTION TO GALATIANS

The book of Galatians is a centerpiece of New Testament theology that had a great influence during the Protestant Reformation. (Martin Luther's *Commentary on Galatians* ranks with the most influential books to come out of the Reformation.) Galatians is the only one of Paul's letters addressed to a group of churches rather than a single location. The epistle has been called a spiritual Magna Carta, due to its masterful explanation and defense of justification by faith alone.

AUTHOR

The style of writing and method of thinking is so true to that of Paul that few scholars throughout the centuries have questioned his authorship. The early church held a strong and unwavering belief that Paul was the writer.

PURPOSE

The Epistle to the Galatians was written to emphasize the complete sufficiency of justification by faith alone in one's relationship with God. The Galatian churches (where many new believers were Gentiles) were being strongly influenced to add traditional Jewish beliefs and practices to their newfound faith. While it was quite natural for Jewish believers to continue to worship as they always had in the past, to require the same for Gentiles was, to Paul, tantamount to promoting a different gospel (1:6).

OCCASION

Paul had established a number of churches in Galatia during his missionary travels (1:8, 11; 4:13–14, 19–20; Acts 13–14). When he left, the believers were holding up under suffering (3:4) and doing well (5:7). But not long afterward, Paul had received word that they were being influenced by a group requiring circumcision for salvation, and he was disturbed and dismayed to hear how quickly the Galatians had forsaken his teaching of salvation by faith through grace (1:6–9; Acts 15:1). So Paul wrote this letter to circulate through the churches and call the believers back to the truth of the gospel of Christ.

THEMES

In Galatians, Paul doesn't move from topic to topic as he does in some of his other letters. His focus is on a single theme throughout: Faith in Christ *alone* is all that is necessary for one's justification before God. It had been true for Abraham, and has been God's plan all along. While the law has its purpose, attempting to require *anything* for salvation other than by God's grace through faith in Christ is a serious distortion of the gospel.

HISTORICAL CONTEXT

A centuries-long debate has taken place as to whether Paul was writing to churches in the northern part of the province of Galatia, or to those in the south. The different options allow for different dates for the letter. We know from the book of Acts that Paul took his first missionary journey through southern Galatia, establishing churches in Pisidian Antioch, Iconium, Lystra, and Derbe, before returning to his home base in Antioch, Syria (Acts 13-14). According to the South Galatia theory, Paul wrote his letter to these churches that were established on his first missionary journey. After this journey, Paul attended the Council in Jerusalem (Acts 15:1-35), and then went on a second missionary journey that included the regions of "Phrygia and Galatia" (Acts 16:6). According to the North Galatia theory, on this journey Paul established churches in northern Galatia, and it is to these he is writing his letter. Unfortunately, no specific cities in north Galatia are named in the account in Acts, and no details of events are provided.

A greater number of modern scholars favor the South Galatia option for various reasons: (1) The southern churches are named (Pisidian Antioch, Iconium, Lystra, and Derbe), while the northern are not; (2) Those southern churches were on a route that would have taken Paul through Tarsus, his hometown (Acts 15:41); (3) Paul writes about Barnabas without introducing him (Galatians 2:9, 13), and they had only traveled together on Paul's first journey; and (4) It seems unlikely that the Judaizers would have ignored the more prominent southern cities to go to the north instead.

The various options make it difficult to establish a date for the writing of Galatians. Proponents of the North Galatia theory suggest it was written during Paul's third journey, around AD 53 to 57. And those who hold to the South Galatia theory aren't agreed as to the date of the epistle. If written before the Council of Jerusalem, as some believe, the date could be as early as AD 48-49, making it one of the New Testament's earliest books. Others feel a more accurate date is AD 51 to 53.

CONTRIBUTION TO THE BIBLE

The Epistle to the Galatians should be perceived as each believer's emancipation proclamation. For all the attempts of others to impose a yoke (5:1) of some kind in regard to church practice, Galatians insists that faith is the only instrument needed to free us.

And while spiritually oppressed believers can find great freedom in the teachings of Galatians, it doesn't take much reading between the lines to see that the people attempting to restrict freedom were those who believed themselves to be more mature spiritually. Paul both exposes their error and points out the potential of sin to affect the most devoted believers—even Peter and Barnabas (2:11-13). Galatians reminds us that no one should ever presume to be beyond the effects of sin and the danger of losing sight of the wonderful grace of God.

Along these lines, as Paul contrasts the actions of the human, sinful nature with the qualities provided by God, he lists the fruit of the Spirit (5:22-23), and assures his readers that the exercise of such characteristics will never oppose any spiritual law.

OUTLINE

GALATIANS 1:1–24
THE THREAT OF A DIFFERENT GOSPEL

Setting Up the Section

Paul's epistles have a standard opening that usually include a note of thanksgiving for those reading the letter. However, those complimentary words are absent from his letter to the Galatian churches. The Epistle to the Galatians has a sense of urgency. Paul gets right to the point: His readers are facing serious problems.

📄 **1:1–9**

NO OTHER OPTIONS

Since Paul will be addressing weighty problems in the church, he begins by identifying himself as an apostle. He would open other letters with a similar reminder that he was one who had been sent (Romans 1:1; 1 Corinthians 1:1; Ephesians 1:1; etc.), but here he places special stress on his authority and the fact that he is speaking for God (1:1).

In other epistles, Paul acknowledges all the people with him, but not here (1:2). Every indication is that there was no time wasted in opening this letter.

Paul's salutation addresses the churches (plural) in Galatia (1:2), while later he refers to the church as singular (1:13). This demonstrates how there is but one church, although it is composed of various bodies of believers. Paul's language also suggests that this epistle was intended to be encyclical—read in one congregation and then passed along to another church in the area. Paul had traveled through southern Galatia during his first missionary journey (Acts 13–14) and again during his second (Acts 16:1–6). If those church members were his intended readers, the letter would have gone to places such as Derbe, Lystra, Iconium, and Pisidian Antioch. Other scholars believe Paul was writing to churches in northern Galatia that were not mentioned in the Acts account or elsewhere.

Twice in his opening Paul notes the connection between—but distinctive identities of—God the Father and Jesus Christ (1:1, 3). In this context, he summarizes the essence of the gospel in a single sentence (1:3–5). It was easy for the early church (as it is for the contemporary church) to begin to place emphasis on things other than the sin of humankind and the need for redemption. Paul makes clear that deliverance from sin is God's doing, not ours, and that He deserves the glory for it.

Paul's opening is something like an overture that contains elements he will return to. And then he goes right to the point of his letter: Certain people within the church were perverting the gospel (1:6–7). The people hadn't been given an option about *which* gospel to believe. Anything that opposed what Paul had taught was not the gospel (1:7). No human credentials were strong enough to discredit the truth of the gospel, and for that matter, no divine credentials either (1:8). Anyone who attempted to teach things contrary to the gospel of Jesus Christ was to be eternally condemned—*anathema*, in Greek. Paul felt so strongly about this offense that he states the curse twice (1:8–9).

Paul is disturbed that the Galatian believers had so soon forsaken their faith (1:6). They had heard Paul preach mere months before. They had seen him perform miracles with their own eyes. They had witnessed the power of the Holy Spirit. How could they have forsaken so much so soon?

Critical Observation

No mention is made of Paul's appeal to the elders of the Galatian churches. Surely elders had been appointed (Acts 14:23), but were likely (by necessity) young believers who may have succumbed to the persuasive but false teachings being introduced. In his later writings, Paul would make it known that no inexperienced Christian should be given the responsibility of church leadership (1 Timothy 3:6–10).

📖 **1:10–24**

THE DIFFERENCE THE TRUTH MAKES

Paul is writing with the authority of God, by revelation of Jesus Christ, yet he also draws from personal experience. His question in verse 10 suggests that he had been accused of tailoring his message to please his audience. To an extent, the charge was true. He believed in becoming "all things to all people" (1 Corinthians 9:22 ESV). When around Jewish believers, he could join them in their traditional, ceremonial, God-given rites. But he did not attempt to demand such practices of Gentile believers. When traveling with Timothy, a half-Jewish believer who was ministering to the Jews, Paul had him circumcised. But when traveling with Titus, a Gentile believer, he didn't require circumcision. People who lacked Paul's Christian sensibilities might well view his actions as vacillation, moral weakness, or a penchant for playing to the crowd. It has been an age-old tactic to attempt to undermine a message by undermining the messenger.

So Paul goes into further detail about how the gospel had affected his own life. His readers would have equated the meaning of the words *servant* and *slave*, so Paul's reference to being Christ's servant (1:10) was stronger to them than many modern translations suggest. Paul had previously known the slavery of the law (5:1) but had been freed of that yoke. In response, he willingly made himself a slave (servant) to Jesus Christ.

It was no man-made philosophy that turned Paul's life around. Rather, he received the truth of the gospel by direct revelation of Jesus on the road to Damascus, where he was summoned to both salvation and apostleship. It would have been easy enough for him to *say* he had experienced divine revelation (1:12), but the subsequent change in his life was *proof* of what he had experienced.

Paul's critics would have others believe that he was out of step with the genuine apostles because he welcomed Gentile converts into the church without first having them be circumcised. The Council at Jerusalem had sent out letters to Gentile churches about some who went to them without authorization and disturbed them (Acts 15:24), and Paul himself had delivered the letter (Acts 15:25). Yet Paul's critics had the audacity to claim the authority of church leadership and suggest that Paul was among those purporting a false doctrine.

In defense, Paul simply summarizes his life story. He never attempts to hide his sinful past—and especially his zeal as a practicing Jew and early persecutor of the church. In his understanding, the change in his life only magnified the grace of God. However, his comment in Galatians 1:13 suggests that Paul's enemies were telling his story with a different purpose in mind. They hoped to convey that he was still a shady and unreliable character.

Yet Paul's personal history was exactly what made him an expert in the very questions being raised in Galatia. He knew the Jewish mind-set inside and out, as did others. But he also knew the gospel from firsthand experience. As a result, his zeal was redirected. While he had previously gone after the advocates of Christianity, now he used the same passion to promote the truth he had come to know.

Paul's newly discovered Christian truth had come into direct opposition with the traditions of his ancestors (1:14). The beliefs and practices of the rabbinical schools had shaped the Law of Moses into a legalistic system. The problem was not with the law of God, but with the many interpretations that had completely altered its fundamental spirit. Over the centuries the law had become, according to Peter, an unbearable burden (Acts 15:10). In spite of all the zeal and devotion to the law that men like Paul held, it was not a means to salvation. So when Paul discovered the truth of the gospel of Jesus Christ, he wasted no time in responding.

Paul's phrasing in verse 15 is strongly reminiscent of Jeremiah 1:5—another example of God's watchful eye over someone from birth until the time was right for a summons to faith, new life, and new purpose. Paul's original vicious and misdirected hatred of the gospel was no match for God's power and plan. God was pleased to reveal His Son to Paul (1:16), and that's all it took to change Paul's life from that point onward.

Paul's comment about the other apostles in verse 17 may sound a bit arrogant at first, but is not intended to be. He would soon express respect for the other apostles' ministry as equal to his own (2:7-10). Yet since his apostolic calling and commission had been questioned, he made it clear that he did not derive his authority from the other apostles, but from God (1:15-17). It was *not* true, as his critics were seemingly suggesting, that Paul had first been taught by the apostles, but had then broken ranks with them on the issue of circumcision and had begun to follow his own path.

Demystifying Galatians

Paul's mention of going to Arabia (1:17) has generated much speculation. At the time Arabia bordered much of Judea and stretched from an area near Damascus to include most of the Sinai Peninsula. The text does not say that Paul spent three years in Arabia, as some teach. Nor does it say he went there to contemplate his new faith and to meditate for awhile, although that is certainly possible. All we really know for sure is that three years elapsed between Paul's conversion and his first journey as a Christian to Jerusalem, and during that time he made a trip to Arabia.

Paul's return to Jerusalem as a Christian (1:18) is described in Acts 9:26–30. The believers in Jerusalem were understandably suspicious of their former enemy, but Barnabas helped them overcome their fears and introduced Paul to them.

Paul took fifteen days to get to know Peter (1:18). The word translated "get acquainted" can also mean "interviewed," which is almost certainly just as accurate in this context. It is easy to envision Peter providing Paul with firsthand information about Jesus, and to imagine Paul's active mind interrupting, questioning, seeking clarification, and so forth.

Again, Paul makes it absolutely clear that he received no special training from the apostles. He didn't even meet anyone other than Peter and James on his first contact with them (1:18–20).

Cilicia (1:21) was the Asian province where Paul's home city of Tarsus was located. Again, the information he relates to the Galatians agrees with the account of his conversion in Acts 9:1–15. And even with his reputation of terrorizing believers and attempting to prevent the spread of Christianity, the people who first heard him present the gospel were fully convinced of his sincerity and genuine faith (1:23–24). From the beginning, no one had ever questioned his credentials. So the church members in Galatia had no reason to doubt his motives or ministry—especially since they were aware of his additional years of serving faithfully as an apostle and had personally witnessed how much he cared for their church and the others he worked with.

Perhaps more than anyone else in the New Testament, Paul demonstrates what a difference God's revelation of Jesus Christ can make in a person's life. Paul is a consummate example of conversion and repentance from sin, and of what God can do with someone willing to turn from his or her old sinful ways to seek His righteousness.

Take It Home

The Galatian believers' rapid abandonment of their faith in the gospel (1:6) didn't just affect them—it created great disappointment and inner turmoil for Paul, as well as anger toward those who were leading them astray. But at least Paul was willing to confront the Galatians directly and instruct them to ignore the lies they had been hearing. While most people today don't fall away so quickly, it's not unusual for them to lose some of the devotion they had as new believers. Some settle into a pattern of regular growth with normal highs and lows of life, while others seem to continue to drift farther and farther away from the relationship with Jesus that once seemed so vital. Did you undergo any kind of slipping away after your initial commitment to Christianity? How did you work through it? Did you have someone like Paul, who took to heart what you were going through?

GALATIANS 2:1-21

THE DIFFICULTY OF LIVING IN FREEDOM

Setting Up the Section

Paul has been dealing with a charge by his critics that he is out of step with the Jerusalem apostles as he promotes Gentile freedom without requiring adherence to Jewish ceremonies. Paul's opponents have suggested that his apostleship was derived from those in Jerusalem and should be subordinate to the other apostles, yet his critics accused him of teaching the Gentiles something entirely different. So far Paul has emphatically shown that his gospel and his commission to preach came directly from Jesus, and not from the other apostles.

📄 **2:1–10**

THE TRUTH OF THE GOSPEL

The book of Acts mentions two different visits that Paul and Barnabas made to Jerusalem (Acts 11:29-30; 15:2). Scholars are divided as to which of the trips is referred to in Galatians 2:1, yet evidence is strong for the earlier visit. It seems likely that if Paul had written Galatians after his second visit, he would have made reference to the Council in Jerusalem that had reached the very conclusion about the Gentiles that he was attempting to defend in this epistle. It would have been the coup de grace against his opponents and would have publicly unmasked them as pretenders who falsely claimed to have the support of the apostles.

Paul had been working in Gentile communities and witnessing God's grace among them. On his trip to Jerusalem, he took an uncircumcised believer named Titus along as an example of his position that Gentiles did not have to be circumcised as a requirement for salvation. The fact that no one in Jerusalem complained of Titus's presence was proof that Paul's position was not out of step with that of the Jerusalem apostles.

Paul always attempted to do things properly. Although he was responding to a revelation he had received, he first met privately with the church leaders to minimize public disagreement and friction that might impede the work he had already accomplished among the Gentiles. It appears from Paul's wording in Galatians 2:4 that the issue of Gentile freedom didn't even come up during this visit to Jerusalem. After all, Peter had had similar encounters with Gentiles that led to their belief in Jesus (Acts 10).

Galatians 2:4-5 seems to be a parenthetical thought. Paul has already dropped some strong hints about his critics and their accusations against him. Here he adds that they had actually infiltrated the church as spies in order to discredit Paul and enslave believers by imposing legalistic restrictions on them. Yet Paul successfully resisted them and continued to hold fast to the truth of the gospel that allowed Christian freedom.

Demystifying Galatians

Although the word isn't used in this epistle, Paul's opponents came to be known as the Judaizers. Most of the early believers in Jesus were Jewish. Some seemed to believe that Christianity should be just a continuation of Judaism with the same adherence to the law and the requirement of circumcision as a sign. The Judaizers had become a vocal group advocating this belief. Paul was never against the law or the practice of circumcision as such, but strongly insisted that such things had nothing to do with one's salvation that was possible only as a result of God's grace through faith (Ephesians 2:8–9).

Paul acknowledges the roles of the Jerusalem apostles (2:6), yet refuses to revere them as some were wont to do. He knew that any wisdom or power that *he* had came from God, and was aware the fact would be true of the other church leaders as well. He realized they all had their callings to attend to. His was among the Gentiles—the uncircumcised. Peter's was among the Jews. Many other apostles were not mentioned, although Thomas, for example, is believed to have gone to India to minister.

The James that Paul refers to (2:9) is not the apostle—he had been put to death by Herod (Acts 12:2). The James of the early church was the brother of Jesus whose faith had led to a leadership role in Jerusalem. Paul would not be swayed by his critics, nor was he unduly impressed by the titles and credentials of the Jerusalem apostles. He had his own sure and certain calling, and his goal was to be faithful to the truth of the gospel (2:5).

📄 2:11–14

AN EMBARRASSING SLIP

The fact that the apostles were human beings with their own frailties and weaknesses became apparent with Paul's next comment (2:11). Paul and Barnabas had been ministering primarily to Gentile believers in Antioch, a prominent city in Syria. Peter had visited and witnessed the unity between Jewish and Gentile believers. Then, later, more people from Jerusalem arrived, claiming to be sent from James. However, several among them were in the militant group who thought circumcision should be required for salvation.

Although previously meals had been shared between Jews and Gentiles, the members of the "circumcision group" segregated themselves. Other Jews soon joined them, followed by Peter, and even Barnabas. It was with clear apostolic authority that Paul corrected these fellow church leaders.

As acting head of the church, Peter should certainly have known better. But Barnabas was a bigger shock. Throughout the book of Acts he appears as an encouraging figure in all circumstances. In addition, he and Paul had been instrumental in founding the Galatian churches. Seeing this entire group distance itself from the Gentile believers must have created both dismay and outrage in Paul.

Paul doesn't attempt to soften the offense of the circumcision group members. He calls it hypocrisy and writes of how Barnabas had been led astray (2:13). He even confronts Peter publicly and challenges his attitudes and actions (2:14). Peter had been living like a Gentile in that he (rightly) didn't feel obliged to follow all the old Jewish ways, including dietary restrictions. Yet suddenly he was positioning himself with the Jews as being somehow superior to the Gentiles.

Some have criticized Paul's public display, suggesting that instead he should have dealt with the matter privately (Matthew 18:15). But later Paul writes that the sin of church elders should be a public matter so that others will witness and take warning (1 Timothy 5:20).

📄 2:15–21

JUSTIFIED BY FAITH IN CHRIST

Paul would soon write that among those who have placed their faith in Christ, there is no distinction between male or female, slave or free, or Jew or Gentile (3:28). At least, God doesn't make such distinctions. Yet the leaders in the early church were forced to deal with the distinctions of these different groups.

Jews by birth (2:15) were those who had grown up with the Mosaic Law, the Old Testament covenants, temple worship, and the promises of God. Some, like Paul, had come to realize that the law was insufficient to accomplish salvation. It had taken Paul a long while to realize that both Moses and Abraham taught justification by faith and not by works. The Jewish people who had not come to that conclusion were still looking for justification by observing the law (2:16)—the equivalent of legalism before they had a word for it.

"Gentile sinners" (2:15 NIV) were those outside the Jewish faith. The term was probably an often-used derogatory phrase among the law-abiding Jews of Paul's day. As an attempt to belittle Him, Jesus had been called a friend of sinners (Matthew 11:19).

It is at this point in his letter where Paul finally gets to the main point. He has let his readers know that the dispute he is addressing concerns the freedom of Gentile Christians from Jewish ceremonial regulations, but not precisely what he understood to be at issue in that dispute.

Here Paul reveals that at issue is how a person is *justified*. It is his first use of the terminology of justification in Galatians. The Judaizers had been teaching that justification was by works—by holding fast to the law, by getting circumcised, and so forth. They would probably have insisted that they believed in justification by faith *and* works, but Paul saw it as just another form of justification by works. It is not correct to say that someone believes in justification by faith if he or she does not mean justification by faith *alone*.

Paul does not deny that good works should be evident in a Christian's life (6:9–10). But nothing—not good works, adherence to the law, circumcision, or anything else—contributes to a person's justification. Anything people attempt to add to justification by God's grace only serves to diminish God's perfect plan of redemption. Therefore, any attempt to require Gentiles to first become Jews in order to become Christians is a denial of the sufficiency of Jesus' atoning work on the cross.

The brevity of Galatians 2:17–18 makes the passage difficult to interpret. Some believe Paul was anticipating the antinomian response to the idea of justification by faith. Antinomianism is at the other end of the scale from legalism. The doctrine perceives that since salvation is indeed by grace through faith, the gospel gives Christians freedom from all other laws and requirements—civil, moral, and even scriptural. Paul refutes this way of thinking in various places, such as Romans 3:31, and it may have been his intent to do so here. Yet if so, his next statement (2:18) makes little sense.

Paul is probably suggesting that if believers forsake all thought of justification by their own works of the law and turn instead to Christ's righteousness, they are likely to be considered sinners by others who have a legalistic mind-set. Although the first-century believers were breaking no biblical mandates, they were going against a lot of Jewish traditions. It might *seem* as if leaders such as Paul were invoking Jesus' name in support of sinful practices, when in actuality they were taking a stand for Christian liberty. So if they decided to rebuild the hindrances they had destroyed (2:18)—as Peter had done by first receiving the Gentiles and then distancing himself from them—*then* they would be perceived as lawbreakers.

Paul is being tactful. Rather than pointing a finger at Peter's discriminatory behavior, he speaks only of himself in making his argument. The Judaizers could charge him with being sinful, but their accusations meant nothing to Paul. However, if he gave in to their pressure, he would indeed have committed a sin against God.

What did Paul mean by saying he had died to the law (2:19)? He isn't suggesting that the law is useless. His defense and admiration of the law is clear in Romans 7:7-13. What Paul means by this is "dying to sin." He had died to the law as a means of justification, of peace with God, and of acceptance by God. He had died to the self-righteousness that had come from knowing the letter of the law and not the Spirit of God. And he had determined to live his life for the Lord, not to fulfill the requirements of the Jewish laws and traditions.

Paul's statement that he had been crucified with Christ (2:20) can be interpreted a couple of different ways. Taken one way, it could mean that believers share in Jesus' crucifixion, death, and resurrection. Just as Jesus underwent suffering and death prior to eternal glory, so shall those who believe in Him.

Yet more likely is the explanation that the old, self-righteous Paul, who based his hope on obedience to the law, had been executed and was dead. It was a new Paul, a new man, who now lived for God. He uses this concept in Romans 6:6, and will come back to this point later in Galatians (5:24; 6:14).

Whatever the particular nuance, Paul's general meaning is clear. Having died with Christ to the law and all thoughts of justification by keeping the law of God, Paul was living according to new realities. No longer driven by self-effort, his purpose and strength now come from a present Christ living in and with him. He had died to the law, so he no longer lived. Yet now Christ lives in him, so in response he lives for God (2:19-20).

Paul makes little distinction between Christ living in him and the Holy Spirit working in him. The Spirit is the Spirit of Christ (Romans 8:9-10). Here Paul assures his readers that Christ lives in him (2:20); later he will say it is the Spirit of God's Son (4:6). Living by faith in Christ is the same as being controlled by the Spirit.

Paul is not promoting some sort of mysticism where two personalities merge—his and Christ's—until Christ takes full control with Paul as merely a vessel. Note all the personal pronouns (*I* and *me*) in verses 19–20. Paul still has his earthly existence. Yet his faith makes possible a real and personal union with Christ, and Christ's presence with him provides power in Paul's life and being.

Critical Observation

Notice that Paul isn't just making a theological argument. It is personal. Paul is responding to the God who lovingly gave His life (2:20). It is one thing to believe that God died for the sins of the world, but when believers comprehend that God died for individuals, allowing for personal relationships with Him, they can experience (as Paul did) a more intense passion and joy in response to their salvation.

Finally, Paul observes that since it required the death of Jesus Christ to purchase his peace with God, then clearly salvation has nothing to do with his own effort or acts of righteousness (2:21). It was the grace—the free gift—of God that achieved his justification. The law had nothing to do with providing righteousness.

Take It Home

This passage has much to consider in regard to personal application. But perhaps one of the weightiest concerns is how even mature church leaders like Peter and Barnabas fell into habits of prejudice and hypocrisy when prompted by a crowd of spiritual-sounding peers (2:11–13). Can you think of a time in your spiritual journey when you were guilty of a similar offense? Is it possible that even now there are times when you aren't as consistent as you need to be?

GALATIANS 3:1–25

A CLOSER LOOK AT THE LAW

Setting Up the Section

Paul has been making the case that the gospel of grace and justification by faith alone is, in fact, the true and only gospel. In this section he will begin to demonstrate his point using a biblical, theological argument. As he does, we need to keep in mind that when he makes references to the scriptures, he is referring to what we know as the Old Testament. When he speaks of grace, freedom, and righteousness, he does not present them as new ideas, but as concepts that should have been evident to anyone who was familiar with the law and the prophets.

📄 3:1–9

A NEW LOOK AT AN OLD STORY

The Galatian believers had experienced the freedom of Christ, but were being influenced by the Judaizers to consider a much more legalistic lifestyle. Paul says this was tantamount to being hypnotized (bewitched). After they had personally witnessed what was possible through faith in Christ, it was most unwise of them to consider an alternative. The fact that Jesus died for their sins should completely eliminate any consideration of justification by obedience to the law. Otherwise, they disregarded the weight of His sacrifice on their behalf.

Paul doesn't doubt that their conversion had been genuine, or that they had received the Holy Spirit (3:2). He poses his question, knowing that they would have to answer, "By believing," and in doing so would concede his argument and abandon the Judaizers' viewpoint.

Paul intentionally left no middle ground between justification by faith and justification by works (2:15–16). The inclusion of any works at all as a prerequisite for salvation becomes justification by works. Here Paul provides clearer insight into the Judaizers' error: Whatever they might say about faith and the cross, they really believed that their own effort alone made possible the fulfillment, consummation, and completion of salvation (3:3).

If it were possible to be justified by closely observing the Jewish ceremonies prescribed in the law, believers in Christ would not have suffered the reproach of the Jews. Paul doesn't specify in what ways the Galatians had suffered, yet the message of salvation through Christ's death was offensive to everyone in their culture: The Jews thought it blasphemous and irreverent; the Gentiles thought it ridiculous. If the Galatians were to give up now, their suffering would have been for nothing (3:4). But Paul didn't feel they were beyond help and believed they would come back to the truth.

After all, they had seen God's miracles and received God's Spirit in response to their belief (3:5). It is not likely that the message of the Judaizers had been accompanied by any kind of special signs. The Galatians should have had no trouble detecting which was the authentic gospel.

Critical Observation

Throughout this section it may seem that Paul is taking a strong stand against the law, and indeed he is making a powerful argument against its sufficiency to provide justification before God. But it is in this sense *only* in which law stands in opposition to faith.

At 3:6, Paul begins his biblical argument by quoting from Genesis 15:6. It is very likely that the Judaizers placed much emphasis on Abraham and their relationship to him (as Jewish traditionalists had done in their dealings with Jesus [John 8:33–41]). So Paul reviews the life of Abraham to prove the opposite of what the Judaizers were promoting. He shows that Abraham was an obedient person, on which they all agreed. Abraham believed God, and as a result of his faith was a child of God and was found righteous before God. The crucial difference that Paul wants to convey is that scripture says it was Abraham's *faith* that justified him and produced a life of obedience. It wasn't his obedience that gave him proper standing before God and made him righteous. And in that respect, Abraham stands as the quintessential believer—an example for both Old Testament and New Testament people of God (3:7).

Paul's phrasing in verses 8–9 is remarkable. By saying that scripture foresaw justification by faith and spoke to Abraham, he really means God did it. But what better example is there to demonstrate that the Bible is the Word of God? Paul also says that God announced the gospel to Abraham. Again, something we tend to think of as exclusively a New Testament concept (the gospel) actually predated the giving of the Mosaic Law. Additionally, Paul reminds his readers that all nations were to be blessed through Abraham. Throughout the centuries, the Jewish people had tended to separate themselves from non-Israelites, but it had been God's intention from the beginning to reach out to the Gentiles through them. The writings of the prophets had much to say about God's outreach to the Gentiles—not least among them Jonah's message of repentance to the Ninevites (Jonah 1:1; 3:1–10) and Isaiah's messianic prophecies (Isaiah 2:2–3; 40:5; 42:6; 49:6; etc.).

📄 3:10–14

REMOVING THE CURSE

In Paul's next section he exposes a spiritual dilemma. The law pronounces a curse on those who do not do everything it requires (Deuteronomy 27:26). Yet he implies (with no expectation of disagreement) that no one does everything the law requires. Therefore, everyone is under the curse of the law.

So there are only two options for getting out from under the curse. Paul quotes Leviticus 18:5 for those who promote a works approach to righteousness. If someone argues that it is by obedience to the law and good deeds that God justifies people, then everything depends upon *doing what the law requires*. Obedience must be perfectly consistent with the person committed to keeping every single one of God's laws. Otherwise, the law condemns him as a sinner and lawbreaker; it does not justify him.

But Paul also quotes Habakkuk 2:4, which provides a second option: Those who are righteous live by faith (3:11). Their faith is in Christ, who redeemed them from the curse of the law by personally becoming a curse.

Redemption is one of three great metaphors used in the Bible to describe the work of Jesus as our Savior from sin. One is *propitiation* or atonement, a sacrifice offered for sins that turns away the wrath of God. Christ's death on the cross accomplished this by paying the price of humankind's sin and guilt. The second is *reconciliation*, a bringing together of estranged parties, which Christ achieved by taking away the sin that created separation between humans and God. And *redemption* is buying someone out of bondage by paying a price (ransom). Jesus paid the ultimate price by giving up His life on the cross.

However, the reference to one who is hung on a tree (3:13) originally had nothing to do with crucifixion (Deuteronomy 21:23). Crucifixion was neither an Old Testament nor a Jewish practice. The original reference was to the practice of hanging up, or impaling on a pole, a body *after* execution, with the humiliation of exposure and denial of a proper burial. Yet if the practice of hanging the body of a criminal up *after* death was a shame and curse, how much worse was the experience of being killed on the tree itself and exposed through the entire process of death!

Such was the price of Jesus' redemption of the human race. As a result, all who were under the curse—even Gentiles—can now avoid the just punishment for sin and instead receive peace with God and a righteous status before Him. The Holy Spirit is God's pledge of everlasting life as well as the source of power by which believers can live new lives for God. This justification before God is the "blessing of Abraham" (3:14) that Paul has been describing.

📄 3:15–25

THE BINDING PROMISE OF GOD

Paul next uses an argument based on the nature of covenants (3:15–18). When two people sit down and write out a legal agreement, one of them does not have the right to change the terms of the contract at some future date. Even more binding are the covenants of God. After He made a covenant with Abraham, He wasn't going to renege. And God's promise wasn't just to Abraham, but included his descendants as well (3:16). Abraham's faith had been credited to him as righteousness (3:6), and that arrangement was not going to be annulled or modified—not even by the Law of Moses that came afterward.

The word *seed* (a metaphor for "descendant"), even when in singular form, can refer to a single seed or many seeds (descendants). In one sense, the seed of Abraham includes all believers (3:29). Yet Paul points out that the single most significant seed of Abraham was Jesus Christ (3:16). The promise that God made to Abraham was based, from the beginning, on the work that Christ would do as Redeemer. So from the time of Abraham onward, forgiveness and peace with God were available by faith—faith in what God had promised to do through Christ.

The 430 years (3:17) refers only to the amount of time the Israelites had spent in Egypt (Exodus 12:40–41). From the time of Abraham to Jacob/Joseph would have been about another 215 years. Perhaps Paul chose to use the shorter period of time in order to understate his argument, knowing his critics would realize the covenant with Abraham predated the law by an even longer period of time. Or perhaps Paul considered that God's promise to Abraham applied to all the patriarchs, and dated it from the time Jacob went down to Egypt with his family (Genesis 46). Other places in scripture deal with Abraham, Isaac, and Jacob almost as if they were a single unit.

Then Paul reiterates his point: God had made a promise to Abraham and his descendents. The promise preceded the law by centuries. So when the law was given, it in no way negated or affected the lasting promise of God (3:18).

In addition, Paul connects the law with sin. The law increased transgression (Romans 5:20) in a number of ways: (1) Due to its specific requirements, it produced many more specific violations; (2) Its rules provoked the rebellious spirit within people and produced a more vigorous disobedience (as when a parent tells a child *not* to do something); (3) Like a magnifying glass reveals previously unknown dirt, the law disclosed sin; and (4) It created a far more complete way for people to assert themselves against God by giving sophistication to the perception of works-oriented righteousness.

Demystifying Galatians

What Paul means by the law being put into effect through angels (3:19) is uncertain. There is no explicit Old Testament reference, although Stephen refers to the event as common knowledge (Acts 7:53), as does the author of Hebrews (Hebrews 2:2). We do know that God was accompanied by angels during the giving of the law on Sinai (Deuteronomy 33:2), yet their role in the process is not stated.

The law was also provided by God for the people through a mediator (3:19–20), most likely a reference to Moses. So the promise of God directly to Abraham again takes precedence because the presence of a third party suggests a certain distance.

The fact that the law came later and had a less-direct manner of revelation than God's promise to Abraham was one of Paul's arguments for why it did not supersede or set aside the promise of justification by faith. But Paul then adds that the function of the law was actually to serve the interests of God's promise to bring people to faith in God and in Christ, the Son of God (3:21–25).

Paul again states emphatically that God's law is certainly not in opposition to God's promise. God doesn't contradict Himself. Yet while placing one's faith in God is life-giving, obeying the law is not. (When Paul refers to the law, he almost always means the keeping of the law.) If the law *could* have imparted righteousness, then that method would certainly be preferable to having God's Son die a horrible death (2:21). But God had to step in and do what the law could not do (Romans 8:2–3).

Still, the law has great value. Even though it cannot impart life, it can and does reveal the uselessness of every human effort to save oneself. And it points sinful people to the grace of God and sacrifice of Christ as their only hope of salvation. Being bound by sin

(3:22) is the same as being bound by the law (3:23). People are prisoners because the law shows their helplessness to put themselves right with God on account of sin. The law does not allow escape into fancies of justification by good works. No one is good enough.

So in one sense the law is like a prison warden. In another sense, it is like a pedagogue (*paidagogos* in Greek [3:24]). We tend to use *pedagogue* as a fancy word for teacher, but in Paul's day it meant something more specific. A pedagogue was a slave assigned to attend to the family's son from age six or so until puberty. It was the slave's job to provide moral training and protect the child from the evils of the world. Frequently, the discipline imposed could be quite strict. In that sense, the law provides helpful (though sometimes seemingly harsh) direction for a time.

Yet people need not remain under the law's supervision (3:25). Here Paul shifts the emphasis of his theological argument to become more personal. He includes himself among the Galatian believers as he reminds them that the law was provided to lead *us* to Christ (3:24), and that *we* are no longer under the supervision of the law (3:25). While the law is not a good master and is inadequate to provide justification, it is certainly a helpful servant. Thankfully, God provided a much better way for people to attain righteousness. Paul will have more to say about that in his next section.

Take It Home

While Paul frames his argument in theological terms (*the law* vs. *the promise*), contemporary believers may not be so specific. Yet that doesn't mean they are any less susceptible to the problems Paul addresses. When the topic is salvation, any attempt to justify oneself becomes problematic. Until we learn to trust God in faith, we remain slaves to a legalistic system. But God is willing to bestow His grace and freedom whenever we're ready to turn to Him in simple faith. Can you think of anything people do today to attempt to make themselves seem more worthy before God, or even before other church members? Are you possibly guilty of such behavior from time to time? If so, what can you learn from Paul's advice to the Galatian believers?

GALATIANS 3:26–4:31

CHILDREN OF GOD

Setting Up the Section

Up to this point, Paul has been stating that from the beginning, the message of the gospel has been the promise of righteousness before God through faith in Christ (Abraham's "seed"). Justification never had anything to do with good works or obedience to the law. The law, in fact, is a servant of the promise as it exposes people's sin and guilt and points them to the righteousness that God provides as a free gift through faith in Christ.

🖹 **3:26–4:7**

HEIRS ACCORDING TO THE PROMISE

In the previous section, Paul had begun to personalize what he was saying by applying God's justification and freedom both to himself and the Galatian believers (3:23–25). He continues with his personal application here (3:26–29) by using second person (*you*).

The believers in Galatia (primarily Gentiles) were true children of God and true seed of Abraham—not because they observed the requirements of the law that the Judaizers were demanding of them, but rather because they had placed their faith in Christ and had been baptized into His family. The Judaizers believed that Gentiles needed to become Jews before they could become Christians, but the good news of the gospel is that Christ makes *all* who believe children of God. In Christ, Jew and Gentile are already one. Through baptism, all believers are clothed with Christ (3:26–27).

Galatians 3:28 is one of the greatest verses in the Bible on the liberating power of the gospel and its ability to break down walls that formerly divided. Judaism in many ways was a religion of exclusion, where women, Gentiles, and slaves did not have the same rights or access to God as men. The temple in Jerusalem itself was a series of concentric courtyards. Gentiles could not go further than the outer "court of Gentiles," and women could go no further than the next "court of women." Jewish men were allowed the next step in to the "court of Israel," but only priests could enter the temple building itself. Paul's point here is that the gospel breaks down all such boundaries, allowing equal access to God's presence and equal access to salvation for all people, regardless of their race, gender, or social status.

While this verse is a powerful statement of the liberating power of the gospel, its wider significance is debated by Bible scholars. Some see it as affirming the full equality of women and men in terms of church offices, leadership, and family roles. Others claim that this is going beyond what Paul says. Paul is not presuming to say there should be no distinctions between men and women, Jews and Gentiles, or slaves and free people.

His topic has been justification, and continues to be, so that should be the context in which this verse is understood. In other words, while there is but one way to find justification before God, this does not eliminate distinct roles for men and women in the church and the home. Those who hold this latter perspective point to other portions of scripture—including Paul's writings—which include instructions directed specifically to males, females, slaves, Jews, etc.

Whichever view is taken on this difficult question, Paul himself would certainly be dismayed if differences of opinion provoked division in the church. After all, Paul's main point here is that we "are all one in Christ Jesus" (3:28).

Critical Observation

A common morning prayer among Jewish men included thanks to God that they had not been born a Gentile, a slave, or a woman. The reason was not necessarily to demean the other groups, but an acknowledgement that those people didn't have all the same rights and privileges available to free Jewish males. Paul's choice of terms in verse 28 was probably intentional to precisely counter the viewpoint of the Judaizers.

Paul's clear statement (3:29) is the very thing the Judaizers would not admit. They were tied to rules and regulations, but Paul continues to logically and meticulously explain why the justification of God is so accessible and rewarding.

Paul refers to the law as both a prison warden (3:23) and a pedagogue to lead people to Christ (3:24). Now he presents it as a guardian who controls an heir until the time of his or her inheritance (4:1–2). Even though God designates believers as heirs, they must wait a while before collecting what He promises. In the meantime, they are still subject to rules and restrictions. The situation may *seem* little different than being a slave (4:1), yet the difference is most significant.

Thanks to Jesus, our period of slavery has ended. When God deemed that the time was right, He sent His Son (4:4). The world had been spiritually ready and in need of a Savior for centuries. But in the first century, it was physically ready as well. The Greek civilization had established a common language across much of the world. The Romans had established peace and built roads. And at a time when the seemingly insignificant Jewish culture intersected with these great empires, Jesus came to earth and the good news of His life, death, and resurrection spread rapidly.

Paul's short and simple description of Jesus (4:4) is surprisingly complete. He was God's Son—preexistent and divine. He was born of a woman—fully human. He was sent—He didn't just happen to arrive; He came to fulfill a mission. And He was born under the law—submissive to the law's demands as He fulfilled the promise of God. It was Jesus' redemption of those under the law that entitled them to full rights as God's children (4:5).

Paul also acknowledges the contribution of the Trinity in the process of salvation (4:5–6). Not only did God send His Son, He also sends the Spirit of His Son. Believers receive not just peace with God—though that alone is a priceless gift—but also become God's sons and daughters. They are actually brought back into a family relationship with

God as He originally created people to be. Believers are privileged to address God the Father as *Abba*—an intimate and personal title. In addition, their adoption into God's family bonds them with one another both now (in the church) and eternally, as they discover what it really means to be an heir of God (4:7).

📄 **4:8–20**

PAUL'S PERSONAL PLEA

In verse 3 Paul mentions "the basic principles of the world" (NIV); here he warns of "those weak and miserable principles" (4:9 NIV). He is referring to the basic principles of unregenerate human life that are at the root of all false religion. Here he refers specifically to the idolatry and paganism from which the Gentile Christians had turned, but the Jewish legalists were just as much in error for attempting to use *their* principles to earn God's righteousness. It was a daring thing for Paul to suggest that first-century Judaism and pagan idolatry were resting on the same foundation! His comments would have infuriated Jews who saw their faith as the complete repudiation of idolatry.

Paul had already made reference to some of the Judaizers' demands of Gentile converts, including circumcision (2:3) and dietary restrictions (2:11–14). Here he adds yet another: observance of the Jewish calendar and celebration of special events (4:10). Again, there was nothing wrong with observing the Sabbath or noting Passovers and years of jubilee. Paul continued to celebrate Jewish events as a Christian. But it was wrong to think that doing so made someone more righteous than another (specifically, a Gentile believer). The Judaizers continued to insist on all the things that tended to separate Jews from Gentiles, and ignored the more important work of God that was attempting to bring them together.

The Galatian Christians had been delivered from the falsehood and futility of legalistic religious ideas and practices. They had experienced the glorious freedom of the knowledge of the living God, of justification by faith in Christ, and of a life founded on love and gratitude. Why would they give all that up to return to the bondage and futility they had escaped? It was almost enough to make Paul give up on *them* (4:11).

As both the prophets and Jesus had done before him, Paul mixes warning (4:8–11) with affectionate appeal (4:12–16). Paul's challenge for the Galatians to become like him (4:12) isn't meant to be boastful. They would have known of Paul's legalistic and anti-Christian background, yet he had experienced the grace of God and had found his purpose and ministry. He had left behind the "credentials" he had once been so proud of, and was now simply living for Christ. Paul wasn't going to hold the Galatians' spiritual reversal personally, yet he was pleading with them to reconsider for their own good.

Demystifying Galatians

Paul occasionally makes reference to personal physical problems in his letters (4:13), yet never specifically identifies his struggle. Some suggest that he may have contracted malaria in the lowlands of Pamphylia, and went to drier, cooler, higher altitudes to recuperate. Others read his comment in 4:15 and believe he must have had a vision problem. Some think he may have suffered from epilepsy. But we aren't likely to ever know for sure.

Paul had problems and trials just as everyone else did, and he greatly appreciated the reception he received in Galatia during an illness (4:13–14). Even though Paul was quite sick, the Galatians had hung on to his words as if he were Jesus Himself. His illness was a trial to them in the sense that they proved they loved the truth so much that they gladly received it from someone they had to physically care for.

Yet it hadn't taken long for them to abandon the joy they initially felt (4:15). Although Paul felt a bit of resistance from them at this point (4:16), a real friend speaks the truth even when it hurts—and especially if that truth is a matter of life and death. The frankness of scripture passages such as this one can be encouraging. Contemporary readers can see that biblical churches were not perfect by any means, even with leaders like Paul, so they should not be surprised when modern churches face similar problems and struggles.

It's easy to label the Judaizers as terrible people, but we need to remember that they were professing Christians. They believed Jesus was the Messiah, that He had risen from the dead, and that it was necessary to have faith in Him. They were also quite evangelistic, and Paul notes their great zeal (4:17). But where they went astray from the gospel was in their insistence to also require obedience to certain ritual requirements and connect that obedience to one's peace and acceptance with God.

The Galatians had been influenced by the zealous efforts of the Judaizers, which dismayed Paul. He challenges them to be just as faithful to the gospel when he is absent from them as when he is present (4:18). Paul's imagery in verse 19 is powerful. He would have at least had the attention of all the mothers in the church by comparing his ministry to childbirth. Giving birth is a joyful experience, because once the trauma is over and the pain has subsided, the parent has a child to be proud of. But in Paul's metaphor, he was being forced to start over and "birth" the same child. It's no wonder he was feeling perplexed (4:20).

However, by expressing his honest feelings (and accusations), Paul is exhorting change. People and groups (such as the Judaizers) often get by with more than they should because nobody says anything in their presence. Paul wrote the truth in a letter that would be read to crowds in the church that would surely have included some of those guilty of exactly the things he describes. Their hypocrisy would become instantly apparent.

📄 **4:21–31**

SLAVE VS. FREE

After making his personal appeal, Paul returns to a theological argument against the Judaizers' position. The allegory of Hagar and Sarah (4:21–31) continues the line of reasoning he began at Galatians 2:15. It is yet another reference to the founder and hero of their faith, Abraham. The patriarch's first two sons are the focus of Paul's attention. The first was born to Abraham by Hagar, Sarah's maidservant. The second, Isaac, was the product of Abraham and his wife, Sarah. In this culture, the status of the son depended largely on the status of the parents, so Isaac was entitled to far more than Hagar's child, Ishmael.

In addition, there was nothing special about Ishmael's birth. Abraham impregnated Hagar and she delivered the child in the usual way. But Sarah's delivery was much different. She had been barren all her life, yet had God's promise that she would have a child. God waited until she was ninety years old before fulfilling His promise, so Isaac was always special to his parents as a reminder of God's greatness.

Since Paul recalls this story and mentions two covenants (4:24), many believe he is contrasting the covenant God had with Moses and the Israelites with the new covenant that was established through Jesus.

It may well be that Paul is using the term *covenant* with powerful irony, just as he defines the Judaizers' teaching as a different gospel (1:6) when it was no gospel at all. This is another way for Paul to reiterate the point he has been making: There is the way of self-effort and the way of faith in God. Only those who remain faithful and receive the grace of God will experience His powerful and holy love.

Take It Home

Today's Christian community is not so different from the Galatian church. Some people forget the kindness that others have shown them. Some keep going through the motions of worship, but without the joy they previously experienced. Have you witnessed any similar problems of this sort? What do you think Paul would have written to such people if he had been told of their behavior?

GALATIANS 5:1–26
TRUE FREEDOM AND SPIRITUAL FRUIT

Setting Up the Section

Paul continues the ongoing argument he has been making to refute the restrictive and destructive philosophies of the Judaizers. He has just made a contrast between slavery and freedom, and now continues with a call to the freedom that only Christ can provide. He will also explain how the Holy Spirit influences the lives of believers in a way that no law can possibly countermand or contradict.

📄 5:1–6

THE ONLY THING THAT COUNTS

It is one thing to acknowledge that freedom is better than slavery, but intellectual assent is not enough. So as Paul concludes his contrast between Sarah and Hagar (or more accurately, Isaac and Ishmael) in 4:21–31, he calls for the Galatians to stand firm in their freedom (5:1). Trying to adhere to the law as a means of righteousness is akin to choosing to wear a yoke of slavery.

Paul was circumcised, and when working among Jewish believers he even had his coworker, Timothy, circumcised (Acts 16:1–3). But in Galatia, where his opponents were insisting that circumcision was a requirement for the salvation of Gentile believers, Paul insists even more strongly that it wasn't. In fact, he says, getting circumcised would be like a personal offense to Jesus (5:2). Adding *any* human requirement to the work of salvation accomplished by Jesus is wrong.

Critical Observation

What Paul seems to suggest in his ongoing response to the beliefs of the Judaizers is that the most troublesome divide in religious thinking may not be between those who call themselves Christians and those who don't. It is likely that an even more egregious division exists between those whose hope of salvation is based on Christ alone and those who think that, in one way or another, salvation is partially based on their own efforts. This latter division is particularly disturbing because it exists largely *within* the church.

Either Christ provides our justification or the law does. There is no middle ground. If it is Christ, it is Christ entirely. If it is the law, it is the law entirely. The latter option would entail performing *all* the demands of the law—not picking and choosing as the Judaizers were doing (3:10; 5:3). They focused on circumcision, diet, and observing special events, yet the law included so much more. Paul becomes emphatic in this section, reverting to first person singular (*I*) to project his personal presence and apostolic authority as much as possible.

Those who don't stand firm in the freedom and grace that Christ provides (5:1) are in danger of falling away from grace (5:4). That doesn't mean God writes off such people, but that they voluntarily give up their freedom by seeking justification by the law—exactly the reason it is such an offense to their Savior (5:4).

The hope Paul writes of (5:5) is not a vague wish, but rather a confident expectation of eternal deliverance based on the presence of the Holy Spirit in believers' lives and His communication of the gospel to their hearts. Christians are already assured of a "not guilty" verdict at Judgment Day, so they can look to the future with eager anticipation rather than fear. In the meantime, issues such as circumcision are irrelevant (5:6). The focus of God's people should remain on faith in Christ, expressed in love. That, writes Paul, is the only thing that counts.

📄 **5:7–15**

A CHOICE TO MAKE

Why is faith crucial to salvation by grace alone? First, the nature of faith is to look away from itself to another. Only as believers divert attention from themselves to God are they able to maintain a clear focus on His grace. And second, faith is God's gift to those who are being saved (Ephesians 2:8–9), and therefore cannot be regarded as the believer's own contribution to his or her salvation.

Initially, the Galatian believers had understood this. Paul compares their spiritual journey to a race where things were going quite well until someone cut in on the runners and got them off track (5:7). Clearly, the interference was not from God (5:8).

Paul uses the same proverb to awaken the Corinthian church to the problem of tolerating sexual sin in their midst (1 Corinthians 5:6) that he applies here (5:9) to the insidious effect of legalism. If the Galatians allowed works-oriented justification to penetrate their church at all, soon it would crowd out grace altogether.

Paul didn't have many positive things to say about the Galatians in the opening of his letter, and he had recently expressed both fear that he was wasting his time on them (4:11) and perplexity about why they made the decisions they had (4:20). Yet at this point, he is willing to give them the benefit of the doubt that they would do the right thing. The Galatians were making bad decisions when they should have known better, yet Paul realizes they were victims of people who were eloquently promoting untruthful things. It was those people who would be responsible to God (5:10). Paul expects the Galatians to reject the error of the false teaching and return to a genuine, faith-based relationship with God.

Although a *group* of Judaizers had created the trouble in Galatia, Paul uses a singular pronoun in verse 10. Perhaps he was simply alternating between singular and plural (as he had done in 1:7 and 1:9), or maybe he was aware of (or suspected) a specific ringleader and chose not to mention names.

As was stated in connection with 5:2, Paul tolerates (and even endorses) circumcision as a valued Jewish symbol of faithfulness—just not as having anything to do with salvation. Yet his critics could accuse him of inconsistency. They would say either circumcision was right or wrong; Paul couldn't have it both ways.

Yet *they* were trying to have it both ways. If indeed Paul were preaching circumcision as they accused (5:11), then he would have *agreed* with them, so why did they continue to give him a hard time? He would have been their ally, not their enemy. Clearly, that was not the case.

To Paul, the cross of Christ meant everything as the validation of God's great love and the source of grace, mercy, and forgiveness. But to many other people, the very thought was offensive (1 Corinthians 1:23; Galatians 5:11). Anyone who endorsed the validity of circumcision as a way to God negated the importance of the cross—something Paul would *never* do.

Paul is so intent on refuting the Judaizers' views on circumcision that he effectively evokes a curse (imprecation) on them (5:12). In the style of the imprecatory psalms— those where the writers prayed that God would break the teeth of their enemies (Psalm 58:6), dash evil people's babies against the rocks (Psalm 137:8–9), and so forth—Paul wishes castration upon the Judaizers. He isn't specifically asking God to do something bad, yet he wouldn't have minded seeing their misdirected zeal bring harm to themselves rather than the spiritually immature believers in Galatia.

Paul's specific intent is debated. Perhaps he didn't want the Judaizers to reproduce. Maybe it was a spiritual issue, because eunuchs were not allowed to participate in worship (at least, not in the Jewish system [Deuteronomy 23:1]). Or it could be that Paul was adding sarcasm to logic: If a little bit of cutting meant such a big deal to them, then why not be really spiritual and cut a lot? In Paul's extremism, it becomes clear that circumcision truly had very little to do with one's spiritual relationship with God.

In contrast to Paul's feelings toward the Judaizers, he tenderly implores the Galatians to remain free, but not to misuse their freedom (5:13). It would be quite natural for some people, after hearing someone repeatedly emphasize that following the law is not what God expects, to go to the other extreme and ignore all spiritual rules (antinomianism). But Paul immediately clarifies himself and challenges the Galatians to celebrate their freedom by serving and loving one another.

In this context, Paul's reference to "the entire law" (5:14 NIV) means more than just a list of dos and don'ts. Rather, it is the entirety of the spirit, intention, and direction of all the commandments of God. As strongly as Paul had just stressed that the law is *not* the means of justification, it is interesting to note how much he continues to value it as the guideline for how we are to live.

Here, at this late point in Paul's epistle, is the first indication we have that the Galatian church was experiencing divisions and conflicts (5:15). However, the disclosure should come as no surprise. When *any* new teaching is introduced into a group—whether true or false—it is not uncommon for responses to be divided, frequently with controversy, quarreling, and fits of temper. Paul's mental picture of the disharmony in Galatia is quite graphic: wild beasts charging at one another, biting, and hoping to prey on the others (5:15). Paul calls for them to make peace before the damage became irreversible. The choice was theirs, but as he is about to explain, they would have help if they chose wisely.

IN STEP WITH THE HOLY SPIRIT

It would appear to be obvious which of Paul's two options—to either serve one another in love (5:13) or to continue devouring one another (5:15)—is his preference for the believers in Galatia. Yet Paul also knew the frustration of *wanting* to do something one way, but somehow failing to accomplish what he knew was right (Romans 7:14–20). So he reminds his readers of the continual inner struggle between the desires of the sinful nature (the flesh) and those of the Holy Spirit.

As long as believers are still human, they never fully outgrow the lure of the sinful nature to respond to wants, drives, and matters of self. Moral conflict in the Christian life is an ongoing reality. However, the more a believer learns to live by the Spirit, the more his or her self-centered desires are diminished.

Demystifying Galatians

Essentially what Paul means when he writes of living by the Spirit and being led by the Spirit (5:16, 18) is the doctrine of sanctification. When someone becomes a Christian, a process of transformation begins. The Holy Spirit works within to change the heart, which in turn affects behavior. The education, illumination, conviction, and love for God that come with sanctification are ultimately the result of the work of God within believers. Yet people are still responsible for making the right decisions and working out their own salvation (Philippians 2:12–13). So believers won't be able to avoid spiritual conflicts and crises from time to time, but they can always count on the Holy Spirit to help them prevail.

Paul's list of sins (5:19–21) addresses four distinct problem areas. The first three terms refer to sexual immorality, the next two to false gods, the next eight to various sins of personal conflict, and the final two to drunkenness. It also appears that this is not intended to be a complete list, but rather a representation of common problem areas (5:21). This list is quite similar to those Paul provides in other epistles (see 1 Corinthians 5:9–11; 6:9–10; 1 Timothy 1:9–10; and especially 2 Corinthians 12:20–21). The striking similarities have caused Bible scholars to wonder if these lists were circulating among Jewish and Christian ethical teachers, and Paul incorporated them into his letters.

In addition, it is most likely that the sins he lists here would have been specifically targeted to the Galatian Christians. Several of the sins—especially the sexual sin, idolatry, and drunkenness—had become so rampant in the Roman culture that most people tolerated them unless carried to real excess.

Then, in the starkest of contrasts, Paul shifts from the acts of human, sinful nature into a list of the qualities that result as the fruit of the Spirit in a believer's life (5:22–23). Love is first on the list, which makes sense because Paul has already said love is how genuine faith expresses itself (5:6). Some Bible expositors have written that love is actually the only item on the list, with the other named characteristics being how love is expressed in a believer's life. Experience would suggest that where there is true love for God and fellow human beings, joy and peace cannot be far behind.

Unlike the *gifts* of the Holy Spirit that are separate and dispersed among various believers, the *fruit* of the Spirit is found grouped together in a Christian heart and life. Where one is found, the others will likely be found as well.

It seems odd that Paul finds it necessary to add that there is no law against such noteworthy qualities (5:23). Perhaps the best explanation is that Paul's remark is an intentional understatement for rhetorical effect. It forces his readers to think, *Of course these qualities fully meet the demands of the law!* (This is Paul's point in verse 14.)

Note Paul's smooth and natural shift from the Holy Spirit (5:22–23) to Christ (5:24), and then back to the Spirit (5:25). Those who belong to Christ are influenced by the Holy Spirit, and keeping in step with the Holy Spirit helps believers live a more Christlike life.

In another beautiful pairing of God's blessing and personal responsibility, Paul makes it clear that the Holy Spirit directs our course in life, yet believers must also choose to keep in step with the Spirit (5:25).

Finally, this wonderful fruit of the Spirit is available for all believers. Therefore, there is no need (or place) for vanity, jealousy, or competition (5:26). Indeed, such feelings cannot exist in a life filled with love, joy, peace, patience, kindness, goodness, faithfulness, gentleness, and self-control.

Take It Home

It is somewhat sad that Paul felt the need to spell out such a specific list of no-no's for the believers in Galatia (5:19–21). Yet many of those things had become tolerated in Roman society and very possibly were being accepted in the church as well. What, if any, behaviors can you identify in contemporary society that you feel are potential threats to the church? How do you think the church should respond to them?

GALATIANS 6:1–18

DOING GOOD WITHOUT BECOMING WEARY

Setting Up the Section

Paul, in a section about the challenges and benefits of Christian freedom, has just made a thought-provoking contrast between the acts of the sinful human nature and the fruit of the Holy Spirit. Clearly, his readers knew the preferable choice, yet Paul was also aware of the power of sin and the grip it could have on people. So as he continues, he provides practical advice for how to deal with existing sin in the church.

📄 **6:1–5**

INDIVIDUAL AND SHARED BURDENS

Although Paul exhorts the Galatian believers to be led by the Holy Spirit and to refuse to gratify the desires of the sinful nature, he knew that would not always be the case. It is no surprise that Christians will occasionally be caught sinning, even committing habitual sin. So Paul immediately addresses how to handle situations where someone is already beset by sin.

Paul's instructions in verse 1 may not apply to every situation. While all sin is problematic and separates believers from God, there is a difference between more common, tolerable faults (being quick to judge, an unkind word, gossip, tardiness, forgetfulness in some duty, etc.) and sins of far greater consequence to the reputation of Christ and the well-being of others. So Paul isn't encouraging Christians to become nitpickers in regard to the quirks of other believers, but rather to be bold in taking action to help those in serious trouble.

From the beginning, Paul makes a number of assumptions. He readily admits that some members of the congregation are more spiritual than others. At any given time, some will be living by the Holy Spirit while others are out of step. In each person's life, spiritual maturity waxes and wanes. Some people continue to mature throughout their lifetimes, while others may be quite spiritual at some point and then decline (Solomon, for example).

Paul also warns of potential danger to the spiritual, seemingly successful Christian. Believers tend to make assumptions as to who among them is above temptation, yet it is all too common to hear of people who seem to be above reproach being drawn into some sort of sin. Being "spiritual" is an ongoing challenge throughout a person's journey as a Christian. When attempting to help pull someone up from the depths of sin, it is essential for the helper to be careful not to be pulled into the sin as well.

Although Paul prescribes that those who are spiritual help those who fall into a sin, he doesn't provide specifics. He does not say precisely how restoration should take place or what recovery will look like. What works well in one situation might not in another. Those who are "spiritual" should, by definition, remain under the control of the Holy Spirit to know how best to handle each circumstance.

When Paul says to carry one another's burdens (6:2), the word he uses almost certainly means "to bear" or "support." However, the same word is translated one time (Revelation 2:2) as "tolerate" or "put up with." Some people take that to mean that Paul is saying we who are more mature should *bear with* the sins and shortcomings of the weak (similar to what he writes in Romans 15:1). Yet in the context of what he is writing here, surely Paul intends for spiritually mature people to assist (not overlook) weaker, growing believers.

The latter option is certainly what Paul taught by example. After enumerating his personal sufferings in 2 Corinthians 11:23-27, he goes on to describe his additional sympathetic suffering on behalf of the believers he knew in various churches (2 Corinthians 11:28-29). He had his own concerns and responsibilities, to be sure, yet was always aware of and affected by the weaknesses and needs of others.

Paul had previously shown the futility of the law in regard to salvation, yet here acknowledges that it is still the law of Christ (6:2). The Law of Moses had the authority of Christ behind it. Jesus Himself had confirmed that He was the fulfillment of the law (Matthew 5:17). As a result, people should be able to see that the Law of Moses was always intended to be a law of love (5:14).

Unfortunately, spiritual maturity is frequently accompanied by spiritual pride, so Paul warns against arrogance (6:3). He is not suggesting that believers amount to nothing. On various occasions, Paul had found it helpful (if not necessary) to list his own accomplishments and achievements, yet was always quick to give the credit to Christ. God chooses to use people to accomplish great things at times. Yet Paul knew that many other times believers begin to think too highly of themselves when they have no right or reason.

A person's sense of purpose in the Christian life should come solely from his or her relationship to Christ. People who know they are doing what God is calling them to do find great satisfaction regardless of other factors (6:4). It is when they start comparing their own accomplishments and situations to those of others that problems begin to arise. The key to contentment is to respond to one's calling without perceiving the Christian life as a competitive event.

Although Paul had been making a strong argument in favor of justification by faith alone, he still acknowledges the importance of personal responsibility. Not only should each person carry his or her own load (6:5), but believers could take pride in themselves. Indeed, there was a future aspect to what Paul writes here; perhaps he was thinking in terms of believers being judged according to their works. When Judgment Day comes, the evaluation won't be based on how well one person did in comparison to another, but how well each person did in light of God's calling and provision.

Demystifying Galatians

This passage seems to be contradictory. Paul first says to carry each other's burdens (6:2), and then almost immediately says each person should carry his own load (6:5). The similarity is probably intentional, although different words are used. The latter instruction has to do more with one's personal responsibility in life. Believers aren't to coast through their spiritual journeys while others do all the work for them. The former burden has more of an emphasis on morality. So when someone gets mired down in a serious sexual or ethical quagmire, mature fellow believers should be willing to step in and help.

📄 6:6–10

SOWING AND REAPING

Paul was never one to demand payment for his work as a minister. There were times in his travels when he didn't have enough money to support himself, so he went to work in the area in which he had been trained: tent making (Acts 18:1–4). Yet his belief was that churches should take proper financial care of those who were investing their time and spiritual gifts into church leadership (6:6).

Paul was in an ideal position to make such a statement. Because he personally didn't demand financial support from the churches he had founded, he made a good spokesperson on behalf of others in his position. And when churches *did* sacrifice to ensure that Paul could continue his ministry, he always tried to acknowledge their gracious gifts (as in Philippians 4:14–18).

Verses 7–10 may seem out of place after Paul has made such an exhaustive argument defending justification by faith alone. Others of Paul's writings make numerous exhortations to persevere in good works and to expect to give an account for one's actions on Judgment Day, but the message is not expected here at the conclusion of Galatians.

And the full force of Paul's remarks should be noted. He is not making a distinction between people who had professed faith and those who hadn't. Rather, he describes two alternatives: either destruction or eternal life (6:8). And he seems to say that those who persevere in good works get to heaven, while those who fail to persevere get hell instead. In other places he had differentiated between believers and nonbelievers (2 Thessalonians 1:8–10), but here he suggests that the principle of reaping what one has sown applies also within the Christian life and with how Christians will be judged.

Critical Observation

The truths of the Bible are sometimes found at opposite ends of a continuum and juxtaposed, but are not synthesized or harmonized. For example, scripture teaches God's sovereign grace and election (choice) of believers on one hand, and the freedom of human will on the other. We find the assurance of salvation by grace alone contrasted with Judgment Day parables, where Christ's final separation seems to be based on whether or not those involved had done good works (Matthew 25:31–46). There are passages about the reality of the continuing sinfulness of Christians as well as the call for them to be perfect (Matthew 5:48). Such perceived polarities are not really opposites or in conflict with one another, yet they are difficult to harmonize. That is the point. Many spiritual errors develop as a one-sided assertion of "truth" uncorrected by a corresponding truth that would bring balance. So part of spiritual maturity is learning to live with the tensions as we continue to grow in the knowledge of Christ.

The weight of what Paul is saying is intensified based on everything he had written the Galatians to this point about justification by faith alone. Having established that point, clearly he wants his readers to know that love-inspired actions are also important to a believer's life and faith.

And regardless of how Paul's meaning is interpreted, his command is clear: Believers are to commit themselves to good works—especially among one another. A commitment should be made that allows them to continue without giving up (6:9–10).

6:11–18

THE ONE REASON TO BOAST

Paul usually dictated his letters to a scribe rather than write the entire epistle himself. But it was common for him to take over at some point and write a portion of the letter in his own handwriting. Apparently he wanted to personally emphasize this closing section, so he uses large letters (6:11)—either for emphasis, or due to an eye ailment or some other physical problem.

Paul wants to assure the Galatians one more time that he is concerned about their inner, spiritual growth. In contrast, the Judaizers remained focused only on external conformity and their own reputation (6:12–13). They wanted to be accepted by the Jewish community and were unwilling to face the hardships and rejection of those who followed Christ completely. (If the Judaizers could persuade the Gentile converts to be circumcised, those new believers would appear no different than any other Jewish proselytes, and perhaps the Judaizers—who were also Christian converts—would be less likely to be persecuted by the traditional Jews.)

While the Judaizers took great pride in external religious symbolism, Paul's only "boast" was in the reality of Jesus' crucifixion and its results (6:14). Paul once had a list of honors and accomplishments (Philippians 3:4–6). Although religious in nature, they had drawn his heart away from God, so now he considers them crucified. They had lost their charm and allure to Paul, just as he had lost the respect of many who once admired him. For those who rejected Jesus, Paul was an object of either complete disinterest or active contempt.

For Paul to boast in the cross of Jesus was not something many people could understand. We don't find much about crucifixion in classic literature because it was so barbaric and horrific that even the Romans didn't much care to talk about it. As Paul writes elsewhere, it was foolishness to the Gentiles and a stumbling block to the Jews (1 Corinthians 1:23). Yet Paul isn't referring to the actual cross, the literal pieces of wood, but rather to the Savior who was crucified there to bear in our place the punishment of our sins. Nothing else that the world finds important can stand up to the reality and consequence of that event.

No one but God can make someone a new creation, which is really the intent and goal of religious faith. Circumcision in and of itself contributes nothing to one's peace with God. What matters is the supernatural work of grace by which, in Christ, men and women are transformed into new creatures by the Holy Spirit (6:15). Those who are justified by faith in Christ rather than attempting to work toward their own justification—whether Jewish or Gentile—can find God's peace and mercy (6:16).

Although Paul was circumcised, that was not the mark he took pride in. Just as slaves traditionally bore brands or other identifying marks, Paul wore the marks of Jesus—surely a reference to the scars he had received from beatings, stonings, and other such experiences he had endured. Those marks identified who he served and to whom he belonged, so anyone who resisted his message (caused him trouble) was an opponent of Christ Himself (6:17).

And although Paul had shared a message with the Galatians that was probably hard to write and certainly hard to hear, he closes with the final encouraging affirmation that he and they are brothers. He believed they would heed his appeal and remain true to the gospel. And in doing so, they would experience the true grace of Jesus (6:18).

Take It Home

In today's Christian culture, we may do well to consider what Paul meant when he wrote that God cannot be mocked (6:7). There is a tendency to think that we don't always reap what we sow. Many people believe that they will somehow be spared the consequences of their actions. Can you think of examples in your own circle of acquaintances where someone reaped an unwanted result of an action? Such self-deception can frequently be corrected. But what can you learn from such an experience to keep from being deceived about spiritual—and eternal—sowing and reaping?

EPHESIANS

INTRODUCTION TO EPHESIANS

The book of Ephesians is a powerful and uplifting contribution to the canon of scripture. Lacking any specific rebuttals of false doctrines, and addressed primarily to Gentile believers, it has long been beloved by seekers and new believers. Its doctrinal foundation has made it a favorite of Bible scholars as well.

AUTHOR

Paul's authorship was not questioned until the early nineteenth century, at which time certain Bible scholars began to speculate that Ephesians was historically, theologically, and stylistically inconsistent with Paul's other writings. Paul had spent much time in Ephesus (Acts 19:1, 8-10), yet his letter to the Ephesians is impersonal. The discrepancy is easily explained if Paul were addressing a different group of Gentile believers (perhaps newer ones he hadn't yet met), or if he intended the letter to be circulated to different churches. As for theology, Paul never even refers to justification in Ephesians, and his references to reconciliation pertain more to unity between Jews and Gentiles than humankind and God. Yet simply because he emphasizes a different aspect of God's grace in Ephesians is no proof that Paul didn't write the epistle. Any opposition to Paul's authorship is subjective and speculative. Indeed, the logic, the structure of the book, the emphasis on the grace of God, and the full acceptance of Gentile believers are distinct indications that Ephesians was written by the apostle Paul.

PURPOSE

Although some of Paul's epistles address specific problems within a particular church, Ephesians doesn't. Rather, it challenges the reader to set a higher standard for living—the imitation of God (5:1). Paul was writing to a prominently Gentile church, and makes clear that its members have been fully reconciled to God and are entitled to every spiritual blessing that He offers (1:3; 3:16-19).

OCCASION

Paul was a prisoner when he wrote this letter—most likely under house arrest in Rome, awaiting trial before Caesar (Nero). If so, his had been a long, arduous journey, including false arrest in Jerusalem, a series of trials (with ongoing imprisonment) for more than two years, a harrowing shipwreck on the way to Rome, and the current uncertainty of what would happen to him. Yet his letter is filled with enthusiasm, faith, and confidence.

THEMES

A number of topics are repeated with some frequency in this epistle. One is the *Trinity* of God the Father, Jesus Christ the Son, and the Holy Spirit. Where Paul mentions one member of the Trinity, many times he will specify the others as well.

The *mystery* of God is mentioned throughout the letter. Paul explains that, at his writing, it is a revealed mystery—a reference to the gospel of Jesus Christ that can now be understood even though its full meaning had been hidden for centuries.

Ephesians has much to say about the *heavenly realms*, as Paul regularly shifts his readers' attention from their personal, earthly concerns to the spiritual conflict they are involved in.

And Paul's focus remains on the *church*. Although he provides both a theological basis for how to live and practical applications for what to do, his intent is to build up the body of Christ—not a random assortment of spiritually mature Christians.

HISTORICAL CONTEXT

Ephesus was a major city in the Roman Empire. The book of Acts details a number of events that took place there, including passionate opposition to Paul by silversmiths who made their living from the great number of visitors to the temple of Artemis (Acts 19). In spite of the heavy influence of idolatry and sexual promiscuity connected with the temple and the culture, a predominately Gentile church had arisen. Although Paul has nothing bad to say of the church there, John would later report that it had forsaken its first love (Christ) and needed to repent (Revelation 2:1–7).

AUDIENCE

Many scholars believe that Paul did not send this letter exclusively to the church in Ephesus, but that he meant it to be an "encyclical" letter to circulate among various churches. We know from Acts that while ministering in Ephesus, Paul and his disciples started churches throughout the Roman province of Asia (Acts 19:10).

Arguments supporting a circulating letter:

1) Some ancient manuscripts omit the words *at Ephesus* in Ephesians 1:1.
2) There are no personal greetings at the end of the letter. This is particularly surprising since we know from Acts that Paul worked in Ephesus for nearly three years on his third missionary journey (Acts 19).
3) There seems to be no treatment of *specific* church problems. When Paul is writing to an individual church he usually addresses issues and problems specific to that church.
4) Paul writes that he has "heard" of the readers' faith (1:15) and they have "heard" of his ministry (3:2). But Paul knew firsthand of the faith of the Ephesians.
5) In Colossians 4:16, Paul tells the Colossians to read the letter from Laodicea. Some scholars speculate that this is our letter to the Ephesians, and that it is circulating among the churches in Asia Minor.

Together this evidence makes it possible, though not certain, that Paul originally sent this letter to circulate among various churches. Such a possibility does not affect the theological or practical importance of the letter.

CONTRIBUTION TO THE BIBLE

Ephesians in its entirety is a grand epistle of spiritual richness. Yet several of its components have been singled out as favorites of Bible students. One such passage is Ephesians 2:8-9, Paul's clear and concise affirmation of the absolute sufficiency of salvation by grace through faith—and nothing else.

Another favorite selection for memory verses comes at the end of Ephesians 3, where Paul uses physical measurements (wide and long and high and deep) to describe the love of Jesus, and follows that with the assurance that Christ can do immeasurably more than people can ask or imagine.

The submission teachings of Ephesians (5:22-6:9) have generated much discussion throughout the centuries since they were first written. And the closing description of spiritual qualities as the armor of God (6:10-18) is another often-cited section of this epistle.

OUTLINE

EPHESIANS 1:1–23

THE ALL-SUFFICIENCY OF CHRIST

Every Spiritual Blessing   1:1–14
A Glorious Inheritance and Incomparable Power   1:15–23

Setting Up the Section

Paul's letter to the Ephesians has long been considered a masterwork of doctrine and critical thinking. In this epistle, Paul does not address specific problem areas, but directs the thoughts of his readers toward the things God has done for them, and then to what they should do in response. This section will remind believers of many things for which they should be thankful.

📄 **1:1–14**

EVERY SPIRITUAL BLESSING

Paul begins this epistle, as usual, by identifying himself (1:1). He also uses the title of *apostle*, as he frequently did, as a reminder that he was sent from God. His message is not merely opinion or casual conversation, but carries the authority of the Lord.

As noted in the introduction, several of the oldest manuscripts of Ephesians do not include the mention of Ephesus in the opening of the letter. It is addressed simply to the saints rather than the saints in Ephesus, adding to speculation that this might have been intended as a circular letter. Additionally, Paul does not deal with any specific heresies as he does in other letters, nor does he greet people by name, even though he spent nearly three years in Ephesus (Acts 19:10).

Though *grace* and *peace* (1:2) were traditional greetings, both terms had a personal spiritual significance to Paul and reappear throughout the letter.

At verse 3, Paul begins a sentence that, in the original Greek, doesn't end until verse 14—over two hundred words. One clause builds upon another as Paul loses himself in enthusiasm over what he is writing. As many scholars have noted, this extended paragraph is a doxology. It opens with praise to God the Father, and Paul attempts to keep directing the readers' attention to Him throughout the letter (1:17; 2:18; 3:14; 4:6; 5:20; 6:23).

Ephesians maintains an emphasis upon the person of God the Father and His role in salvation. As Paul opens his letter, he reminds the believers of their rich heritage. He wants them to appreciate what extraordinarily great things had been done for them and given to them, and they had God the Father to thank for it all. He is the source of all good things—peace, joy, hope, love. As believers begin to dwell on what God the Father has done for them, they find inspiration and determination to love Him in return and demonstrate that love through service.

Yet Paul's opening doxology also acknowledges the work of the triune God: the Father, the Son, and the Holy Spirit. Before the creation of the world, before the human race even existed, God was already laying the plan for its salvation from the death and doom humans would bring upon themselves (1:4–8), and that plan would include both Jesus (1:5, 9–10, 12–13) and the Holy Spirit (1:13–14). It is as if the Father, Son, and Holy Spirit met and conferred before the creation of the earth, agreeing on what part each would play in the salvation of the human race. The Father was the planner, choosing those to be saved and determining the way of salvation. The Son was the executor of the Father's plan, bringing it to pass by His incarnation, suffering, death, and resurrection—all on behalf of the ones the Father had given Him. The Spirit would be the communicator of the Father's plan, accomplished by the Son. The Spirit calls the elect to faith in Christ and communicates to their hearts the knowledge of God, of Christ, and of their own salvation.

The salvation of humankind was no afterthought. God knew that human beings would be guilty and inveterate sinners, so He provided a way for sin to be removed, the record cleansed, and perfect righteousness reestablished. Still, that was not all. God loved human beings so much that He chose to include them in His family—not only as servants or friends, but as His sons and daughters (1:4–5). And God is by no means a stingy Father. Believers are lavished with wisdom and understanding. They are made privy to the mystery of His will. While they may not know all the specifics, they can have absolute confidence that all things are proceeding according to God's plan and will ultimately conclude with a universal demonstration of the glory and divine dominion of Jesus Christ (1:7–10).

This passage is rich with theological terms and biblical doctrines: predestination, election, justification, adoption, salvation, sanctification, and more. In addition, the family aspect of God's plan is significant. The connection to Jesus brings all believers together; they are not solo entities. They belong to a family—the church.

The same plan that enables any person's forgiveness and adoption embraces the farthest reaches of the cosmos and everything that happens in it. The salvation of each and every believer is subsumed into God's larger, greater plan for the world and for humankind (1:11–12). The God who planned, accomplished, and applied Christ's salvation to each believer is the same God who now controls the march of history as, day by day and event by event, it makes its inexorable way toward the consummation of all things.

Then, finally, at the conclusion of his long, meandering sentence, Paul relates this mélange of grand, sweeping themes to the daily lives of God's people. The believers in Ephesus were recipients of everything God had promised, and well aware of their inheritance. Yet they could not yet see or experience those things fully. Paul instructs them to wait and look to the future in confident hope (1:13–14). To prevent them from becoming discouraged in the meantime, the Holy Spirit is present among them to assure them that God would someday deliver everything He had promised.

Demystifying Ephesians

The word *redemption* in this instance (1:14) does not mean Christ's payment of His life as a ransom to deliver people from the bondage of sin and guilt (as it usually does in scripture), but rather refers more broadly to the ultimate issue of Christ's redeeming work—the full and absolute deliverance of His people from all the consequences of sin and guilt when He brings them at last to heaven.

In his opening salvo, Paul traces humankind's salvation from its inception in the plan and purpose of God to its ultimate fulfillment in the eternal inheritance of the saints in the world to come. Yet he does not fill in any details. Everything is summarized. Doctrine after doctrine flows among Paul's cascading clauses in this, the longest single sentence in the New Testament. It is God's plan of salvation in a single breath.

Verses 3–14 are a thesis statement—a table of contents for the letter. There is no need to stop and delve into any of these magnificent themes in depth because Paul will come back to them later in the letter. Yet before going any farther, Paul provides a controlling perspective, a theological viewpoint of the sovereignty of God and His grace to sinners. It is this viewpoint that will bring the rest of the letter into clearer focus.

📖 1:15–23

A GLORIOUS INHERITANCE AND INCOMPARABLE POWER

The section that follows (1:15–23) is another long, single sentence. In this case, the passage begins with Paul's thanksgiving for the believers to whom he is writing, his prayer for them (in three parts), and an elaboration of his prayer regarding the power of God.

Paul had spent years in Ephesus (Acts 19:8–10), yet his phrasing (1:15) makes him sound like a stranger. This may be attributed to regular growth in the church, to the point where many new converts would not have known him. Or, as some believe, if Paul intended for this letter to be circulated to numerous congregations, he might have intentionally downplayed personal bonds to address the church as a whole.

Here, as in a number of other places in the New Testament, the point is made that true faith in Christ is evident by showing love for fellow Christians (1:15–16). Paul would soon go on record with his insight into the faith-works debate (2:8–9), but as the Ephesian believers already demonstrated, faith and works *should* go together. Paul wasn't there to see for himself, yet hearing of their actions gave him confidence that they were in fact Christians (1:16).

The report Paul had received about the Ephesian church had inspired thanksgiving, and he responds with prayer on its behalf (1:17–19). When Paul writes of hope (1:18), he isn't referring to a fingers-crossed wish for God to come through. The biblical concept of hope is confident assurance that God will do as He has promised. Christ's work is finished and the Holy Spirit has been given as a deposit and guarantee of a future inheritance (1:14).

Paul desired to see the Ephesian believers grow in the grace and knowledge of the Lord—in wisdom, revelation, and enlightenment (1:17–18). As they grew, they would first see more clearly what God had in store for them. Second, they would learn to appreciate what a wonderful thing it is to be part of the people of God. And third, they would comprehend God's mighty power that assures, secures, and inspires those who realize that it is always available to them and working for them.

The Ephesian believers already possessed the Holy Spirit (1:13), yet Paul writes of a deeper knowledge of Him as well as subsequent wisdom and power available to them. As God's truth more fully captures their hearts, as only the Holy Spirit could make happen, they would live in abounding joy, perpetual thanksgiving, and confident effectiveness.

Critical Observation

It has been written that the mature and holy Christian life has three dimensions: (1) doctrine (the knowledge of the truth about God, man, sin, Christ, the Holy Spirit, salvation, etc.); (2) experience (the life-transforming force of the truth in the heart, producing sorrow for sin, hunger and thirst for righteousness, love for God, joy, and peace); and (3) practice (obedience by keeping the commandments of God and serving Him in the body of Christ). Paul's writings affirm the importance of these spheres of Christian life. Yet while some people tend to minimize the importance of doctrine, that was certainly not Paul's view. Experience and practice are not authentic or effective unless they begin with the knowledge of truth. Awareness of Christian doctrine is imperative.

It should be noted, however, that Paul is not writing about a new or secret knowledge that requires great effort to decode or unveil—a teaching that certain cultic groups would soon promote in the early church. Rather Paul refers only to a deeper awareness of what the Ephesian believers had already been taught. From their introduction to Christianity, they had heard of heaven, the world to come, the grace of God, their inclusion in His household, and His limitless power. These were not brand-new discoveries. Yet as the Ephesians grew in Christian maturity, such truths would become more important to them and begin to burn in their hearts. *That* was the knowledge Paul desired for them.

Believers have access to the same power of God that Jesus had (1:19–23). At one point, Jesus appeared to be at the mercy of Pontius Pilate; now He is King of kings and Lord of lords. Here, Paul hints at spiritual forces of darkness as he writes of authority, power, and dominion. He will later be more specific (3:10; 6:12). Yet whether human or spiritual, current or future, no ruler can ever compare to the power and authority of Jesus Christ.

Paul will also go into more detail about the definition of the church and its relationship to Christ, although his explanation in verses 22–23 is nicely compact. And just as he had done in the previous paragraph, Paul acknowledges each of the three persons of the triune God. Faith in Jesus (1:15) inspires prayer to the Father (1:17) for the sending of the Holy Spirit (1:17). The result of the Spirit's work is that believers are even more certain of the power of God the Father that was demonstrated in raising Jesus from the dead and placing Him over the church (1:19–23).

God has already acted on behalf of believers. It is now important that believers remember that an effective Christian life is built on establishing regular communion with the Father, the Son, and the Holy Spirit.

Take It Home

How often do you take the time to really think about how much God has given you? If indeed He has given His people every spiritual blessing (1:3), how many of those blessings have you thanked Him for lately? Even while offering thanks to God, many people limit their thinking to the more tangible things of life. Paul, however, tends to dwell on truly valuable gifts such as redemption, grace, forgiveness, and the knowledge of spiritual mysteries. It is in recalling the greatness of God's love for us that His Spirit helps us shift from being aware of His work among us to really *knowing* Him.

EPHESIANS 2:1–22

DEAD IN SIN, ALIVE IN CHRIST

Sin and Salvation	2:1–10
Brought Near to God	2:11–22

Setting Up the Section

After a magnificent opening section reminding his readers of the work of God the Father, Jesus Christ, and the Holy Spirit, Paul critiques the believers in Ephesus and explains how they have come to connect with such a holy God. He describes their transformation as a move from death to life, and his intention is to be more literal than symbolic. His words to the first-century Ephesians are just as relevant for the church today.

📄 **2:1–10**

SIN AND SALVATION

Paul begins this section by reminding the Ephesian Christians of what they once were. Theirs was a church of mostly Gentiles who had placed their faith in Jesus. They had not been raised in godly, believing homes. They could recollect very easily what their lives had been prior to their Christian experience. According to Paul, they had been dead (2:1)—a highly controversial and offensive statement to many who are not believers, but a statement of fact from Paul's perspective.

Many places in scripture portray the absence of faith in Christ as "death." To be dead in a biblical, spiritual sense is not nonexistence, but rather a condition of inner disintegration, of thorough brokenness as a human being. It is an existence devoid of the true purpose, character, and fulfillment of human life created in the image of God. Unbelievers are alive physically, emotionally, and intellectually, yet they are dead.

God had told Adam in the Garden of Eden that if he ate of the fruit of the Tree of the Knowledge of Good and Evil, he would die. After his sin, Adam did not cease to be physically alive, yet he died in a more significant way. From that point forward, the biblical concept of "life" was not understood as simple existence, just as "death" involved more than physical annihilation or destruction.

The reason for the Ephesians' spiritual death, writes Paul, was their trespasses and sins (2:1). Elsewhere Paul makes clear that the wages of sin is death (Romans 6:23). And since all people have sinned (Romans 3:23), they all remain spiritually dead until faith in Christ makes them alive again.

Critical Observation

The understanding of the biblical concepts of life and death, side by side with the more contemporary meanings of the terms, helps us better understand numerous phrases in scripture. For example:

- " 'Let the dead bury their own dead' " (Luke 9:60 NET).
- "It is no longer I who live, but Christ lives in me. So I live in this earthly body by trusting in the Son of God, who loved me and gave himself for me" (Galatians 2:20 NLT).
- "Whoever does not love abides in death" (1 John 3:14 ESV).
- "This lake of fire is the second death" (Revelation 20:14 NLT).

The ruler to whom unbelievers submit so willingly (2:2) is the devil (Satan), whom Paul later identifies more specifically (4:27; 6:11, 16). Paul also will specify the domain of the evil spirits as the heavenly realms (3:10; 6:12), yet here refers to a kingdom of the air (2:2). Perhaps his intent is to emphasize the lower reaches of the devil's influence—and the proximity of evil to the people on earth.

The original sin that permeates human existence is no small problem. It is human nature to sin—to rebel against God rather than trust Him or please Him (2:3). Sin comes from deep within and leaves no part of the person untainted, including his or her desires and thoughts. Sin is not just a matter of misdeed, but also of an unrighteous state of mind, attitudes, and motives. People are born in this sinful condition, and even if they desire to escape are unable to do so in their own power.

But Paul is not out to depress his readers. Quite the opposite. Only by seeing clearly their status of sin, death, and the reality of evil could they truly appreciate the great love, mercy, and grace of God (2:3–5). It was because of sin that the Ephesians had been dead, but then they were made alive because of Christ (2:5). Just as God the Father had raised up Jesus Christ and established His position securely in heaven, so He will for each believer (2:6–7).

Clearly, people can do nothing to deserve this grace of God, which is exactly what makes it grace. Nothing more can be said in explanation of salvation other than God is love and, loving us, He intervened to give us life when we were dead. Such truths of Christianity are not only realistic, but they provide the only truly hopeful teaching to be found.

Salvation is only by God's grace, which Paul emphasizes with repetition (2:5, 8). Some people try to dissect Paul's wording in verse 8 to suggest that while grace is certainly from God, the faith aspect of salvation comes from people. In any reasonable reading of Paul's words, and in any understanding of Paul's teachings, he also takes the origin of faith in Christ out of people's hands and places it within God's graciousness. Believers owe God the entirety of their salvation, both its provision by God and Christ, and its appropriation by the individual.

Paul further emphasizes his point by restating his positive message from the opposite perspective (2:9). Paul's mention of works is to a predominately Gentile group, in which context it would mean simply human effort or human achievement. From beginning to end, salvation is God's doing, which is why boasting is eliminated. No one has any basis for self-congratulations.

Paul has written of predestination and God's sovereignty (1:4–6); here he confirms that God prepared in advance for His workmanship—those He created and who responded in faith to His Son—to do good works. Yet Paul points out that good works are a *result* of salvation, not the *reason* for it (2:10).

📄 **2:11–22**

BROUGHT NEAR TO GOD

At this point in the letter, Paul confirms that most of his readers are Gentile believers (2:11) as he begins to apply what he has been saying specifically to their experience of salvation. Their situation had been bleak. Not only were they separated from God, they were also excluded from any kind of community of faith (2:12). The Jews at least had their covenant with God and the promise of a Messiah (even though Israel was equally guilty of unbelief).

That's not to say the Gentiles didn't have multitudes of gods. Many Gentiles were intensely religious, and some were proud of their accomplishments and hoped to improve their world. Yet Paul says their gods and all their hopes were false, amounting to nothing. Only in Christ can God and hope be found.

Paul's description of first-century circumstances is not much different from the church of today. The same point he makes about the Gentiles could be made for unbelievers: It could be said that they are separate from Christ because they do not belong to the Christian church. As long as people remain strangers to the covenant of promise (in the Old Testament) or the gospel of Christ (today), they are without God and without hope. Yet recent trends suggest that more and more believers want to allow for people of other faiths to find a way to God that bypasses the sacrifice of Jesus Christ. It's a culturally tolerant view, but a spiritually inaccurate one. Paul would never have agreed.

Now, as then, Jesus is the source of hope for all people. From all appearances, the Gentiles in Ephesus were far away from God, yet they were instantly brought near to Him through the sacrifice of Christ. Jesus came to save the world, not only the Jewish nation (2:13). And again, the proof of God's grace was that the Gentiles had done absolutely nothing to warrant God's love and salvation.

Paul writes about the reconciliation of the Gentiles to God, yet the work of Christ also accomplished reconciliation between the Gentiles and the Jewish nation—the two that Paul refers to in verse 15. This was no small achievement. Hostility between the Jews and

Gentiles had been long, deep, and abiding. Fueling the conflict was the exclusiveness of Judaism. Their customs and self-consciousness as a set-apart people led Jews to regard Gentiles as inferior and unclean (spiritually defiled). Not surprisingly, the Gentiles fostered a reciprocal animosity toward the Jews, their religion, and their way of life that seemed so bizarre and offensive. The barrier between the two groups (2:14) is both a metaphoric and literal divider: Gentiles were only allowed into the outermost courts of the temple, and entering the places prohibited to them was punishable by immediate death. (Paul had once been accused of this very offense, attempting to take a Gentile beyond the barrier [Acts 21:27–29].)

If taken out of context, Paul's statement about abolishing the law with its commandments and regulations (2:15–16) can easily be misinterpreted. Some suggest that Paul is saying that Christ did away with the entire law so, therefore, Christians need not obey *any* commandments. The principle of love has made the expectation of obedience obsolete. But clearly, this is an invalid interpretation.

Paul himself is on record saying that upholding the law is part of Christian faith (Romans 3:31). And he is simply reflecting Jesus' teaching: Love for Christ is to be demonstrated by keeping His commandments (John 14:15; 15:10). Later, in this very letter, Paul will quote from the Ten Commandments to make a specific point about keeping the Old Testament law (6:1–3).

So if Paul isn't referring to Jesus' abolishment of the whole law in verses 15–16, what is his meaning? By comparing his statement to the Ephesians with a parallel thought in Colossians 2:13–17, his intent becomes clearer. Christ, by His death on the cross, did away with the *curse* of the law (Galatians 3:13). He did away with the law in the sense that He removed the regulations of Jewish religious life that placed a barrier between Jew and Gentile. (Really, very few laws did so. Most of the separation was due to rabbinical innovations rather than the Law of Moses.) A few of the Mosaic laws needed to be adapted in order to bring the Gentiles into the church without prejudice as members in completely good standing. One example Paul uses in Colossians is the explicit mention of the laws regarding clean and unclean food—laws that Jesus had already revised as He sent disciples out to minister to others (Luke 10:8).

The Old Testament laws regarding clean and unclean food, observance of religious festivals, and certain other rites had a temporary and revelatory purpose. But after Jesus had come to establish a new and better way to approach God, those laws were no longer necessary. It was *those* laws that Jesus abolished, and His purpose was to make peace between the Jews and the Gentiles, forming one united body (2:15–16). So the fruit of the Cross was not only the reconciliation of sinners to a holy God, but also the reconciliation of Jews and Gentiles. Thanks to Jesus' sacrifice, writes Paul, peace is now available to both groups. The same Spirit works through both Jews and Gentiles to provide access to God the Father (2:17–18).

This is not to say that Gentiles received "membership" into Judaism. The unity created by Jesus established oneness among believers that transcended Israel and Judaism. Gentiles are no longer outcasts, but neither are they Jewish proselytes. Rather, they are fellow citizens with the Jews and equal members of God's household (2:19). All believers are part of the same structure, where Jesus is the cornerstone that both supports and unites all the other components. And that structure, or building, as it turns out, is a temple where God resides (2:20–22).

Demystifying Ephesians

The reference to *prophets* as a foundation of this new building (2:20) may evoke images of solitary and eccentric Old Testament figures, but that was not Paul's intent. Most likely he was referring to New Testament prophets who played a vital role in perceiving the will of God in the context of the early church. When apostles and prophets are paired in Ephesians, the apostles are listed first (2:20; 3:5; 4:11). Furthermore, Paul may not have been emphasizing people or their roles, but rather the instructional aspects of both positions. In other words, the foundation of this new temple that unites Jews and Gentiles is the *teaching* of the Word of God by the apostles and prophets.

Once again, Paul brings together the members of the Trinity as he describes this temple of God, where Jesus is the cornerstone and the Holy Spirit dwells among God's people. Believers in Christ—whether Jew or Gentile—have access to God's presence. Yet the biblical image of salvation is lifted up beyond individual redemption and renewal to its corporate dimension. Believers are integrated into the body of Christ, made a living part of something far larger than themselves. No individual Christian can fulfill God's purposes in his or her life without contributing to the life and ministry of that body. People are saved to become part of the church and Christian community—to participate in the life, worship, and ministry of the house of God.

It is helpful to remember that Ephesus was the site of another temple—the renowned temple of Artemis, a stunning marble building that was one of the seven wonders of the ancient world. It would have been natural for Paul's readers to think of this other temple as they considered his words. Artemis resided in her temple in the form of an impressive statue, but God dwells in His in the form of the Holy Spirit who gives comfort and direction to His people. God's temple is less visible and less tangible than the one dedicated to Artemis, but His is just as real and much more lasting. As impressive as the marble structure in Ephesus seems to be, the temple of God that Paul describes to the Ephesians is still standing—stronger than ever.

Take It Home

Do you think Paul's terminology is still applicable to believers and nonbelievers today? For example, would you say the unbelievers you know (or yourself prior to becoming a Christian) are dead (2:1)? What makes you say so? In what ways are unbelievers still foreigners (2:19) to God and His people? In what ways are believers God's workmanship (2:10)?

EPHESIANS 3:1-21
REVEALED MYSTERY AND GLORIOUS RICHES

Setting Up the Section

Paul has been reminding the predominantly Gentile body of believers in Ephesus of the spiritual blessings that have been provided for them, and he continues to do so in this passage. After just completing a section about how God had brought together Jews and Gentiles, in Christ, into one body, Paul's thoughts seem to turn to the "mystery" of God that had become much clearer in light of the life, death, and resurrection of Jesus.

📖 3:1-6

MYSTERY AND REVELATION

In order to better understand the message of God's grace being communicated to the Gentile believers in Ephesus, it is important to remember who is writing. Paul (Saul of Tarsus) was a former Pharisee and persecutor of the Christian church. Moments before becoming a Christian, Paul couldn't stomach the name of Jesus Christ. He had recently witnessed the stoning of Stephen and was glad to see it happen—the groans and blood coming from that righteous man hadn't affected Paul at all.

Paul would eventually suffer a similar end, but in the meantime he was rejoicing to be counted worthy to suffer for his Lord. He never lost sight of the fact that his dramatic conversion on the Damascus road and subsequent transformation occurred only by the grace of God. He was more amazed than anyone that he had been called to be the missionary of Jesus Christ to the nations. The well-educated and proud Jew who had been conditioned to look down on Gentiles had become their encouraging and devoted servant.

Even as Paul wrote, he was in prison for the sake of the Gentiles (3:1). During his most recent visit to Jerusalem, a group of zealous traditional Jews had accused him of opposing their people, their law, and their temple (Acts 21:28). Paul was also accused of taking a Gentile into the temple beyond the established barriers (previously referred to in connection with 2:14). Paul's message in Jerusalem probably wasn't much different than what he had written the Ephesians so far—that God, in His grace, was bringing together Jews and Gentiles who believed in Him. So the charges against him were false, yet Paul had already been tried before various officials (Acts 21:27–28:31), been threatened with death, spent years imprisoned, undergone a harrowing shipwreck en route to a higher court in Rome, and was currently awaiting trial before Nero. Even so, he didn't consider himself Nero's prisoner, but rather a prisoner of Christ (3:1).

Paul's imprisonment was an honorable one, and proof of his commitment to the Gentiles. So as he writes to the Ephesians, he stops in mid-sentence to remind his readers of his own experience with God's grace (3:1-2).

Paul's use of the word *mystery* has an important distinction from the way the word is used today. To modern ears, a mystery implies something uncertain and vague—a secret only known by very clever people or perhaps a puzzle for which no answer can be found. In New Testament usage, a mystery is still hidden and secret, but only temporarily, and in time is revealed by God so that it can be known and understood. In numerous instances the word *mystery* can almost be a synonym for *revelation*.

Paul uses the word so frequently in this letter that it is not difficult to determine his meaning. He writes of the mystery of God's plan of salvation in its entirety as now revealed in Christ (1:9), the mystery of the gospel (6:19), and here, the mystery of Christ (3:4). In each of these instances, the mystery is clearly the way of salvation for sinners through Jesus Christ. Paul confirms this meaning in Colossians 1:27, where he defines the mystery as "Christ in you, the hope of glory" (NIV). The mystery has become known and is no longer hidden from the world.

Paul frequently emphasizes that he receives his insight into the gospel by direct revelation from Jesus (3:2-5). He is not being boastful, but rather defensive. He knew he had critics who disputed his authority as an apostle. They falsely claimed that he had been taught by the other apostles, yet had strayed from their teaching by opening the gospel to the Gentiles. So Paul inserts regular reminders that he writes and speaks with the authority of Christ.

Although the mystery of Christ had only recently been fully revealed (3:5), God had provided clues for centuries. Long before the ministry of Paul or the incarnation of Christ, the Old Testament prophets had foretold the salvation of God and even the inclusion of the Gentiles in His plan. Paul refers to the gospel in connection with the belief of Moses and Abraham. Yet their understanding could not possibly be as clear and detailed as the comprehension that came *after* Jesus had fulfilled the promise of salvation and unlocked the mystery. Although the ultimate mystery is salvation in Christ, one surprising aspect of the mystery is that salvation would be lavished on the Gentiles as well as the Jews, resulting in a single unified spiritual body (3:6).

📄 3:7–13

CONFIDENCE BEFORE GOD

As soon as Paul really began to comprehend the mystery of God—the gospel—he became its servant (3:7). Like an efficient service person in a restaurant, Paul was pleased to present the gospel to whomever he could. He had received the gift of God's grace and was more than willing to pass it along to others. He knew the message and the power came from God, and it wasn't up to his own strength and capability to spread the word. In fact, he considered himself the very least of all God's people (3:8).

Critical Observation

The Latin word *Paulus*, from which Paul's name is derived, means "little" or "small." Tradition also suggests that Paul was short of stature. Yet Paul had no Napoleonic complex. His ego was also small (3:8). He realized that with God's power he would be plenty big enough to take on any task and endure any trial.

In Paul's case, this was not false modesty. Everyone knew of his pre-conversion reputation. Paul had more than just a message of God's grace; the fact that he was the front person responsible for bringing Gentiles into the church was *proof* of God's grace. Paul, who had once been so protective of the Jewish way of life, was now the primary spokesperson promoting the mystery of God to *everyone* (3:9).

"The unsearchable riches of Christ" (3:8 NIV) refers to God's love, sacrifice for sin, present intercession, promise to come again, and gifts of joy, peace, love, and hope. Even in a Roman prison, Paul is thankful for such riches and confident that they are available to the Ephesian Gentile believers as well.

The church does not exist for itself, but for the glory of God. It serves that purpose by demonstrating the wisdom, grace, goodness, justice, and holiness of God as sinners are transformed by the gospel of Christ and become unified in love. Such a magnificent transformation is bound to be noticed—not only by people who see the changes that the love of Christ can make in a believer's life, but also by rulers and authorities in the heavenly realms (3:10). Paul probably meant that both good and evil beings take notice. We know from 1 Peter 1:12 that holy angels witness matters of human salvation with amazement and wonder. It stands to reason that evil angels see as well, although their response to the progress of the kingdom of God would certainly be different.

Perhaps one of the church's most overlooked privileges is the right to approach God freely and confidently (3:12). For centuries God's people had to offer blood sacrifices and go through priests for access to God. And closeness to God evoked great fear. Modern believers tend to take for granted the perpetual nearness of God they have through prayer and the Holy Spirit. Such access to God greatly diminishes worry and discouragement (3:13). As believers realize that God is working His gracious and perfect purpose out in the world and that all that happens is somehow setting an example for other people and heavenly powers, they can learn to rejoice in their sufferings instead of becoming discouraged by them.

📄 3:14–21

THE WONDER OF SALVATION

In verses 14–19, Paul returns to the prayer he had begun in verse 1. The prayer is similar in content to the one he records in 1:17–19. In between is his description of the wonderful aspects of God and salvation that Paul wanted the Ephesian believers to appreciate more and more. The two prayers serve as bookends for Paul's first section of Ephesians. He asks God to enable those Christians to grow in their understanding of salvation—to deepen their experience of the Father, Son, and Holy Spirit. He wants their transforming experience to be more complete, more powerful, and life transforming.

Paul continues to acknowledge all three persons of the Trinity. He prays to the Father, asking for power from the Holy Spirit and the presence of Christ in the hearts of the Ephesians (3:14–17). Father, Son, and Spirit are intertwined, each relating to the believer in a harmony of grace and love.

Demystifying Ephesians

Paul's reference to heaven and earth (3:15) is sometimes taken to mean both angels and people, with God presiding over both. But a better interpretation may be based on what Paul had just written about Jews and Gentiles forming one body (3:6). More likely, what Paul means is that some of that "family" had already died. So the use of heaven and earth would be his way of referring to the saints above, already in glory, and those still living in the world below.

Paul's mention of glorious riches (3:16) echoes his previous phrase, "the unsearchable riches of Christ" (3:8 NIV). Perhaps there were people in the church then, as now, who would rather have their ministers speak of other, more relevant things: money, marriage, politics, raising children, and so forth. Paul would address those topics, and would do so in helpful and practical ways. Yet he always did so in the context of presenting God's glorious riches.

People can learn to handle money, have a good marriage, raise good kids, etc., and still be dead in sin. So Paul keeps his focus on what Jesus Christ had done on behalf of the Ephesians in providing peace with God, forgiveness of sins, sure hope of everlasting life, and a perfect life after human death. None of those things would ever come from money, marriage, children, politics, or any other source. For Paul, Jesus Himself was the center of everything, the meaning of everything, the way to everything good. (In his Epistle to the Colossians, he makes a classic argument for the supremacy and preeminence of Christ.)

Paul identifies the Holy Spirit as the active agent of the believers' sanctification (3:16). It is His influence within that leads them deeper into godliness. And through the Spirit, Jesus Christ is said to dwell in the hearts of Christians (3:17). Believers need divine insight and power to begin to understand the intensity of God's love—how wide and long and high and deep it is (3:18). Even with God's help, it is a love that cannot be fully understood. Who can really describe what it feels like to be filled with all the fullness of God (3:19)?

Yet Paul also prays that the Ephesian believers would understand (3:18). God empowers believers and helps with their ability to comprehend, but He doesn't download such knowledge into their minds. When it comes to the grasping, comprehending, and proper perception of spiritual truth, scripture teaches that such things are both the gift of God and the responsibility of seekers.

The more believers discover of God, the more they experience His presence, witness His holiness, splendor, love, and grace, and become more holy and loving. Someday they will see Jesus as He really is, face-to-face (1 Corinthians 13:12). Until then, they learn to see more clearly by *trying* to see Him more clearly.

Paul wraps up this first half of his letter with a short doxology (3:20–21). As he reflects on the things he had written about all that God has poured out on His people, Paul could not help but stop and give Him the glory for it. No matter how much believers can comprehend and imagine what God has done for them, He has actually done even more (3:20).

And lest his readers forget, as Paul was finding himself so carried away with all that God had done, he was writing from prison! He demonstrates that the blessings of God and Christ by the Holy Spirit can transcend the troubles of life. Everyone will certainly experience his or her share of trouble, of course, and should feel justified in expressing true feelings that may not sound overtly spiritual. David did. Jesus did. Paul himself was quite open about his "thorn" (2 Corinthians 12:7–10). But even in the midst of their deepest sorrows, believers can realize that their sufferings are minor in comparison to their knowledge of God's glory and the joy and fullness of life that are certain to exist in their future. It is sometimes during their greatest tribulations when Christians actually experience the ecstasy of such knowledge of God.

Paul concludes with the desire that God would receive glory throughout all generations (3:21). That includes modern believers! Today's Christians have access to the same glorious, unsearchable riches that Paul describes to the Ephesians.

Take It Home

It should be impossible to read Paul's prayer (3:14–21) in light of all he had written in Ephesians 3 and come away unaffected. A closer look confirms how right the prayer is and how happy and holy people would be who saw it fulfilled. Spend some time reflecting on what it would be like to be filled with all the fullness of God (3:19) and thinking about all God has done for His people. What can you do so that you will come to an even greater knowledge of the glory of God on a regular basis?

EPHESIANS 4:1–32

A GOOD WALK

A Call to Unity   4:1–16
Putting on the New Self   4:17–32

Setting Up the Section

The first three chapters of Ephesians have been theologically based. In this section, Paul turns from theology to ethics. From this point onward in his letter, Paul will focus on the Christian walk. Now that he has shown what God has done on behalf of believers, he addresses practical ways in which believers should respond.

📄 4:1–16

A CALL TO UNITY

Paul's outline of Ephesians is exactly opposite of what it would be for any other religious philosophy. Most world religions would open with the necessity of being good and doing what God requires, followed by salvation as a result. But as Paul clearly perceived and explained the truth of Christianity, he spent the first half of his letter detailing the salvation of God, the grace that made it possible, and the complete inability of anyone to achieve it on his or her own merit. Only then did he turn to the section on how to live.

Some Bible translations lose the emphasis, but in Greek, Paul opens Ephesians 4 with a strong "therefore." Everything he is about to write from this point forward should be viewed in light of what he had already written. The behavior he will prescribe is based on what God has already done, His great love and power exercised on behalf of humankind, and the sacrifice Jesus made even when people were enemies of God due to their sin.

Verses 1–3 are a single sentence in Greek, so should be considered a single thought. In other words, the qualities of humility, gentleness, patience, and love—as well as efforts to maintain unity with other believers—are all part of the calling believers have received.

The biblical concept of humility, or meekness (4:2), has nothing to do with weakness. As personal experience will attest, it can take great inner strength and the help of God's Spirit to set aside one's rights in favor of a weaker party or the common good. Yet this is the model set by Jesus (2 Corinthians 10:1; Philippians 2:5–8), and one that believers should determine to imitate.

Another significant biblical theme is the connection between personal qualities and ethical choices, as seen in Ephesians 4:2–3. Only someone who is humble will be willing (or able) to lovingly bear with someone else when disagreements arise. Only a gentle and patient person will be successful at preserving the unity of God's people. Secular philosophies suggest that it is possible to maintain spotless public behavior regardless of one's personal character, but the Bible makes clear that right living requires virtue and character. Even godly believers will struggle from time to time, which is why Paul challenges them to make an effort (4:3). Even though the Holy Spirit makes unity possible among people, it requires determination on their part as well.

But Paul is not asking too much of the Ephesians. Unity is God's desire and God's design (4:4–6). Believers *are* one. They are a body, whether they act like it or not. They have the same God, the same experience of salvation, the same future, and the same calling.

Yet at the same time, Christian unity is not a matter of imposing a dreadful sameness upon all believers or reducing individuals to the status of a single cog on a large wheel. When properly understood and experienced, Christianity is anything but monotonous. When individuality and personal initiative are encouraged rather than crushed, the church experiences beautiful harmony, not monotony. Believers receive various gifts apportioned in different ways (4:7–8). As each person applies his or her individual gifts, the resulting variety produces complex and magnificent harmony.

Ephesians 4:8–10 appears to be a parenthetical comment by Paul, yet this short passage has generated countless discussions, debates, and controversies. For one thing, Paul makes a reference to Psalm 68:18, and then appears to misquote it. David's psalm describes the Lord who *received* gifts from men, ascending as a victor loaded with the spoils of his conquests. Paul applies the psalm to Jesus, yet writes that He *gave* gifts to men. His thought seems to be that the Lord distributed those spoils among His people. Paul would have known other biblical passages such as Isaiah 53:12, foretelling that the Messiah would divide His spoils with the strong, and Paul's understanding of the gospel would have allowed him to properly interpret such prophecies.

Paul's mention of the "lower, earthly regions" (4:9 NIV) is another frequently questioned phrase. Some have posited that he is referring to hell (Hades), but that opinion doesn't seem likely. It is probably simply a reference to the earth, intended to emphasize how far away from heaven the Lord Jesus came to fulfill God's plan—Paul's way of acknowledging Jesus' incarnation. Or maybe Paul is noting that Jesus descended into the grave, after which He ascended and bestowed gifts on the church. The common thread among all of the speculations is that Jesus indeed voluntarily lowered Himself for the good of humankind.

And still another debated interpretation: In what way did Jesus' ascension fill up the whole universe (4:10)? Since Paul had been describing the gifts of the risen Savior, maybe his point is that Christ filled the universe with His blessings and His gifts. Then again, he might have been attempting to convey a message similar to that of Philippians 2, about how Jesus came to earth, humbled Himself, and then ascended to receive His reward from God. With every knee bowed to Him and every tongue confessing Him (Philippians 2:10–11), the universe would be filled with His praise.

Paul's statement amounts to saying that the Lord did all that He intended to do in this world. He routed every enemy that enslaved His people. He destroyed every obstacle to their everlasting life and happiness. He completed His work and ascended back to heaven. Now, as head over all things connected with the church, He fills the whole universe with the blessings He brought back with Him as spoils of His holy war.

It is through the grace of this triumphant Christ that each person receives spiritual gifts (4:7), and Paul mentions a few of them. Yet it should be noted that the gifts Paul names (4:11) are those having to do directly with the life of the church as a body. They are the gifts that Christians benefit from when they meet *together*.

Paul raises the topic of spiritual gifts here (4:11–13), yet doesn't stop to make much comment or enumerate the various gifts to the extent that he does in other epistles. We can safely presume that his list of gifts in verse 11 is clearly representative—only a sampling. Other lists are found in Romans 12:6–8 and 1 Corinthians 12:7–11, and what Paul says in those passages contributes to the understanding of this brief passage.

These church leadership gifts are essential to the integrity and growth of any body of believers. Some Bible versions translate the responsibility of church leaders as preparing God's people for works of service (4:12). Other versions express the role of church leaders more strongly, as bringing believers to completion for the work of ministry. Although *all* believers receive gifts and have a ministry to perform, everyone is also accountable to those with the leadership gifts. The result should be unity in the faith, deeper knowledge of Christ, and maturity (4:13). Believers will always have something more to strive for, because the ultimate goal is attaining the whole measure of the fullness of Christ.

Paul provides both a positive and negative image of spiritual maturity. Spiritually immature people are like small children who are easily deceived by false teachers and flit back and forth, responding to every new philosophy that comes along (4:14). It doesn't take much to distract them from what they need to be doing and learning.

In contrast, mature believers continue to grow up, becoming more and more like the head of the church, Jesus Christ. Their ongoing commitment is to love one another. They bear with one another in love (4:2). They speak the truth, but do so in love (4:15). And they grow and build up the body of Christ in love as each person does his or her work (4:16). Paul portrays spiritual maturity as a corporate rather than an individualistic vision, as did Jesus when He promised to build His church. In New Testament thinking, believers are almost always addressed in a group (church) rather than as individuals.

📄 4:17–32

PUTTING ON THE NEW SELF

Paul begins this section with another note of transition ("so," "therefore," or some similar translation). This serves as a reminder that he is still building on what he had already written in Ephesians 1–3. He insists on a connection between doctrine and life. What a believer does on any given day should be that person's reflection on who God is, what He has done for the person, and what the person understands His purposes to be. As Paul teaches repeatedly, the Christian life flows out of salvation and forms its character from it at every turn. When people truly begin to comprehend what God has done, they also see more clearly what they must do in response.

One thing Paul insists that the Ephesian Christians do is reject their old way of life, even though many of their peers were still involved in such things (4:17). Paul suggests that the darkness of unbelievers (4:18) is not necessarily due to lack of knowledge about God or inability to understand. Rather, it is a hardness of heart and unwillingness to repent that prevents their salvation, which in turn makes the things of God seem strange and wearisome to them.

The problem with unbelief is that it has lost touch with reality—a fatal flaw. God is in control, and those who acknowledge the fact and respond in faith discover that reality is human existence as created, defined, and judged by the living God. Those who deny God or resist His leading must establish a different reality, one that is not built on truth.

As Paul goes on to describe unbelievers (4:19), he paints their world in very dark colors. No doubt the Ephesians would have lauded the achievements of their civilization in art, building, and government. Thousands of years later, their aqueducts still carry water. Their literature still moves people's hearts and minds. Their buildings remain as inspirations to the world. Yet Paul says nothing at all about those aspects of their lives. When it comes to what is truly important—the moral and spiritual dimension of life as viewed from God's perspective—many would be found wanting and judged accordingly. They weren't even attempting to be disciplined and felt no qualms about indulging in every impure opportunity that came along (4:19). Paul tells the believers in Ephesus to walk away from such people and behavior.

Paul explains that even after placing one's faith in Jesus, a struggle continues between the old self and the new (4:20–24). Although believers die to sin, change their priorities, and begin to live for Jesus, the complete transformation doesn't take place at once. Paul refers to the old self as dead and destroyed (Romans 6:2), because Christ effectively removed people from the sentence of sin and death. Yet the influence of sin continues, and believers must *choose* to ignore the evil desires that remain within them (Romans 6:11–14). Those choices must be made every single day, no matter how long a person lives as a Christian.

To ensure everyone understands what he is saying, Paul gets more specific about exactly what should be discarded as believers begin to live as new creations (4:25–32). First on his list is falsehood. Truth is of utmost importance in Christian doctrine and practice. Lies distort the gospel and poison personal relationships. Yet the deeper such habits have been embedded, the more difficult they are to eradicate.

Quotation marks are around Paul's admonishment against allowing anger to lead to sin (4:26) because he is citing Psalm 4:4. Anger should never be allowed to linger and fester—not even overnight. Paul would soon comment that a believer's struggle is not so much against other people as it is against spiritual forces (6:11–12). Anger, though a common emotion, is one potential avenue to allow spiritual enemies a foothold (4:27).

Critical Observation

The behaviors that Paul extols in this section (4:25–32) are not exclusively Christian concepts. Other philosophies and most civilized societies have promoted truth over falsehood, self-control rather than unleashed anger, and honest work over stealing for a living. Yet Paul places these common, everyday behaviors in the context of a Christian's relationship with God. To him, the difference is more than simple choice, and is instead the result of the old self being replaced by the new self. It is not a matter of simply giving up what is wrong, but also requires replacing the sinful behaviors with godly ones. Paul's ethical teachings are distinctly spiritual, and are based on a genuine experience with the Father, Son, and Holy Spirit.

As believers respond to God's transforming them from old to new, other changes are just matters of common sense. They need to stop stealing and instead work—not just for themselves, but also for the good of others (4:28). They need to start watching their language, realizing that their words can be more harmful than they realize (4:29). And although such instructions make sense, for some people change is much easier said than done.

What many people don't realize is that sin in a believer's life brings grief to the Holy Spirit (Isaiah 30:1; Ephesians 4:30). Not only are Christians wrong to think their sins don't affect others, they are also foolish to suppose that God doesn't notice or doesn't care. The Holy Spirit's very presence in their lives is a sign of their redemption (1:13–14; 4:30). To revert to their old sinful ways is naturally an offense to Him.

Finally, Paul isn't recommending a mild improvement in one's behavior. He says to get rid of *all* bitterness, rage, anger, brawling, slander, and every other form of ill temper (4:31). Those traits should be replaced with ongoing kindness, compassion, and forgiveness (4:32). Thanks to Jesus, God demonstrated such love and grace to humankind. Believers should do no less to one another.

Take It Home

Although everything Paul wrote to the Ephesians applies to believers today, one issue seems particularly relevant—spiritual maturity as a corporate (church) matter rather than an individual one (4:13). Most church members are accustomed to being challenged to become more mature on an individual level, but how does your personal spiritual maturity affect the church as a whole? Can you detect a current influence? If you were to become more spiritually mature, how might the church—either your current body of believers or the worldwide church of Christ—benefit?

EPHESIANS 5:1–33

LIVING CAREFULLY

Setting Up the Section

In the previous section, Paul had shifted from a theological perspective of spiritual life to writing about applicable and relevant ways that such a perspective plays out in everyday life. In this section, he continues his instruction concerning daily living, including guidelines for sexual propriety, speech, drinking, and marriage.

📄 5:1–7

A HIGHER STANDARD OF LIVING

In Ephesians 5, Paul continues what he had started in Ephesians 4, as he spells out practical ways to live a more righteous life. He had already said to put on the new self that was created to be like God (4:24). Here he states the same concept in a different way by saying to imitate God (5:1).

Again, he encourages believers to walk appropriately—this time exhorting them to walk in love (5:2). He had made this point in various ways throughout the letter and restates it here: The Christian life is the believer's outworking of God's salvation. There is one acceptable standard of living for God's people; many other standards are not appropriate (5:3).

Paul's intent in verse 3 is most likely that certain things shouldn't even be *mentioned* in Christian company. Rather than being regularly exposed to and beginning to tolerate common sins, Paul recommends that believers keep themselves removed as much as possible, remaining tender and sensitive.

His instructions on speech (5:4) reinforce what he had just written (4:29), because they would have gone against the beliefs of his culture. Paul forbids believers from speech about coarse topics. In contrast, Aristotle considered it a virtue to be skilled at suggestive language and double entendres. So while it is clearly inappropriate to engage in "gutter talk," it is equally wrong to envy the quick-witted, sexually suggestive quips of sophisticates. Neither option is an attempt to imitate God (5:1).

In place of these common sins, Paul says to practice thanksgiving (5:4). By regularly thanking God for what He has provided, people come to see that He is the source of everything good and perfect (James 1:17). Sexual immorality, greed, and rough language direct one's focus away from the goodness and holiness of God; thanksgiving redirects a believer's attention to where it belongs.

Although many sins are common, they are not minor by any means. As Paul continues with his epistle, he connects sinful behavior with idolatry, God's wrath, and future judgment (5:5-7). People don't need wooden or stone images to be idolaters. The biblical definition of idolatry is worship or loyal service to *any* person or thing other than the living God. The human heart—particularly the heart of the old self—is prone to idolatry.

Peer pressure also comes into play in regard to the sins Paul has been describing. He warns of being deceived by the empty words of others (5:6), and of partnering with such people (5:7). Believers are to follow the example of Jesus, who lived and ministered among sinful people. Yet they are also to be ever watchful that they don't fall into the same sin that grips the lives of unbelievers.

📄 **5:8-20**

OUT OF THE DARKNESS, INTO THE LIGHT

When believers remember the state of their lives before their faith in Jesus, they become less likely to fall back into that sinful lifestyle. Paul challenges his readers to walk as children of light (5:8) and experience the benefits of pleasing God (5:9). Paul doesn't say how to find out what pleases God (5:10), but he suggests that it isn't difficult to discern God's will in such matters. Anyone whose intention is to please the Lord will have no trouble knowing what to do.

Paul had already said to not even speak about the common sins of the world (5:3) and reiterates that thought in verse 12. Yet he also says to expose such sins (5:11). Most likely his meaning is to remain close to the light of God. When believers live as God instructs, their lives reflect His light and reveal fruitless deeds of darkness. The light exposes sin for what it really is (5:13-14).

Paul's citation in verse 14 is probably a portion of an early Christian baptismal hymn. (He will refer specifically to hymns just a bit later [5:19].) If that is the case, it is probably an attempt to remind the Ephesians of the transformation that had taken place in their lives and had been affirmed at their baptisms.

It is far too easy to fall into patterns and habits that don't necessarily lead to sin, yet don't accomplish much either. Paul is attempting to rouse his readers into making something of their lives by capitalizing on every opportunity and making each day count (5:15-16). When he tells the believers to be careful how they walk (live), it is more than a warning to avoid missteps and sin. His command also includes being aware of every potential chance to improve the world around them. The days are evil, he writes (5:16), because sin is prevalent. Believers ought to walk carefully, determine what God's will is (5:17), and do what they can to represent God's kingdom to those around them.

Paul continues with some specific suggestions for how to walk in light. When desiring a consoling influence in one's life, he says, wine is not the answer—at least not to the point of drunkenness (5:18).

Critical Observation

Drunkenness makes people susceptible to numerous subsequent sins by lowering inhibitions. Paul points out that the next step is debauchery —indulgence in sensual lusts (5:18). His point is that if someone is looking for an experience to help him or her rise above the monotony of ordinary life, being filled by God's Holy Spirit is far more effective and beneficial than filling oneself with alcohol.

Spiritual living is exemplified in a number of ways, one of which has always been singing. Church music has long been a source of inspiration. Paul first acknowledges the importance of psalms, hymns, and spiritual songs as edification and encouragement for believers (5:19), but he immediately adds a vertical dimension. Spiritual singing comes from the heart and is ultimately directed to God.

Paul's Trinitarian thinking is again evident in this section of his letter. Believers are to be filled with the Holy Spirit, giving thanks for everything to God the Father, offered in the name of Jesus Christ (5:18–20). Paul again emphasizes thanksgiving as essential to maintaining a proper perspective on spiritual things.

Some people argue that Paul is expecting too much from ordinary people. At this point, it might be wise to consider whether he was really expecting his readers to adhere to the standards he was setting, or whether he was being a bit rhetorical, exaggerating to make a point. No Christian can read what Paul has written here and come away without a measure of disquiet and concern.

The standard Paul sets is for believers to imitate God! Is that not impossible? Yet Paul doesn't stop there—they are to rid themselves of any hint of sexual immorality, all greed, and any degree of coarse speech. He leaves no room for half-measures. And in addition to ridding every shadow of sin from their lives, Christians are not to miss an opportunity to show the love of Christ however possible.

All people come to God from sinful lifestyles. They are weak and continually bombarded by temptations. Is it remotely feasible to expect them to imitate God?

Yet Paul is not suggesting anything Jesus hadn't taught. Christ, too, set the imitation of God as the standard for believers to strive for (Matthew 5:19–20, 48). They realize they have never met that standard and know they will never do so as long as they remain in this world. Nevertheless, the ongoing goal of every follower of Christ is perfection, an ever more complete imitation of God. They will stumble. They will fail at times. Yet they are to grow stronger through their mistakes and keep trying.

Paul himself would not deny the difficulties involved. He was personally determined to press on toward perfection, yet was honest about his own failings (Romans 7:14–25). And in spite of his personal experience, he exhorts the Ephesian believers (and all those since) to imitate God.

HUSBANDS AND WIVES

In this passage Paul discusses how husbands and wives should live in relationship with one another. Not so long ago, the passage was a favorite at weddings. More recently, it has become a battleground of competing interpretations. Some interpreters claim that Paul is affirming God's universal standards for the roles of husbands and wives. Others claim that Paul's commands have a strong cultural element that must be applied differently today—similar to commands related to head coverings (1 Corinthians 11) and foot washing (John 13).

Paul begins by telling believers to submit to one another out of their reverence for Christ (5:21). So is Paul simply recommending mutual submission, as some interpreters have claimed? The context indicates otherwise, as Paul sets out a particular order of submission in relationships: Wives are to submit to their husbands (5:22), children to their parents (6:1), and slaves to their masters (6:5). This clearly goes beyond mutual submission. Furthermore, in other places the concept of submission is used in regard to Jesus' submission to His parents, demons submitting to the power of the disciples, citizens submitting to governing authorities, Christian submission to God, and so forth. Such relationships involve more than mutual submission.

It seems clear, therefore, that Paul is setting out particular role relationships in the Greco-Roman households of first-century Ephesus. The harder question, however, is whether Paul intended these role relationships to be applied to all Christians for all time. This is the point where good Bible scholars and well-meaning Christians differ.

Those who identify themselves as "Egalitarians" claim that Paul is writing to a specific first-century situation where such relationships would have been assumed. Paul wants husbands and wives to respect the orderly institutions of their day in order to be a good witness for Christ. This would also explain why Paul encourages slaves to submit to their masters, instead of calling on masters to free their slaves. Paul placed the proclamation of the gospel first, realizing that major disruptions to the present social order would impede rather than promote the gospel's spread. Social change would occur gradually, as the gospel took hold in people's hearts.

Those who identify themselves as "Complementarians," on the other hand, claim that Paul is here stating God's divinely sanctioned and universal roles for husbands and wives. These roles are complementary rather than identical, with the wife submitting to the husband as the head of the household. Evidence for this view are similar commands throughout the New Testament (Colossians 3:18; Titus 2:5; 1 Peter 3:1) and Paul's linking of male authority to God's order in creation (1 Timothy 2:11–14). Believers certainly have an obligation to love and serve one another (mutual submission), yet that does not nullify the relationships that God has established for the life of humankind and of His church. Paul wants to sanctify and purify both genders in married life. He expects husbands to be distinctly Christian men in their marriages, and he expects wives to be thoroughly Christian women. Whether male or female, the goal in marriage is to be Christlike. The present author believes this interpretation best fits the overall teaching of scripture and represents God's intention for men and women.

It should be noted that as soon as Paul instructs wives to submit to their husbands, he explains what is expected of the husband in the relationship (5:25–30). Husbands are expected to show the same love for their wives that Christ has for the church (5:25). They are to love their wives as their own bodies (5:28, 33). If marriage were merely a matter of hierarchy, no one would want to leave the comfort of his or her own home to become one flesh with a spouse (5:31).

No one can fully comprehend the mysterious metaphor of Christ as a husband and the church as His bride (5:32). Yet we need not have a full understanding to know what Paul means here. Again, Paul sets an immensely high standard for Christians—in this case, Christian husbands—to live up to.

Just as it requires grace when people fall short in their efforts to imitate God, so too is grace necessary in every marriage where two sinful, fallible people attempt to become one flesh. As they attempt to become holy and blameless, without stain or wrinkle (5:27), much love, forgiveness, and grace will be needed.

Paul wants men to accept the authority of headship, but to exert that authority with love and self-sacrifice rather than selfish domination. Similarly, Paul calls for wives to fulfill their femininity willingly, lovingly, and gratefully. Both parties have a special nature to bring into the marriage, which they share with each other in love and humility. There is nothing ordinary about Christian marriage. It is a relationship that human beings can live only by the grace of God. And it is a relationship that they would *want* to live only by His grace.

Take It Home

After reading Paul's challenging words about marriage, it is only natural to examine one's own marriage—or dating relationships. Do Paul's instructions (concerning the wife's submission to her husband) bother you at all? What do you understand them to mean? Even if this is a sensitive subject for you, how do you feel about the rest of what Paul says in this passage on marriage?

EPHESIANS 6:1–24

STANDING FIRM

Setting Up the Section

As Paul concludes this insightful letter, he has some very important things left to say before signing off. Having just addressed the relationship between husbands and wives, he now turns to parents and children, and slaves and masters. Then he will explain how all Christians are engaged in spiritual warfare, and instructs them on what they need to do to stand firm and emerge victoriously.

📖 **6:1–4**

PARENTS AND CHILDREN

None of Paul's commands in this section would have seemed controversial in his culture. Both Judaism and the Greco-Roman world placed emphasis on the authority of parents (especially fathers) over children, and all would have agreed that it was right for children to obey (6:1).

However, the teachings of scripture stand out by consistently including children in the membership of the church. Jesus had surprised His listeners by saying that the kingdom of heaven belonged to little children (Matthew 19:14). And in this letter, Paul addresses children along with other groups within the church, instructing them of their obligation to serve the Lord by obeying their parents (6:1). Children did not always get as much respect in other segments of society.

Honoring parents (6:2) involves more than mere obedience. It is possible to obey grudgingly, moodily, or only because one has to. Such responses do not honor parents. The one commandment with a promise is the fifth of the Ten Commandments (Exodus 20:12; Deuteronomy 5:16). This is only one of many places in the New Testament where a law is cited from the Old Testament as something believers must obey. Some people promote the idea that the commandments of God have been supplanted by a vague and general law of love. Such an idea never occurred to Paul.

Paul doesn't leave his instructions one-sided. After asking wives to submit to their husbands, he had then clearly instructed husbands how they were to act within the relationship (5:22-33). Similarly, after telling children to obey their parents, he does not leave room for fathers to take license and mistreat their children (6:4).

MASTERS AND SLAVES

In the ancient world, slavery was a way of life. Cruelty on the part of the masters was common enough, yet virtually no one (including the slaves themselves) ever considered abolishing the institution itself. And the lives of many slaves were comparatively good—sometimes better than those of freedmen. Some slaves owned land and even owned other slaves.

Masters who treated their children well tended to also treat slaves with dignity. It was common for masters to grant legal freedom to slaves after a time, although that could involve a lower standard of living for the slave. In fact, some people would even sell themselves into slavery in order to climb the social ladder. In many ways, slavery in the first century was not unlike a boss-employee relationship in the modern world. Some philosophers believe the Western world has only replaced an obsolete form of slavery that was no longer economically viable with a new version. In addition, sin continues to produce slaveries of all kinds, and always will.

Paul follows his pattern of first addressing the group in the subordinate position: wives before husbands, children before parents, and now slaves before masters (6:5). And as there has been much written about the behavior of children outside of the Bible, so also there is plenty of comment about how slaves should conduct themselves. The difference in this case is that Paul addresses the slaves as ethically responsible agents.

Paul makes a strong argument, pointing out that believers all have the same Master to whom they will someday give an account (6:6–8). By faithfully serving their earthly masters, slaves also please their Lord in heaven.

Both slaves and masters are instructed to keep their focus on Jesus. Slaves were not to obey simply because doing so might ingratiate themselves with their masters. And slave owners were not to mistreat their slaves, because in one sense, they were actually fellow servants (6:9). Paul's exhortations are very general; he doesn't provide a long list of dos and don'ts. As in many other places in scripture, it is assumed that if the conscience is awakened and love is ruling in the heart, people will know what to do and how to behave.

Critical Observation

One of the most striking evidences of the difference the gospel made in a culture where slavery was a way of life appears in the catacombs. In a typical ancient Roman cemetery it is very common to find references to the deceased as either a slave or a freedman. But in the Christian tombs there are only names along with an ascription of Christian hope—with no reference as to whether the person was slave or free. In addition, there are numerous cases of slave owners turning to Christianity and, as a result, freeing their slaves. On occasion, thousands of slaves were set free at the same time.

THE ARMOR OF GOD

As Paul approaches his final point (6:10), he turns to a logical question. He has already presented a theological explanation for *why* believers should live for Christ (1–3), as well as *what* they should be doing in various practical ways. Now he turns his attention to *how* they are able to rise above the secular standard of living and devote themselves more fully to God.

He begins by acknowledging adversarial spiritual forces that are under the control of a dark and scheming spiritual leader (6:11–12). Paul has already referred to the devil a couple of times in this epistle (2:2; 4:27), and here he gets more specific.

The existence of evil spirits is taken for granted in much of the world today, and throughout human history people have devised ways to deal with them, mollify them, or defeat them. However, there is a tendency in modern society to dismiss them as superstition and as incompatible with a scientific and sophisticated view of reality. The devil—described by Paul as a very real and dangerous opponent—has become the subject of jokes and cartoons rather than given serious consideration. Even among many evangelical Christians there is a reluctance to express belief in Satan as a personal being. Consequently, the severity of scripture passages such as this one is minimized.

However, the Bible is very clear about the reality of evil spirits, and weaves that teaching into the sum and substance of its doctrine. It was Satan who was instrumental in engineering the fall of humankind into sin and death. It was Satan who did his best to seduce Jesus through various temptations, hoping to hinder or prevent His saving work. It is Satan who, according to Jesus Himself, snatches away the "seed" (the Word of God), attempting to keep people from believing (Matthew 13:19). It is Satan who blinds the eyes of men and women to keep them from seeing clearly the truth of God. As a result, hell was created for the devil and his angels.

If one is to dismiss such biblical teachings about the devil, is it not also necessary to do the same for all teachings about the spiritual realm? If there is no devil, why should we believe there are angels? And if we rule out the devil and angels, why should we think there is a heaven or hell? If we question the teachings of Jesus about Satan, do we also question the other things He taught? And how do we explain the foolishness, empty pride, cruelty, and selfishness of human beings that exceed anything else found in the animal kingdom? Like it or not, what the Bible says about Satan is important to a complete understanding of human and spiritual reality.

As Paul introduces the concept of God's armor (6:11), he is reinforcing what he has already written about putting on the new self (4:24). Whatever people lack that makes them weak, vulnerable, and incomplete, God will supply. They are not strong in themselves, but can become strong with God's power (6:10).

Although Paul describes armor similar to that which a Roman soldier might have worn, his explanation for each piece relates to a spiritual quality. Satan is described as a liar (John 8:44), a lion stalking his prey (1 Peter 5:8), and here as a schemer (6:11). He does not fight fair. A believer's real enemies are not going to easily be dispatched (6:12).

Demystifying Ephesians

It may seem strange that Paul would use the weapons and dress of war to enumerate qualities befitting a Christian—someone called to be a peacemaker. However, it should be noted that Paul was under arrest in Rome when he wrote this letter. He would have been very familiar with the appearance of a Roman legionnaire. It is not unrealistic to think he might have looked up at his own guards as he was writing this passage, noting their uniform piece by piece, and comparing each component to a believer's spiritual armor.

So while Roman soldiers would prepare themselves for battle with a helmet, breastplate, belt, foot guards, shield, and sword, the armor for believers is less tangible. They are to arm themselves with truth, righteousness, readiness, faith, salvation, the Word of God, and prayer. These are metaphors, of course, and there is no need to attempt to make strong and indisputable parallels to a soldier's equipment. Much of Paul's language throughout this section is influenced by Old Testament passages (compare Isaiah 52:7 to Ephesians 6:15).

Taken as a whole, Paul's exhortation to put on the armor of God is intended to convey the fact that all the resources needed by a believer to oppose the devil and his powers have been provided in the gospel of Christ. Putting on the armor means living according to the new life that God has provided in Jesus Christ by the Holy Spirit.

Paul's main thought throughout this section is the importance of standing firm (6:11, 13–14), because the battle will be close and intense at times. For instance, the sword Paul makes reference to in verse 17 is not a large broadsword but rather the short, sharp sword carried by Roman soldiers—their primary offensive weapon for close contact.

As the sword is a weapon, so is prayer. In fact, prayer is given the most prominent place and the most space in Paul's description of a fully armed Christian soldier. The importance of prayer is seen in verse 18, with the repeated emphasis on *all*: *all* petition at *all* times with *all* perseverance for *all* the saints. To pray in the Spirit (6:18) means to pray with the guidance and assistance of the Holy Spirit. While continuing to stand firm, a believer is also to pray and to keep alert.

One possible interpretation of Paul's statement is that prayer is not simply the final piece of a Christian's armor, but also the means by which all the other pieces are made useful. Everything else—truth, righteousness, peace, faith, salvation, etc.—is effective only when employed in a spirit of dependence on God.

The mystery Paul refers to (6:19) means, as before, the gospel itself (1:9; 3:3-4, 9; 5:32). It is something that would not be known unless God had revealed it. Now it is able to be embraced by both Jews and Gentiles alike.

Paul is aware of his own need for prayer (6:19). Writing during his first imprisonment in Rome, he wasn't beyond fear and worry—for others, if not for himself. Yet he was committed to keep going as long as God gave him the words.

The reference to an ambassador bound in chains (6:20) would have been interpreted as an oxymoron. An ambassador was entitled to diplomatic immunity. The arrest of an ambassador would have been a grave insult to the king who had sent him as well as reflect poorly on the leader of the country who had imprisoned him.

CLOSING COMMENTS

Much of Paul's closing (6:21–22) is verbatim to what he writes in his closing statement to the Colossian church (Colossians 4:7–8). The two letters were probably written at about the same time and were possibly both carried by Tychicus to different groups of Christians living in the Roman province of Asia.

Paul had opened his letter with the words *grace* and *peace* (1:2); here he closes with the same sentiment (6:23–24). If this closing sounds a little less personal than some of his other letters, perhaps it is because Paul intended for this one to circulate among several different churches in the same area—to people whom he hadn't even met. Still, his wish for all who read it is an undying love for the Lord Jesus Christ. It is more than a sign-off. Indeed, it would be difficult to think of a more relevant blessing—and challenge—for all who profess faith in God.

Take It Home

What can be done to help you stand firm in your faith? Consider each piece of a believer's armor, and see which, if any, of them could use some reinforcement:

- The belt of truth
- The breastplate of righteousness
- Feet fitted with the readiness that comes from the gospel of peace (6:15 NIV)
- The shield of faith
- The helmet of salvation
- The sword of the Spirit (The Word of God)
- Prayer on all occasions

PHILIPPIANS

INTRODUCTION TO PHILIPPIANS

Paul's letter to the church in Philippi is remembered for its joyful tone of gratitude against the stark background of the fact that Paul was in prison while writing. Paul writes about the peace, joy, and contentment he finds in Christ, no matter what his situation or circumstances.

AUTHOR

According to Philippians 1:1, the apostle Paul is the writer of this letter. The theology and personal comments fit with what we know of Paul from other writings in the New Testament. Early church fathers and historians also affirmed Paul's authorship.

THE ESTABLISHMENT OF THE CHURCH IN PHILIPPI

Philippi was a city in Macedonia (northern Greece), ten miles from the Aegean Sea. The city was named for Philip II of Macedon, father of Alexander the Great. Though a relatively small city, Philippi was a Roman colony, which meant it received special rights and privileges equivalent to those given to the cities of Italy. Many retired Roman military and other colonists from Rome lived there, creating a sense of prestige and civic pride. When Paul says our true "citizenship is in heaven" (3:20 NIV), this meant something in a place where citizenship was of great value.

The story of the founding of the church in Philippi appears in Acts 16. On Paul's second missionary journey he had a vision in Troas, which prompted him to cross the Aegean Sea (Acts 16:8–12). Philippi was the first town in which Paul preached after he crossed the Aegean Sea, making this the birthplace of European Christianity. Paul's normal pattern was to preach first in the Jewish synagogue, but Philippi had few Jewish residents and no synagogue. So Paul began his ministry at a place of prayer beside the river (Acts 16:13). There he met Lydia, a merchant in purple cloth, who became the first convert in the city (together with her household). Lydia subsequently gave Paul and his missionary companions (Silas, Timothy, and Luke) hospitality and a place to stay (16:15). It was also in Philippi that Paul cast out a demon from a fortune-telling slave girl. This provoked the anger of the girl's owners, who were making a tidy profit from her gifts, and they had Paul and Silas arrested, beaten, and imprisoned as troublemakers. That evening an earthquake miraculously opened the prison doors, and Paul led his Philippian jailer to Christ (Acts 16:12–40). In this way, the church at Philippi was founded (about AD 51).

OCCASION

Paul wrote this letter while in prison (1:7, 13, 19). The place of Paul's imprisonment is not clear from the letter, but the ambiguity doesn't affect the interpretation of the book. Some have suggested that this imprisonment was in Caesarea (Acts 23:33; 24:27) or Ephesus (1 Corinthians 4:9-13; 15:32; 2 Corinthians 1:8-10; 4:8-12; 6:4-11), but the evidence points most strongly to Rome. Paul refers to the "praetorian guard" (1:13 NASB)—Caesar's personal guard—and sends greetings from "those of Caesar's household" (4:22 NASB).

Paul was arrested in Jerusalem after completing his third missionary journey (Acts 21–22). He spent two years in a prison in Caesarea before he made his appeal to the emperor and was sent to Rome (Acts 23–28). The year was AD 59 or 60. Most believe that the Philippians heard Paul was in prison in Rome and, wanting more specific information about him and desiring to help, they again raised a large gift and dispatched Epaphroditus to Rome with the money. Because Epaphroditus experienced a substantial delay, Paul had been in Roman prison approximately one year when he arrived. The sacrificial gift touched Paul deeply.

PURPOSE

When Epaphroditus visited Paul, he also brought news of troubles in the Philippian church: The Judaizing threat had appeared (Jewish Christians claiming Gentiles must first become Jews in order to be saved), financial troubles and other problems were creating doubts about the Philippians' newfound faith, and discord had surfaced in the church. Knowing they were in need of help, they asked Paul to send them Timothy, but he could not come immediately. However, Paul sent back with Epaphroditus this letter full of thanksgiving and encouragement, instruction and correction, and doctrine and exhortation.

THEMES

Philippians includes themes such as joy, humility, self-sacrifice, unity, and Christian living. Partnership in the gospel is a theme and nucleus of the letter. This partnership includes the fellowship of the church with the Spirit (2:1), and the fellowship of the believers with Christ's suffering (3:10–11).

OUTLINE

PHILIPPIANS 1:1-26

OPENING WORDS

Setting Up the Section

Paul opens his letter to the Philippian church with heartfelt words of gratitude and rich blessings. It is in this section that Paul introduces a main theme of Philippians—partnership in the gospel.

📄 **1:1-11**

CHRISTIAN AFFECTIONS

While modern letter writers put the addressee first, first-century letters typically listed the sender first and the addressees second, then a greeting. Thus, this letter begins (1:1). Timothy is mentioned because of his connection with the Philippian church and because the believers had asked for Timothy to be sent to them (2:19).

Paul's use of the word *saints* refers to all the Christians in the Philippian community of faith rather than a super-spiritual subset, as the term sometimes implies today. Paul also mentions the church officers here (1:1), a distinction from his other letters. These people were perhaps instrumental in raising the generous offering that was sent to Paul. They will also likely be the ones who ensure that the Philippians follow Paul's instructions in the letter. The fact that this church had these types of leaders, particularly deacons, indicates that it was well established.

Paul replaces the typical greeting with more of a Christian salutation, "Grace and peace" (1:2 NIV). He identifies the source of that grace and peace as God the Father and Jesus Christ. Jesus' life and work remains a recurring theme throughout this letter.

Paul's mention of joy is significant (1:3–4). His was not an easy situation, yet he found joy in the midst of it. Joy is another key theme (1:19, 25–26) in this letter.

In verse 5, Paul acknowledges that the Philippians had participated in his work. They did this by their financial gifts and the resulting emotional support. The good work that God would continue in these believers (1:6) is not another reference to *their own* good work in generous giving, but rather a reference to *God's* salvation and His continued sanctification of His children.

The Philippians had shared God's grace with Paul (1:7) by supporting him as an evangelist and defender of the faith. In both verses 5 and 7, Paul uses a Greek word meaning "to share" or "partner with." Sharing in God's grace means they share a common experience of Christ's love (1:7). Through their experiences they formed an unbreakable bond. His affection for them (1:8) is visible evidence of this bond.

Paul and the Philippians have a mutual admiration. Because Paul loves them as he does, it is easy to pray for blessings on their behalf. The beautiful prayer he prays for them reveals his affection (1:9–11). He wants the best for them.

The day of Christ (1:10) is a reference to the final judgment of Jesus. Paul is praying for their blamelessness in their day-to-day dealings, but also that their lives will be lived blamelessly overall.

📄 1:12–17

MOTIVES

Verse 12 begins the body of the letter. In contemporary terms, Paul is a missionary and the Philippians have supported his work. The next few verses amount to what we know today as the report a missionary sends home to his supporters. The first thing Paul tells his supporters is that their investment is reaping returns and that his imprisonment, which could be seen as an impediment to the spread of the gospel, has actually, in the plan of God, advanced the gospel. Here's how:

- The praetorians, or palace guards, were an elite force serving as the emperor's body-guards. As Paul met one after another of these soldiers, the knowledge of the gospel began to spread among them. A number of them became Christians, and as a result they began to spread the gospel themselves (1:13–14).
- Being encouraged by Paul's example, Christians in Rome became more daring and fearless in their witness for Christ (1:14). One implication in verse 14 is that evangelism in early Christianity was the work of Christians in general and not left only to the ordained ministry. Much of the evangelism described in the New Testament is the work of apostles and other church officers. But here it seems clear that Paul is talking about Christians in a general sense.

The Christians mentioned in the previous verse include both the rightly motivated and the wrongly motivated (1:15). Paul is willing to say that those who preach Christ out of envy and rivalry are, nevertheless, Christians. He raises no question as to the integrity of the message itself. These people were preaching Christ, but they didn't all have the same opinion about Paul. The genuinely motivated viewed Paul's imprisonment as a consequence of his work. The other group stumbled over it. A real Christian leader, they reasoned, shouldn't be in jail (1:17). Jealous of his prestige, it seems they were trying to outdo him while he was confined. They were taking advantage of an opportunity to preach when Paul could not, perhaps in hopes that in his absence the church would rally around them.

📄 1:18–26

O HAPPY DEATH!

Paul rejoices because the gospel is advancing and for an additional reason—the hope of his own deliverance (1:18–19). When Paul writes about his deliverance, some take him to mean his release from prison (1:19). However, the language he uses is most likely a reference to salvation, and almost certainly his meaning here. In other words, trials and difficulties are part of the means the Lord employs to carry us safely to the end of our pilgrimage. Most scholars believe Paul is quoting from Job 13:16.

Paul will not be put to shame before God (1:20). The eagerness Paul describes here is translated from words that refer to someone straining his or her neck to see what is ahead. (Paul also uses this word in Romans 8:19.) Paul is not worried about God's judgment, nor is he simply celebrating his achievements—he is saying that he has lived the life of a follower of Christ. Having lived such a life, death is the doorway to that happy triumph.

The effectiveness of Paul's work doesn't depend upon whether he lives or dies. In fact, life in this world lived in fellowship with Christ has incomparable advantages, but death has even greater advantages (1:22–25). Paul no longer lives for his own pleasure or makes decisions based on what would be easiest for him. He doesn't expect to go to heaven immediately—his personal preference—but to remain for the sake of the Philippians (and others), who were still in need of his ministry (1:25–26).

Demystifying Philippians

When Paul wrote his letter to the Philippians, he was under arrest in Rome. We know little of the precise details of his imprisonment, but there is reason to believe that by this time Paul was reasonably confident he would eventually be released. In those days, one could never count on a just outcome—Paul had certainly not done anything remotely deserving of Roman punishment, but he was hopeful nonetheless. He would be released and enjoy several more years of ministry before being arrested again and executed in Rome, almost certainly during the reign of the emperor Nero, sometime in the mid-60s, perhaps as early as AD 64.

In the maturity of his Christian life, Paul has come to the place where he actually welcomes death. If he lives he is with Christ, but if he dies he is much more with Christ. For Paul it is proximity to Christ that is the measure of everything.

Paul's welcoming of death may seem strange, but it is not morbid. He is, in fact, happy to spend his life working for the sake of the gospel, and even expects to do so. He is not worried about being exposed to shame in life or death because he is confident that God will approve of him, first because of Christ's perfect righteousness that is his by faith, but also because he has served the Lord faithfully.

PHILIPPIANS 1:27–2:30

FAMILY BUSINESS

Setting Up the Section

This section marks the beginning of the body of Paul's letter. Greetings and personal information out of the way for now, Paul begins his exhortation about the kind of lifestyle the Philippian Christians are called to live.

📖 **1:27–30**

UNITY AND FAITHFULNESS

The Philippians needed to be reminded of their calling to live holy lives worthy of the gospel. When Paul writes of their conduct or lifestyle, he uses Greek language from which modern English words such as *politics* are derived. Paul is hearkening to the citizenry of the Philippians. Philippi was a Roman colony, so these people were citizens of Rome, though they didn't live there. Paul is pointing out to them that they are also citizens of the kingdom of heaven. He refers to this citizenship more directly in Philippians 3:20, but the foundation of the theme can also be found here.

The Philippians were facing opposition (1:28). There does not seem to have been a large community of Jews in Philippi—there was no synagogue—so local opposition would likely have come from Gentiles. Here Paul makes a statement mirroring a theme that runs throughout his writings—those who wish to live godly lives will suffer persecution. The Philippians' suffering is proof of their belonging to God and of their being identified with the Lord Jesus (1:29–30).

📖 **2:1–11**

HUMILITY

Paul's main point of this section is found in the first four verses—a call to holy living.

While Paul asks his readers to make his joy complete, his own joy is not his main concern. His primary concern is the Philippians' unity in love. Rather than rebuke them for disunity, he appeals to the fact that they love him. Their sacrificial actions on his behalf have recently proven the depth and power of that love.

The four brief clauses that complete verse 2 all amount to emphasis on the same thing: spiritual unity. Often in the Bible emphasis is conveyed by repetition, either by repeating the same thing multiple times or emphasizing the point in various ways. Being like-minded does not mean that they should think precisely the same way about everything, but rather that they are one in intentions.

The true obstacle to unity of heart and mind is not based on differences of opinion but is due to selfishness and vanity. Shifting attention away from oneself to others—which, of course, is what Jesus Christ did—is the key to Christian unity (2:4). The fact that Paul has to tell the Philippians this, and later appeal to some members of the church to get along with one another, is proof that Christian unity does not come without effort and attention. Loving unity is as difficult to fulfill as any other part of sanctification.

Verse 5 serves to set up the following verses. When some translations refer to Jesus' mind, it is likely not an actual reference to how or what Jesus thought, but more to His disposition.

The idea in verse 6 is that Jesus, the Son, had in His possession all the attributes and the prerogatives of Almighty God, the Father, but He did not regard His equality with God as something to use to His own advantage.

Critical Observation

Carmen Christi or "Hymn of Christ" is the traditional title for verses 6–11. It has long been thought that these verses were not original to Paul, but are instead the citation of an already existing Christian hymn.

The Greek words translated as Jesus emptying Himself or making Himself nothing (2:7) have led some to believe that Jesus stopped being divine. However, that is not a principle taught elsewhere in the New Testament, and it cannot be the meaning here. Jesus' deity is affirmed both before and after His incarnation—His taking on of human flesh (John 1:1-2, 14, 18). It is Jesus' humility and obedience in the face of His true identity that brings such meaning to His actions (2:7).

The mention of death by crucifixion (2:8) emphasizes the extent of Jesus' sacrifice. Crucifixion was the most degrading and repellent form of execution known to the ancient world.

In verse 9, the focus switches to God's role. Jesus humbled Himself, but God exalted Him. Jesus' teachings include references to this principle—that when we humble ourselves, God will lift us up (Mark 9:35).

Critical Observation

Philippians 2:9–11 describes a universal confession of Jesus' lordship. That does not suggest, however, that each confession is offered willingly. This is more of a statement that Jesus' identity will eventually be acknowledged by all, whether they like it or not.

Paul's mention of every knee bowing to God (2:10) may be a reference to Isaiah 45:23. Paul cites the same text in Romans 14:11, in reference to the Day of Judgment. Both the doomed and the saved will make this confession.

Few passages in the New Testament, apart from the first eighteen verses of the Gospel of John, are as important to the doctrine of the person and work of Jesus Christ as Philippians 2:6–11. It states the following:

1) Jesus existed before there was a baby named Jesus.
2) Jesus is God. The two expressions—"being equal with" and "being in the form of"—mean the same thing.
3) Jesus truly became a human. This is what Christian theology calls the incarnation. As the living God, Jesus did not and could not cease to be God, but He added to Himself true and authentic humanity.

📄 2:12–18

UPRIGHT LIVING

Verses 12–13 are the first part of a subparagraph that extends to verse 18. In typical fashion, Paul follows a general statement of a principle with specific applications of that principle.

The phrase "work out your salvation" (2:12 NIV) is another way of saying "obey." To work out one's salvation is to apply oneself to living in a manner worthy of the gospel of Christ. It is a theme of this whole section. The idea of obedience also connects this statement to the previous verses, which emphasize Christ's obedience, even to the point of death.

Our obedience depends upon God's prior working (2:13). Our work is only made possible by God's grace. This truth reveals the interplay between God's grace and our responsibility. What matters is not that we harmonize the two or that we choose one over the other, but that we believe and live in the reality of both: working to live obedient lives all the while depending upon God's grace in order to be able to do so.

Take It Home

When Paul told his readers to work out their salvation, this was not an encouragement to become a Christian by doing good works. That would be inconsistent with the teachings of the New Testament. But we *are* to work on our own sanctification—the transformation of our lives—and that is a part of salvation in this context. We have been saved, after all, to be conformed to the image of God's Son, and there is work for us to do to that end, even if it is part of that salvation that from beginning to end is the work and the gift of God. This work must be done in and for the community of believers. Unity in love in the body of Christ is always the result of Christians working out their own salvation.

The "awe and reverence" (NET) Paul urges upon us, which is sometimes translated "fear and trembling," is not the same as dread (2:12). It is not insecurity or alarm at the prospect of failure, nor does it require a dark solemnity. You can be in awe of God and be filled with joy at the same time. This awe involves an awareness of your own smallness before the Judge of all the earth. It requires you to accept your proper place as a servant before your God, and then give yourself to obedience with all your heart and mind and strength.

The background of Paul's statement in verses 14–15 is the grumbling of the Israelites in the desert in Exodus 16. In Deuteronomy 32:5, the Israelites in the wilderness are described as a "crooked generation" (NIV). Their grumbling was against God, to be sure, but it was also against their leader—Moses—and against one another. As elsewhere in Paul's letters, Israel is used here as a negative example. This may be due to the fact that as he is writing, the Philippian church is being troubled by Jewish Christians who fail to see that it is not being an Israelite—but faith alone—that makes a person right with God.

How can Christians be described as blameless (2:15) while remaining sinful and still in need of daily confession? Throughout the Bible, terms like *blameless* are applied to people who, while not sinless and perfect, are faithful. A Christian falls short of perfection, to be sure, but he or she is not content with anything but perfect purity and a faultless life.

Verse 15 recollects Jesus' Sermon on the Mount, when Christians are described as the light of the world (Matthew 5:14). Holding out the Word of life is, again, the idea of the ministry of the gospel to others. We are to be light bearers to a dark world. Paul spoke of this earlier in Philippians 1.

Paul refers to being poured out (2:17). In the Jewish sacrificial system, and perhaps the systems of other religions of the day, wine was poured out as a sacrifice on the temple altar, just as the blood of animals were poured out during the animal sacrifices made there. In verses 17–18, Paul uses this reference to the drink offering to convey that even if he should be martyred, he will still rejoice in those he has led to Christ.

📖 2:19–30

GODLY EXAMPLES

At this point Paul returns to his missionary report with information about Timothy (2:19). Timothy was well known to the Philippians since he had been there on Paul's first visit, when the church was founded. Timothy traveled with Paul and was dispatched from time to time to conduct ministry on his own or to encourage a community of believers. Sometimes he was sent to evaluate the circumstances of a particular church when Paul had received a bad report. (The New Testament letters 1 and 2 Timothy are from Paul to this protégé.)

It seems that Paul decides not to send Timothy (2:19, 23) to the Philippians. Still being in prison, Paul probably relied on this close friend and loyal deputy. Apparently, all of Paul's other dependable aides had been dispatched elsewhere (2:21), and he was left with the sort of men he describes in 1:15.

Paul compares Timothy to a son, but that does not mean that Timothy is Paul's biological son. It was common in those days for the relationship between a rabbi and a disciple to be described as that of a father and a son (2:22).

Paul seems to expect a favorable outcome to his legal troubles (2:23–24), but decides it necessary to send Epaphroditus (2:25), who earlier served as the Philippians' emissary to Rome, to inquire after Paul's welfare and to bring him their gift of financial support. Though the journey between Philippi and Rome took roughly forty days, news had reached the Philippians of Epaphroditus's illness (2:26–27). In sending Epaphroditus home, Paul not only ensures the delivery of this letter, but also tends to the natural desire of Epaphroditus to be with his family and friends.

Critical Observation

If Paul thought it better to die than to live—because to die is to depart and be with Christ, as he says in chapter 1—then why is Epaphroditus's healing attributed to God's mercy (2:27)? There are ways in which death is a blessing and ways in which healing is. It was certainly a blessing both to the Philippians and to Paul that Epaphroditus had not died. Though if he had, his death would have been a home-going as much as a departure.

Scholars have wondered why this section concerning Paul's plans for Timothy and Epaphroditus is located here. Shouldn't it have been part of the missionary report in chapter 1? But both Timothy and Epaphroditus serve as examples of the character traits Paul has just been talking about—loving others and putting others first. Timothy and Epaphroditus illustrate the exhortation to love and live in unity that Paul has just completed.

Take It Home

Whether intentional on Paul's part or not, Timothy and Epaphroditus serve as a window on the Christian spirit. Paul appreciates and compliments their highly developed spirit of service and their practical contributions to the work of the gospel and to the lives of other believers. These men were making a difference, and Paul often draws attention to and praises such men. The intention is to make the readers of this letter want to be like these men, to be worthy of praise in the same way Timothy and Epaphroditus were worthy of it.

PHILIPPIANS 3:1–4:1

KNOWING CHRIST

📄 **3:1–11**

PAUL'S FOCUS

It seems as though Paul is approaching the conclusion of his letter, but one thought leads to another and two more chapters are recorded. In any case, Paul indicates that the Philippians have heard his advice about rejoicing before, but it bears repeating (3:1).

Paul warns the Philippians about dogs. Today, calling someone a dog can be an insult (3:2). But in this first-century context, the term was often used by the Jews to discriminate against the Gentiles. Here, though, Paul twists that usage, referring to the Judaizers who tried to make all new converts live according to Jewish law rather than by simply following in the ways of Christ.

The evil men, or "evil/bad workers" (3:2), Paul refers to is a reference to the Judaizers' emphasis on doing the works of the law. They were demanding circumcision of the new converts to Christianity, thus the reference to mutilation of the body.

Demystifying Philippians

Circumcision was an important Jewish ritual. Other cultures circumcised their baby boys, but the Jewish nation circumcised on the infant's eighth day of life, ritually connecting the physical procedure with the spiritual covenant God made with Abraham. In that covenant, circumcision became a symbol for the connection between God and Abraham's descendants, the Jewish nation (Genesis 17:9–14). Part of Christ's message, and thus Paul's, was that faith is a heart issue. A person can follow religious rituals but not participate in a faith relationship with God (Matthew 23:27–29; Romans 2:29).

Philippians 3:3 sums up much of Paul's teaching that believers in Jesus, whether Jew or Gentile, are the true inheritors of the covenant God made with Abraham and Israel. When one becomes a Christian, he or she does not abandon the God of Israel—on the contrary, Abraham's God becomes one's own. Paul characterizes true Christians this way:

- They worship in the Spirit.
- They glory in Christ as Lord and Savior.
- They reject all confidence in their own achievements to obtain peace with God (3:3).

In contrast, the Judaizers who were troubling the church in Philippi probably expected their Jewish credentials to add authority to their messages. But Paul points out that he has all those credentials and more (3:4). He was born from a pure family line of Israelites, he was a strict Pharisee, and he was zealous for the Jewish and Pharisaic viewpoint to the point of being a persecutor of the church in his earlier days (3:5–6). But Paul came to see that all this religious status and achievement had left him spiritually bankrupt (3:7). His confidence before had been in himself, in his own religious performance. When he encountered Christ it became perfectly obvious that his confidence needed to be in Christ, not in himself.

In fact, Paul counts his previous assets as a religious man not only a loss but rubbish as far as God and salvation are concerned. Rubbish is a polite way of putting it (3:8). Some versions use the term *dung*, which is closer to the mark.

On the positive side, there is much to gain when one gains Christ (3:9). Paul writes that a person gains justification (righteousness before God), sanctification (the transformation of life), and glorification (the resurrection from the dead).

True righteousness can be obtained only by abandoning one's own effort and turning in faith to Jesus (3:9). Because of humanity's sinfulness, true righteousness can only be a gift; it will never be an achievement. One receives not only righteousness by faith in Christ but the transformation of life. He or she becomes more Christlike, not without pain and suffering to be sure, but more and more each day, rejecting sinful desires. There will be suffering, as with Christ, and for the same reason, because it is by this means that life is renewed and God's will is made perfect (3:10).

And finally, in Christ, one obtains eternal life, the perfection of the body and soul at the last day (3:11).

Critical Observation

Clearly, Paul was convinced that people cannot be right with God in themselves—no matter how hard they work at it. Only faith in Jesus brings about that righteousness. This theme runs throughout Paul's other letters as well, which make up a large portion of the New Testament. Therefore, to be righteous in Christ is a central proclamation of the New Testament, the heart of the good news of the gospel.

Paul refers to the "before" and "after" of his life here in Philippians 3. He uses his own personal history to make his theology clear. What happened to him happens to everyone who is saved. His experience is unique for its drama and its aftermath, but as the experience of a sinner saved by grace, Paul is every sinner and every Christian.

📄 3:12–16

ALWAYS LEANING FORWARD

Paul's wish in verse 12 is clear. What he doesn't yet have but what he very much wants is perfection—to be everything he ought to be as a follower of Christ. But Paul is also careful to say that his striving after what he does not yet have is the result of Christ in him (3:13). Once again, Paul's attention is thrown forward to the end, the prize, the culmination of salvation at the resurrection and heaven itself (3:14). And, as with everything else in his Christian life, Paul presses on in Christ Jesus, depending upon Him, confident of God's grace through Him, and seeking to please Him.

The word *mature* (3:15) belongs to the same word group as the word *perfect* in verse 12. Is there a touch of irony in Paul's remark here—a dig at some in the church who seem to think that they are already perfect, which Paul admits he is not?

The second statement in verse 15 can seem confusing, as if Paul is saying that the Philippians are free to disagree with him. But it is possible that the disagreement Paul is referring to is not with himself but with one another in the church. He is returning to the idea of chapter 2 and the importance of practicing unity in love. So Paul would be saying, in effect, "If disagreements continue among you, I trust that God will soon bring unanimity." Whatever views they hold at this particular moment about this or that, the Philippian believers must live in accordance with the truth that they have already received (3:16).

Take It Home

We all have past failures. Whatever they may be, forget what is past—both your failures and your successes—and look to what is ahead. Paul says Jesus lived and died that you might be rich in the Word of God and in prayer, avid in worship, bold and courageous in witness, pure and undefiled in speech and behavior, a lover of God and humanity, and a humble and selfless servant of the kingdom of God. That is why Christ took hold of you, so that you might eventually become like Him in every good and holy way. Every day you are to press on to take hold of all of that! More today than yesterday; more tomorrow than today.

3:17–4:1

STANDING FIRM

It is a common theme in the Bible, and certainly in Paul's letters, that believers should imitate those who live godly lives and to beware of those who do not (3:17–18). Paul wants his readers to be as conscious of their own failings as he is of his, and as dependent upon God's grace to keep going on as he knows he must be.

Paul's readers no doubt knew of whom he was referring when he writes of people whose god was their stomachs (3:19). But it is hard for us to know today precisely whom he means. They certainly seem to be immoral people. They may have been a group of professing Christians who had given to lax morals and had been troubling the Philippian church. They would be enemies of the cross because they imagined that Christ's atonement and forgiveness of sins gave them liberty to live immoral lives. They disgraced the cross before the eyes of the world.

This group would not have been the Judaizers because they were not morally lax, but were the opposite. Still, because the Judaizers are the only enemies specifically referred to in this letter, some commentators suggest that the description of these people in verse 19 could be applied figuratively to the Judaizers: a fleshly mind, a concentration on the accomplishments of this world, and a betrayal of their privileges as the chosen people of God. Their "god" being their stomach could then refer to the Judaizers' claim that one must keep the Jewish dietary laws in order to be saved. The Judaizers were, in Paul's mind, certainly enemies of the cross.

In contrast, Paul makes the connection between the hope of the second coming of Christ and the believer's resurrection with the believer's present godly living (3:20–21). Paul has already spoken of believers going to be with the Lord at death. The emphasis, though, falls primarily and ultimately on the resurrection of the body at the end of history and the consummation of salvation that will occur then.

Take It Home

All of chapter 3, leading up to the warmly personal and encouraging summation in 3:20–4:1, develops the theme of standing firm, both against legalistic doctrine (3:1–16) and immorality (3:17–19). Paul's own testimony of placing his faith in God rather than in his own accomplishments (3:4–14) is an example the Philippians could follow in order to be able to stand firm. It is the same for us today.

EPHESIANS 4:2–23

BEST AND WORST PRACTICES

Being Like-Minded	4:2–3
Joy and Peace	4:4–7
Keeping the Heart	4:8–9
Credited to Your Account	4:10–23

Setting Up the Section

The previous section of warning and exhortation ends with verse 1 of chapter 4. What follows is a concluding series of more general exhortations quite typical of Paul's letters. He begins here with somewhat of a rebuke, which is unusually personal for Paul's letters.

📄 4:2–3

BEING LIKE-MINDED

The fact that Paul mentions Euodia and Syntyche by name (4:2) is an indication of how seriously Paul perceives the situation to be in Philippi. The disunity in the church, to which these women obviously were contributing, was a problem that needed to be dealt with directly.

Historically, and still today, there is no denying the influence that women yield in a church. These women had proved their mettle in the work they had done for the cause of the gospel in Philippi. Some have suggested that they were deaconesses, an order of women church workers, that may be referred to in 1 Timothy 3:11 (others think this passage is about wives of deacons). In Romans 16:1, Phoebe is called a "deacon," although this may be a nontechnical use of the term, meaning "servant." We can only guess that these women were deaconesses, since we know very little about this church office and have no more information about them than what Paul mentions here.

It's also unclear as to who Paul is addressing as his "true companion" (NET) in verse 3. He may have been referring to Epaphroditus, mentioned earlier as the one carrying Paul's letter back to Philippi, or to some other prominent leader in the Philippian church. Other scholars have suggested Silas or Luke. Clement of Alexandria, in the second century, even suggested that the reference was to Paul's wife. It is impossible to know for sure.

In any case, Paul does not leave the women to overcome their dispute by themselves. He enlists others in the church to help them. In some respects, he pays a compliment to the Philippian Christians and these two women by addressing the issue so bluntly. It is to the credit of the church that Paul feels free to speak so directly, and it speaks to the maturity of these two women that he is able to address them by name in what is a letter meant to be read to the entire church.

Whatever the issue was with the women, Paul exhorts them to come to an agreement and to become one in their attitude and the direction of their motives, as well as their words and deeds. Paul obviously believes the unity of the church is more important than whatever had separated these women from each other.

Take It Home

Paul's dealings with Euodia and Syntyche remind us to put matters right with anyone with whom we are at odds. In whatever forum you can make it happen, apologize and pledge your love and loyalty. And if you think it is more than you can manage to do, ask someone else to help you. Also, look to Christ for help because it is His will that you be unified among other believers.

📖 4:4–7

JOY AND PEACE

The Philippians were facing both opposition from unbelievers and internal tensions in the congregation. Yet Paul tells them to rejoice (4:4). He has already shown them what it is to have joy. On his first visit to Philippi some years before, he and his associate, Silas, had been arrested, severely beaten, and thrown into prison. And yet they spent their night, bruised and aching, singing hymns to God while the rest of the prisoners listened (Acts 16:25–28).

Given these kinds of situations, Paul is obviously after something more meaningful for Christians than mere happiness with their circumstances. Instead, he writes of true joy, a deep-seated delight in life and in the prospect of the life to come. He writes of joy in the love of God and Christ, in the high purposes for which one may now live his or her life, and in the sense of contentment that comes from the knowledge that we are always in our heavenly Father's all-capable hands—nothing in heaven or on earth can separate us from His love. To have genuine joy, a person must have sources of gladness that are not dependent upon anything in this world of temporary and fleeting things. A human being must be able to look forward and backward without his or her joy being blasted by reality.

Critical Observation

Despite being in prison and facing an uncertain future, Paul writes about his joy and urges the Philippians to rejoice.

- He begins chapter 1 by saying that he prays for the Philippians with joy (1:4).
- In 1:18–19 he rejoices on account of their prayers for him, and he continues his work in hopes of increasing their joy (1:24–25).
- He asks them to make his joy complete (2:2).
- He rejoices with them and urges them to rejoice with him (2:17–18).
- He expects their gladness at seeing Epaphroditus again and urges them to welcome their brother home with joy (2:28–29).
- He urges them to rejoice in the Lord (3:1).
- He describes these believers as his joy and crown (4:1).
- He exhorts them to always rejoice (4:4).

It has often been pointed out that joy is a particular emphasis of the Bible, as it is here. From Psalms to Philippians, joy is a characteristic mark of biblical faith. When Paul tells us to rejoice in the Lord always (4:4), it is a command. Christian joy is an act of obedience. This joy of which Paul speaks is something that should be true of every Christian life.

Paul's next exhortation has to do with gentleness (4:5). This carries with it the ideas of patience and graciousness. Given the fact that the church was facing some opposition, Paul reminds the believers to be gentle-spirited, as Jesus Himself was. In 2 Corinthians 10:1, Paul refers to "the meekness and gentleness of Christ" (NIV), using the same word as here.

Why should Christians be gentle? Because the Lord is near. The word *near* can mean near in terms of either space or time. Either would make sense, and both are reasons for Christians to face the difficulties posed by other people with patience and grace.

There is a proper kind of concern for others. The proof of that is Timothy's concern for the Philippians' welfare (2:20). The same word is used in 4:6 and is often translated "anxious." This anxiety that Paul commands his readers to lay aside (4:6), however, is unreasonable worry—worry that distracts and results from a forgetfulness toward God.

If the Philippian believers heed Paul's exhortations in verses 4–6, God's peace will protect them (4:7). The Greek word translated as "guard" is a military term describing an army surrounding a city. God's peace will fill their hearts as they live their lives thanking Him and looking to Him for their needs.

Critical Observation

Don't be anxious, Paul exhorts in verse 6. Being anxious is the practical opposite of the peace of God. But, of course, in those simple words hangs a great tale. Most people imagine true peace to be the condition of having nothing to worry about. For Paul, true peace is *not* being anxious in the midst of problems, difficulties, sorrows, and disappointments that one must face in life. This peace, God's peace, is a condition that fills a heart in defiance of expectations, no matter the existence of reasonable fears and crushing disappointments.

📄 **4:8–9**

KEEPING THE HEART

Now Paul turns to the issue of involvement in God's work. When Paul strings terms together as he does here (4:8), the inevitable question is whether each term bears a distinct meaning or whether Paul is adding one to another for effect. There is a fair measure of overlap in meaning between these terms. The difficulty of making precise distinctions is increased by the fact that five of the words in Paul's list are not words he commonly uses, and two of the eight qualities are mentioned only once in the New Testament. It is safe to assume, though, that this list is not definitive but is representative of the kinds of things a believer should focus his or her mind on. The connotation of the verb used to conclude verse 8 (*think*) is that our minds should *continually* be thinking about these kinds of things.

Paul summarizes by saying that his readers are to live according to the teaching they have received from him and the example he has set for them (4:9). Paul is saying that the virtues here are not only to be pondered and reflected on, but practiced, and practiced in the context of the gospel and of faith in Christ.

Take It Home

In verses 7–9, Paul is saying, in different words and more specifically, what the author of the opening chapters of Proverbs said: "Guard your heart with all vigilance, for from it are the sources of life" (Proverbs 4:23 NET).

And Paul is not simply encouraging the act of guarding one's heart; he is instructing us how to do that. We are to devote our hearts—our thinking, especially, as the end of verse 8 makes clear, but our feelings and our will as well—to do what is good and pleasing to God. The result will be that Christ will come down from His high throne and make His presence known within us.

CREDITED TO YOUR ACCOUNT

Though this book is a first-century letter and is prompted by specific circumstances to the situation then prevailing in the Philippian church, this section contains a beautiful account of the Christian faith and the life that is to flow from it—an account that is timeless in its application.

The section opens with Paul's specific thanks for the financial support the Philippians sent his way. Verse 10 refers to Epaphroditus's journey to Rome with the monetary gift for Paul. While Paul's initial statement can sound a little backhanded in the English translation, verses 11–13 clarify that Paul was not sitting and waiting for the Philippians to bail him out of this situation. God remained his hope, yet he was thankful for the help of this community.

Paul teaches that churches should support those who guide them in the faith, but his first-century role in the Christian church was not one that was regularly funded. He had travel and food costs, which sometimes required him to stop and work. He also depended on the hospitality of church members and the gifts he received along the way. While he was probably well-off before his conversion from Pharisee to Christ-follower, he would have understood both ends of the spectrum.

Paul's claim to have found contentment in every situation is testimony to the fact that he well understood that everything, including himself, belonged to God. His was not a contentment that came from self-will or self-discipline. It came from an understanding that Jesus was his strength, no matter the situation (4:12–13).

To make sure that the Philippians understand the measure of his appreciation for their generosity, Paul tells them that he has not forgotten the unique place they have had in his heart from the beginning, some ten years before, when they generously supported his ministry when no one else did (4:14–16). The significance of the mention of Thessalonica is that it is the next major town on the Roman road from Philippi to Athens. So Paul had scarcely left Philippi before their gifts reached him.

Paul's greatest interest is not in what he could receive from the Philippians' generosity but what they will receive from giving (4:17). The term he uses to describe the return on their investment in him can mean the profit gained in business, and here means something like the interest that would accrue on someone's investment account. While the Philippian church was not a wealthy church, the gifts the believers sent Paul were a great blessing to him and fully met his needs. More important, they were pleasing to God (4:18), and they reflected the Philippians' faith in the truth of verse 19, that God would take care of them.

Verse 20 functions as a kind of doxology, and then Paul sends his final greetings. The "brothers" who were there with him probably included Timothy (4:21). Assuming Paul was in Rome, his reference to all the other Christians refers to all the believers there in the Roman Christian church (Romans 16:1–15).

Paul's mention of Caesar's household reveals a bit of history: The Christian faith had spread even to some who worked for the Roman government (4:22).

Paul gave his life to proclaim the good news of Jesus; he traveled the world with that message. He was Christ's ambassador, preaching to everyone who would listen that God was, in Christ, reconciling the world to Himself. He began this letter with this grace, and he ends with it as well (1:2; 4:23). Only the Bible says that for people to be saved and to rise to eternal life, God has to intervene on their behalf, and in love He did so.

COLOSSIANS

INTRODUCTION TO COLOSSIANS

The New Testament letter to the Colossians presents the person and work of Jesus Christ as the Savior, the Creator, and the Sustainer of the universe and the total solution for humanity's needs, both for time and eternity.

AUTHOR

The author of this letter identifies himself as the apostle Paul (1:1; 4:18). Some modern scholars have questioned this, claiming differences in vocabulary, style, and theology. These differences are minor, however, and are best accounted for by the unique topics covered in the letter. Furthermore, the letter is closely connected to the letter to Philemon, which is widely accepted as authentic, and the two letters were probably sent together (same town, same letter carrier; many of the same companions of Paul are named). No challenges to Paul's authorship were expressed in the early church. We can confidently assert that Paul was the author.

PURPOSE

Paul's purpose in writing Colossians was threefold: (1) to express his personal interest in the Colossians (1:3–4; 2:1–3); (2) to warn them against reverting to their old pagan vices (3:5 and following); and (3) to counteract a particular theological heresy that was being promoted within the church at Colossae (2:4–23). The Colossian heresy wore the mask of Christianity, but it was false.

OCCASION

Several years after the church was established, around AD 61–62, Epaphras traveled to Rome to visit Paul during his first Roman imprisonment. While Epaphras brought some good news regarding the Colossian assembly (1:4, 7–8; 2:5), it appears his primary purpose for visiting was to solicit Paul's help against a certain heresy (or heresies) that was eating its way into the Colossian church.

Paul wrote this letter to counter this false teaching. The epistle was sent to the Colossians by the hand of Tychicus (4:7). In the meantime, Epaphras stayed with Paul, perhaps forced to because of his own imprisonment (4:12; Philemon 23), but surely also for instruction and encouragement from Paul.

THEMES

The main theme of the book of Colossians is the supremacy of Christ and the power of the gospel message. Christ is the object of the Christian's faith because He is God's Son, the Redeemer, the very image of God, the Lord of creation, and the head of the church (1:13–18). It is through Him and because of new life in Him that we are to put away our old manner of life and live according to His grace.

HISTORICAL CONTEXT

Colossae is located about one hundred miles east of Ephesus. At one time the city had been large and populous, but when Paul wrote to the Colossian church, it had become a small town in comparison to its nearest neighbors, Hierapolis and Laodicea (4:13). Though small, Colossae of Paul's day was still a cosmopolitan city with different cultural and religious elements that were mingled together. For the most part, the inhabitants of the area were Gentiles, but there was a considerable quantity of Jews among them.

As far as we know, Paul never visited Colossae, at least not by the time he wrote this epistle (1:4, 9; 2:1). Nevertheless, the community of faith there was a product of his ministry in nearby Ephesus. A young man named Epaphras, who went to Ephesus and evidently heard the gospel from Paul there, is credited with taking the message to Colossae. He was trained and prepared by Paul to go back and plant a church in his hometown (1:7; 4:12).

Though there was a significant Jewish population in the Lycus Valley, the Colossian Epistle suggests that the membership of the church was primarily Gentile. Within the letter to the Colossians, there are not many Old Testament references and almost no reference to the reconciliation of Jews and Gentiles that is found in Ephesians.

OUTLINE

COLOSSIANS 1:1–2:3

THE PERSON AND WORK OF JESUS

Paul's Greeting	1:1–8
Paul's Prayer	1:9–14
The Supremacy of Jesus	1:15–18
The Supremacy of Jesus' Work	1:19–2:3

Setting Up the Section

The apostle Paul follows the customary form of greeting for first-century letters. He first identifies himself as the author, with his associate Timothy, and then identifies his recipients, followed by a brief greeting. However, he seasons the greeting with terms that focus on the letter's distinctively Christian character. These first fourteen verses prepare the Colossian readers for the words of warning and the exhortations that will follow. At the same time, these introductory words provide today's readers with insight into the church at Colossae and their growth in Christ.

PAUL'S GREETING

Paul introduces himself as an apostle by God's will. By doing this, he establishes his authority and the Colossians' responsibility to listen. This description further stresses that Paul's position as an apostle is not something he had sought or earned. It was a calling (1:1; see also 1 Corinthians 1:1; Galatians 1:1; 2 Timothy 1:1).

As for his readers, Paul identifies them spiritually in relation to their position in Christ and physically in relation to their geographical location (*at* Colossae)—a reminder of the two spheres in which believers live (1:2).

When Paul speaks of saints (1:2), or "holy" (NIV) brothers, he is not speaking of a special class of Christians who have achieved a certain level of holiness. This is a term used for all believers because of who they are in Christ.

There is an element of prayerful intercession in Paul's greetings. At the same time, he is challenging his readers to a renewed commitment to know, comprehend, and live by the grace of God.

Note that Paul uses possessive pronouns (*our, we* [1:2-3]). This is a reflection of the unity Paul addresses later in this letter.

Critical Observation

As we move into the body of Paul's letter to the Colossians, we get a glimpse of Paul's prayer life. Somewhere in the early portion of almost all of his epistles, Paul begins with either thanksgiving or praise to God. This becomes even more significant when you stop to realize that Paul wrote this letter while under house arrest.

Paul and Timothy had evidently never been to Colossae and did not know the church personally (2:1-2), but verse 4 reveals that they had heard of the faith that existed among the Colossians and of their love for all the saints.

Colossians 1:5 mentions "hope that is stored up" (NIV). Though centered in the person of Christ Himself (1:27), the place of storage is heaven, a place of security and protection where the corruption of this present world cannot touch it.

The term *gospel* (1:5) is the translation of the Greek noun that means "good news," and the Greek verb that means "to bring or announce good news." The reference to the gospel as "the grace of God in truth" (1:6 NET) is naturally aimed at the false teachers who were seeking to add some form of religious works to the gospel. Paul will deal with this in chapter 2.

Verses 6-8 reveal how the Colossians heard the gospel—Epaphras brought the gospel to the city of Colossae. This not only highlights the ministry of Epaphras and puts Paul's approval on his ministry, but also contrasts it against the destructive heresy being taught by the false teachers. What the Colossians had heard and learned from Epaphras was God's truth.

The name *Epaphras* is undoubtedly a shortened form of *Epaphroditus*. His name is mentioned again in 4:12 and in Philemon 23. This Epaphras should not be confused with Epaphroditus, who is mentioned in Philippians 2:25 and 4:18, and was apparently from Macedonia.

Finally, with verse 8, Paul again calls attention to the love of the Colossians linked to the work of the Spirit. This would again highlight the effectiveness of the teaching and ministry of Epaphras, for it was through him that they had learned about the Spirit-led life (Galatians 5:22–23).

📖 1:9–14

PAUL'S PRAYER

In Colossians 1:9–14, Paul moves from thanksgiving to a very specific petition. Paul's prayers are not only brief and explicit, but they are spiritually strategic in nature. To counter the false knowledge of the heretics, Paul prays for a full and more penetrating knowledge of God's will. Two of the terms he uses, *bearing fruit* and *growing*, suggest the figure of a tree to describe God's desire for the church, the body of Christ. It calls to mind the words of Jeremiah 17:8 and Psalm 1:3.

The content and purpose of Paul's prayer is found in his request that God would fill the Colossians. The idea is that they would be filled up and running over.

Paul prays for two things for the Colossians: (1) that his readers would have a full knowledge of God's will (1:9), and (2) that, as a result, they might live in a manner worthy of the Lord (1:10). Both are necessary. Verse 9 without verse 10 is incomplete and falls short of the will of God, but verse 10 without verse 9 is impossible.

In this context, Paul's request focuses on the impact that a proper understanding of the person and work of Jesus should have on one's spiritual walk. In this case, God's will refers to the complete rule of faith and practice.

The ultimate aim of Paul's prayer is to influence the Colossians' conduct day after day. Paul is not saying that one can become worthy of God's love and grace by good works or manner of life. To walk in a manner worthy of the Lord means to walk in a way that is commensurate, fitting, and consistent with who the Lord is and what the Lord has done, is doing, and will do in the future. The implication is that a Christian's life should bring credit to the grace of God in Christ.

In verses 10–12, Paul describes the results of a walk that is pleasing: bearing fruit, growing, being strengthened, and giving thanks to the Father.

The verb translated "bearing fruit" (NIV) is the same verb used in verse 6. Being fruitful in every good work is a call to be balanced and productive. As a result of that productivity, one must never stop growing (1:10). "Being strengthened" (1:11 NIV) carries the idea of strengthening someone who is inherently weak (Ephesians 6:10; 2 Timothy 2:1). More than that, though, the term is in the present tense and points to the constant source that is available to believers through Christ.

Paul also lists giving thanks as a product of a life that is growing by the knowledge of God. Paul does not just tell his readers to be thankful, but points them to four blessings they possess through the work of Jesus. God has:

1) *qualified* us to share in the inheritance of the saints (1:12);

2) *delivered* us from the power of darkness (1:13);

3) *transferred* us to the kingdom (1:13); and

4) given us *redemption*, the forgiveness of sins, through Christ (1:14).

THE SUPREMACY OF JESUS

From his prayerful concern for the Colossians, the apostle moves quickly into the main focus of this letter—the exaltation and preeminence of Jesus in His person and work. Colossians 1:15–18 has been called "The Great Christology," because it sets forth Paul's inspired conviction and understanding of who Jesus Christ is.

- He is the manifestation of God (1:15). To know what God is like, one must look at Jesus (John 1:14–18; 12:45; 14:7–10; Hebrews 1:3).
- He is the firstborn of creation (Colossians 1:15). This is not saying that Jesus was the first to be created by God; "firstborn" refers instead to Jesus' preeminent position over all creation.
- He is the Creator and Sustainer of the universe (1:16). Paul is describing the all-encompassing scope of Christ's authority—thrones, dominions, principalities, and powers—which includes the invisible world of angels and demons. (With the Colossian heresy in mind, Paul stresses the hierarchy of angelic powers.)
- He is before all things (1:17). Note that Paul says Jesus is before all things rather than *was*. This is Paul's way of saying what Jesus said Himself in John 8:58. It also hearkens back to God's claim to Moses to be the "I Am" (Exodus 3:13–14).

In Colossians 1:18, Paul affirms Christ's superiority and supremacy over a new creation, the church. The Colossians must recognize that the Creator of the cosmos is also supreme head of the church as their Savior. He is the source, power, and originating cause of the life of the church.

The statement that Christ was "the first to be raised from death" (CEV), explains why Jesus is the origin and life of the church. The emphasis by context is on Christ's supremacy in time. He is the first one to break the hold of death in a glorified body by virtue of the Resurrection. As such, He is the beginning of a new creation of God.

THE SUPREMACY OF JESUS' WORK

In verses 12–14, Paul encourages the Colossians to give thanks for what God has done for them through His beloved Son. Here, he moves from the person of Christ to a powerful declaration of the work of Christ.

God was pleased that His fullness dwelt in Christ (1:19). *Fullness* means "the sum total." *Dwell* means "to reside, to settle down." Most expositors understand this as a powerful affirmation of Christ's deity (which it is), but the context of this verse is about the work of reconciliation. It might be better to understand *fullness* in reference to *the fullness* of God's plan of reconciliation. Paul is declaring that the fullness of God's saving provision resides totally in the work of Christ through the blood of the cross. Nothing else can be added to the work of the Son.

In verse 20, the phrase "through Him" (NIV) points to Christ as the sole agent of reconciliation. If there is to be reconciliation to God, it must come from God Himself. In this case, reconciliation is not accomplished through the work of both parties, but only one—God reconciles humanity. This verse also makes the point that the cross is a vital and necessary part of reconciliation.

Demystifying Colossians

What does Paul mean when he says all things—heaven and earth—will be reconciled (1:20)? This is not a reference to universal salvation—that all will be saved in the end. This points to the completeness of the plan of God for the whole universe.

Verses 19–20 focus on how the reconciling work of Christ extends to the whole creation. But with the opening words of verse 21, Paul narrows his focus from all of creation to the believers in Colossae. The emphasis is now on God's purpose and plan of sanctification (spiritual growth and transformation). The purpose of God's plan of reconciliation is personal holiness in His people.

Paul's reference to Christ's physical death (1:22) stresses a vital truth of the New Testament—Jesus is the only one perfectly qualified to deal with the problem of sin by dying in our place. He was undiminished deity. This means He gives not just life, but eternal life and God's imputed righteousness. In verse 22, the phrase "holy, without blemish, and blameless" (NET) pertains to this element of sanctification, and the picture of believers being *presented* refers to the final judgment of Christ.

The purpose of God's work of reconciliation in Christ through the cross is holiness. The holy person is one who is set apart to God from the world. The apostle has in mind the growth in holiness that comes through resting in the accomplished work of Christ.

This leads into both a positive affirmation and a negative warning (1:23). The positive element is the fact that the Colossians don't need to *begin* to be established, they only need to *continue* being established. They are already on the right path. The negative warning is the danger of moving away from the truth.

In this context, the word *established* means "to be built a foundation." Christ's person and finished work constitutes the only rock on which one may build his or her life. The idea of being firm in the faith points to the results of being built on such a foundation. In other words, remaining in the faith, the truth of the gospel as Epaphras had presented it to them, is the only way these Colossian believers, or any believer, can become established and steadfast, and thus protected from the shifting sands of the false teachings found in the world.

The hope that is in the gospel is a living hope through Christ's resurrection. The focus on the term *hope* (1:23) includes the confident expectation of spiritual transformation—the result of the indwelling Christ.

Paul's reference to the words the Colossians had heard is to Epaphras, who brought the message to the Colossians as he had received it from Paul. This once more approves the faithful work of Epaphras and becomes a warning against listening to the wrangling of the false teachers.

By mentioning his own service to the gospel, Paul connects with the Colossians. Epaphras was a servant trained by Paul to carry this message to others, but its path to Epaphras came through the apostolic preaching of Paul, one commissioned directly by the Lord Jesus.

Verses 21–23 stress that the same thing that is true of faith in Christ for salvation is equally true for sanctification—we can't add anything by our own efforts. To add any system of religious works that would somehow serve to justify oneself before God is only to diminish the faith one should have in Jesus.

Paul continues with thoughts on his own suffering. Three things characterize the suffering Paul mentions in verse 24: (1) It was a source of joy; (2) It was for others—for the Colossians and for the sake of the church; and (3) It was related to the sufferings or afflictions of Christ. The false teachers in Colossae may have been claiming that Paul's suffering diminished his ministry, but that was not the case.

Paul claims the preaching of God's message was not an honor and duty that he took upon himself, one that he could either take or leave. Rather, it was an appointment that came directly from God (1:25). The makeup of Paul's message is described as (1) the Word of God, (2) the mystery hidden in the Old Testament but revealed through Jesus, and (3) Christ in the believer, the hope of glory (1:26–27).

What exactly does the apostle mean by "the hope of glory"? It is the confident expectation of the formation of Christ in and through the life of all believers. Glory is the manifestation of the Lord Jesus in us so that we experience Him in attitude, faith, action, and reaction.

How is Christ proclaimed? By instruction and teaching (1:28). Instructing carries with it the idea of warning, counsel, or admonishment. There is a moral appeal for spiritual change, and with teaching there is a doctrinal emphasis. Paul's goal through this instruction and teaching is to present every believer mature in Christ.

The biblical objective of seeing all believers grow and mature in Christ was certainly a captivating force that directed Paul's life, but to accomplish such a goal requires nothing less than God's supernatural power (1:29). "Struggling" (NIV) is a Greek term that means "to engage in an athletic contest." The apostle labored, struggling hard in the task God had given him, but not struggling in his own strength alone.

At the close of chapter 1, Paul declares his struggle to see the Gentiles come to know and grow to maturity in Christ (1:28–29), but as chapter 2 opens, he makes it clear that his message is for everyone (2:1–3). The treasures of wisdom and knowledge are hidden in Christ, but not in the sense that they are concealed. Instead, they are stored up in one place only, and that is in Christ alone.

Take It Home

We can only be truly successful when we learn to live and minister by the unseen presence of the risen Christ and allow Him to work *in*, *through*, and *with* us as the source and power for our ministries. It's often too easy to seek to manipulate, coerce, and force people into spiritual change or Christian service. That may produce some results, but that's not God's method or means. The Lord Jesus, as the unseen power of our lives, works when we relinquish control and draw upon Him through prayer, faith in the truth of Christ, and by means of the control of the Spirit.

COLOSSIANS 2:4–23

THE HERESY

Setting Up the Section

In this passage, Paul addresses the issue of the false teachers among the Colossians. His arguments, however, are never far removed from the doctrinal truth regarding the person and work of Christ. With the exhortation regarding the methods of the false teachers (2:4–5), Paul sets forth the dangers facing the Colossians. With the exhortation to progress in the faith (2:6–7), he sets forth the means of protection: living in Christ. Finally, with the exhortation regarding the philosophy of the false teachers (2:8), his warning focuses on the danger of being tricked by empty philosophy.

📄 **2:4–8**

STANDING AGAINST FALSE TEACHERS

Why would the Colossian believers listen to the false arguments of these heretical teachers when they knew the One in whom all the treasures of wisdom and knowledge are found (2:3)? Because, as Paul says, the arguments regarding the heresy are false, but they are also persuasive (2:4).

The false teachers employed tricky methods—seemingly reasonable arguments. They were probably promoting *some* of the tenets of biblical Christianity, so their system of knowledge sounded reasonable. Nevertheless, these false teachers were failing to hold fast to Christ as the supreme head from whom the body of Christ draws all her resources (2:18–19).

With verse 5, Paul explains his protectiveness toward the Colossians. He is with these believers in spirit. He rejoices over their "morale" and "firmness" in faith (NET). These terms were sometimes used in military contexts and may here bring out the reality of spiritual warfare. The Greek word translated "morale" (NET) can mean "orderly" (NIV), "disciplined" (TNIV), or even "unbroken ranks" (REB). *Firmness* has the connotation of "steadfastness, solid bulwark, or phalanx." In ancient times, a phalanx consisted of a formation of infantry carrying overlapping shields and long spears. The content of the Colossians' solidarity was their "faith in Christ." Though being attacked by the false teaching, they had not broken ranks to follow the false teaching of the heretics pursuing the church at Colossae.

Verses 6–7 reveal a believer's protection against all false teaching—remaining in Christ. Paul offers four descriptions for remaining in Christ:

1) Being rooted. Through faith, there is an organic union established with Jesus from which comes an ongoing source of life.

2) Being built up. This describes the steady growth of the spiritual structure of the believer's life.

3) Being strengthened. This is a call not to merely hold to faith, but to grow in the knowledge of the faith.

4) Being thankful. Constant, overflowing thankfulness directs one's thoughts to God and what He has done and is doing in and through the Savior.

The idea of being taken captive (2:8) here is to be carried off by an enemy army as booty from a conquest. How is the conquest made? Through empty, deceitful philosophy. This does not imply that Paul is against philosophy as a discipline. His use here of the concept of philosophy is humanity's wisdom versus God's wisdom. In humanity's spiritual blindness, our own powers of reason appear attractive, but lead us away from Christ.

📖 2:9–15

THE TRUTH

The Colossians needed to hear and understand the truth of the gospel because they were being told that there is more to being a Christian than just Jesus Christ. In order to counteract this false philosophy, Paul must tell them exactly who Christ is. Therefore, Paul begins with the character of Christ.

Verse 9 says that the full nature of God dwells within Jesus. This means Jesus is completely full of the divine nature; there is not one aspect of His nature that is lacking any divinity. When Christ came to earth, God came to earth.

As a result of Christ's character, believers now are complete in Him because they become partakers of Him. Salvation is not just a philosophy; it is not just an event. It is the partaking of the very nature of Christ. We do not become God, but His righteousness lives within us. In verse 10, the word for "complete" (NKJV) is the same word for "fullness" (NKJV) found in verse 9. Both carry the idea of lacking in nothing, filled to completion. Believers are given all they need at the point of salvation; there is nothing more that one needs to add.

Paul concludes this thought with a description of the authority of Jesus. In essence, all competing thoughts and all competing philosophy must fall subject to Him. Paul is elevating Christ as above all other competing teachings that the Colossians were being exposed to.

Paul then uses three descriptions of what happened at the Colossians' salvation (2:11–15):

- *Circumcision.* Paul probably uses this description because the Colossians were facing Judaizers, those who taught that one must follow Jewish customs—such as circumcision—to follow Jesus. Paul tells his readers that they have been spiritually circumcised already in Christ, and there is no need to be circumcised physically.
- *Burial.* This is the identification with the death of Christ. Paul uses the word *burial* because it signifies the completion of the death process. The death of Christ is the moment that our punishment was lifted, and sin was dealt a death blow.

Critical Observation

Paul also associates this burial with *baptism,* using the word in its figurative sense, as the identification with that moment of death and rebirth. When Jesus took the penalty for humanity's sin, believers were buried with Him.

- *Resurrection.* The resurrection of Jesus signifies the new life of a believer. Because God raised Jesus from the dead, every believer has been given new life. Salvation is complete. We have been forgiven. As a result, believers now have victory over sin because Christ broke the power over sin and death.

Verse 14 goes on to explain just how that victory happened—the certificate of debt was canceled. Paul uses a common Greek expression for a debt certificate, a legal document declaring that one person owed another a certain sum of money. Paul says God canceled our debt of sin by nailing it to the cross. This means Christ paid the debt that we owed by taking on Himself the penalty for our sins.

Take It Home

In truth, every person has a certificate of debt before God—a list of decrees that need to be paid to Him. But through Jesus' death, God canceled our certificate, taking it out of the way. We have complete forgiveness in Christ.

Paul concludes this description of salvation by explaining that believers have complete victory over Satan and the stronghold he once had (2:15). In this verse, Paul develops an image that he touched on in verse 8. It is the picture of the victorious soldiers bringing home the captured troops and parading them around to show that the once feared enemy is no longer a threat. The resurrection of Christ is the public display that Satan has no power over death.

THE OBLIGATIONS OF THE TRUTH

In verse 16, Paul declares no one has the right to judge the Colossians based on religious practices because they have been brought into a perfect relationship with God through Jesus Christ.

The false teachers judged the Colossians on the basis of two things: forbidden practices and required rituals. The forbidden practices probably refer to the dietary laws of the Jewish system (2:16), which required abstinence from certain foods and drink (Leviticus 11 and Deuteronomy 14). These false teachers were condemning the Colossians for not following these practices.

The false teachers were also requiring the Colossians to observe the religious celebrations and observances (2:16). *Festival* refers to the yearly religious celebrations. *New moon* refers to the monthly celebrations. The *Sabbath* refers to the weekly Sabbath celebration.

Simply, the Colossians were facing legalism. Believers are not to follow certain rules in order to maintain their faith; they choose their practices and lifestyle *because* of their faith. Therefore, they are able to live out the intent of the law, rather than just the rules of it. This law represents the "shadow of things to come" (2:17 NIV). What is the reality that the law foreshadowed? The reality of Jesus.

Critical Observation

Verse 17 is one of the key verses in this letter. It defines the heart of the issue and a clear resolution to the problem. The law was not intended to save people or to make them holy. The purpose of the law was to point to Christ, who saves and makes us holy.

Paul warns the Colossians not to be disqualified by the false teachers in their midst (2:18). To allow these people to judge them is to lose the prize God had for them—being complete in Christ.

The picture Paul is painting of the heresy is that of a teaching that requires denial of earthly things in order to achieve a spiritual reality. The humility of these teachers is false because it is a denial of the flesh but has no spiritual substance to it. Though it might appear to be a sign of humility to simply deny worldly pleasures, it is no humility at all if it is not based on Christ. To find spirituality by self-will is not the teaching of Jesus.

Verse 18 indicates these false teachers were involved in some type of angel worship. While the actual practice described here has been debated, it is likely that this heresy taught that God was too holy to be worshiped directly, and therefore, a mediator was needed. These teachers may have considered that the angels' role. This is a denial of Jesus' role as that mediator.

Paul also explains that a false teacher bases his teaching on his own subjective reasoning and personal experiences rather than on the Old Testament and Jesus' teachings. Paul declares that anyone who would elevate his visions as more important than the Word of God is arrogant and working out of a fleshly mind, not a mind controlled by God (2:18–19).

Paul gives the root of the false teacher's problem—he denies the Head (2:19), which in this context refers to Jesus (1:18; 2:10). The mystic teacher ignores Jesus and thus takes away His role of being the teacher and sanctifier of the church.

Demystifying Colossians

Observe the way that Paul describes the body of Christ in verse 19. The significance of this is that we are joined together as one body. The reality of this is that what we do individually affects the entire body. If one member of the body buys into false teaching, the entire body will be affected. Paul is telling the Colossians they are all one body, and Christ is the head of that body—they must reject this false teacher together.

Verses 20–23 summarize the warning Paul has just given. In verse 20, Paul says we have died with Christ to the elementary principles of the world. In this context, the world represents the system that is opposed to Christ and His grace. The elementary principles refers to the philosophy already mentioned in verse 8, the system of human logic that says humanity can right itself, by itself, without the work of Jesus.

Not only are believers free from this godless philosophy, but they are also free from the law. The rules Paul refers to do not have any eternal value; they only deal with the here and now. Notice the way Paul explains it—these rules refer to things that will perish (2:22), not the condition of the heart or the state of the soul.

Paul says that these matters seem to appear wise, but they are of no use in the battle against sinful desires (2:23). One can't, in his or her own will, keep from sinning. That is why Jesus came. The discipline of a person has no ability to change the heart; all he or she can do is modify behavior, and even that is not possible without the help of Christ.

COLOSSIANS 3:1–4:1

THE WAY TO LIVE LIKE JESUS

Setting Up the Section

Paul now shifts gears from the negative to the positive. He tells the Colossians how they are to experience true spirituality in this world. Rather than subjecting themselves to the bondage of the false teachers, they are to understand who they are in Christ, and experience the true freedom that comes from that knowledge.

Instead of thinking that the flesh must be contained by human philosophy, religious legalism, or spiritual mysticism, they are to understand that in Christ, the flesh has been killed on the cross. They must think of themselves as dead to sin and alive to God.

📄 **3:1–4**

THINK LIKE A LIVE PERSON

Paul begins chapter 3 by explaining that the only logical reality for believers is this: Since they have died to the flesh, the world, and the law, then each must be a new creation. And in all reality they are, because they have been raised with Christ.

Paul is declaring in verse 1, that since his readers are now alive in Christ, they will seek those things that belong to Christ and not the things of the world. That is the reality, as well, for all believers.

The word translated "seek" (NRSV) in 3:1 is a present tense imperative (command) in the Greek, indicating that this is a continual, daily practice of seeking; that is why some translations put the word *keep* in front of the word *seeking* ("keep seeking" NET). It is to be a process that occurs all the time as a manner of life.

What are the things above that believers are to seek (3:1)? They are the spiritual realities that are available through Christ. What does it mean to do this seeking? It is cultivating the desire for spiritual food and God's will, rather than the things of earth.

The heartbeat of this passage is that the Colossians must continually, as a way of life, seek Jesus Christ as the source of all of their spiritual victory. The intentions of their life's passions must be to see Jesus as the source of salvation, sanctification, and their future glorification.

Notice the way Paul describes Christ at the end of verse 1: seated at the right hand of God. This helps us understand Jesus' position of authority and power.

Paul writes that the Colossians should also set their minds on the things above, not on the things of earth (3:2). This means they are to set every aspect of their ability and reason to dwell on their salvation in Christ. Understanding Christ, they will understand who they should be—thus they become transformed.

Notice the contrast between things above and things on the earth in verse 2. This image contrasts the wisdom of humanity with the wisdom of God. Throughout this letter, Paul has been comparing human wisdom with God's wisdom, which produces true righteousness through Christ.

In verses 3 and 4, Paul gives the Colossians the fundamental reason they need to seek Christ with such determination. First, their spiritual lives are hidden in Christ. This means they were crucified and buried with Christ. Next, they will be revealed with Jesus when Christ calls believers home and judges the earth. They will be transformed and stand before God, holy and blameless, robed in the righteousness of Christ.

📄 **3:5–10**

LIVE LIKE A DEAD PERSON

The Colossians must, as a result of being alive in Christ, be in the daily process of putting sin to death in their own lives. While through the work of Jesus believers stand righteous before God, they are still responsible to grow into that position of righteousness.

First, believers must set their minds on the pursuit of God (3:1–4). Verses 5–11 are the natural result of living in that pursuit.

The difference between what Paul is teaching compared to the false teachers of Colossae is that these believers need to kill the root of the problem of sin through the power of Christ, not merely control the fruit of sin through the power of their will. Some have read this passage to mean that the believer must physically harm himself, or participate in harsh treatment of the body, as mentioned in 2:23. But that is not the case. Paul is telling the Colossians that they must crucify the root of sin through the spiritual process of renewal.

Paul lists two groups of sin that believers are to put to death. The first group can be described as personal sins (3:5):

1) Sexual immorality: any sexual activity outside of marriage
2) Impurity: the contamination of a person's moral character through immoral behavior
3) Passion: uncontrolled lust
4) Evil desire: the scheming side of a person that makes him or her want to plan to participate in sin
5) Greed: This is the intense desire for physical gratification that comes from longing for things in the world. In essence, it is a form of idolatry because it focuses on pleasing self instead of pleasing God.

Paul gives the Colossians two reasons why they should crucify these passions (3:6–7): first, because God is going to pour out His wrath on those sins; second, because it is not who they are anymore. It is a past-tense reality in their lives.

The second group of sins can be described as public sins, or the sins committed against each other (3:8–9). Paul tells the Colossians to put these sins aside much as they would discard an old garment that is not useful anymore:

1) Anger: violent emotional outbursts, temper tantrums, and indignation
2) Wrath: boiling up of the soul that causes one to become enraged

3) Malice: wickedness that causes one to act in an evil way

4) Slander: speaking about someone in a way that destroys his or her character

5) Abusive speech: foul talk used to purposely hurt others

Paul lists these five sins, and then singles out one more—lying (3:9). Lying is purposefully being deceptive to someone, leading him or her away from the truth. Paul lists this sin separately because it includes all of the vices he's already listed. Every sin mentioned involves falsehood in some manner or another. God is a God of truth, not lies, and when believers lie, they act in the exact opposite of the character of God.

The next reality of the Christian life, after taking off the old, is putting on the new. Christianity is not just a putting off of sin, but it is also embracing Jesus. It is the reality of daily becoming a new person.

Verse 10 describes the new person as being renewed. He or she is in a continual process of being transformed from one state of being to another. This process is going on all the time.

This idea of true knowledge (3:10) is the concept of not just mentally knowing God, but experientially knowing God in mind, will, and emotions.

3:11–17

THE CHARACTER OF UNITY

In verse 11, Paul makes a transition from one's union with Christ to union with one another. Race, religion, and class are no longer a barrier to the body; now everyone is one in Christ.

Demystifying Colossians

Here are the distinctions Paul points out:

- **Race:** Greek or Jew. It does not matter if you are a Jew or a Gentile.

- **Religion:** circumcised or uncircumcised. It does not matter if you came to Christ from Judaism or not.

- **Cast:** barbarian or Scythian. A barbarian was a non-Greek speaking tribal person. The Scythians were a Far Eastern Asian people, even more tribal than the barbarians. But even these extreme cultures both lose their stereotypes in Christ.

- **Class:** slave or free. Even considering the social order of the day, the slave and the free are on the same page in Christ.

Paul's next point: Christ is the only source of a believer's salvation. When he says Christ is all and in all (3:11), he probably means that Christ is in all believers. Christians have a new identity in Christ, and are unified by His presence. We are brought into a relationship with Jesus Christ and, through that, a relationship with each other.

The church's unity, Paul points out in verse 12, is not centered around a cause, but rather the eternal work that God has done for the believers. As a result of what God has done for them, the Colossians are chosen (called out by God), holy (set apart), and beloved (before he or she ever asked for it). In light of how God has loved them, Paul tells the Colossians to *put on* the following character traits: compassion, kindness, humility, gentleness, patience, bearing with one another, and forgiving one another. The idea is that they are to wrap themselves around with these essential traits.

Critical Observation

Paul adds to this last point of forgiveness. We are to pattern our grace by the forgiveness we have received from God (3:13)—God forgave us before we could have ever asked for it. He gave grace, not on the basis of our merit or even our request, but on the basis of His love while we were still in rebellion toward Him. Christ is the standard for forgiveness.

Verse 14 serves as Paul's summary: Of all the things the believer is to put on, the governing agent is love. The love that Paul is talking about is God's selfless love that seeks to do the best for people who deserve only death. It is this kind of love that unites the body of Christ.

When Paul refers to the peace of Christ (3:15), he is not talking about an internal feeling of serenity as much as a result of doing the right thing. When humanity rebelled, God sought to make peace by sacrificing His own Son. That same trait must rule within the body of Christ.

Critical Observation

The idea around the word *ruling* is that of an umpire or judge (3:15). An umpire is a person who calls and enforces the rules of a game. When conflict arises, Christ's peace should be the arbitrator.

Paul writes that Christ's Word must take priority among believers in the church (3:16). The word *dwell* used in some translations means to take up residency, to move in and make a home. The Word of Christ is to take up an abundant residence in the hearts of believers. Since the main issue in this letter is the sufficiency of Jesus over all other man-made attempts at righteousness, Paul is declaring that the commands of Jesus should dwell in believers so they have the wisdom to teach (instruct), admonish (warn), and encourage one another.

When Paul lists the types of music in the church in verse 16, he is simply offering a sample, not an exhaustive list. A psalm may be a poem put to music such as David's psalms. A hymn is a song that, in content, specifically praises God. A spiritual song may refer generally to other styles of worship songs.

Paul closes this section of his letter with an exhortation to the Colossians to do everything in the name of Jesus. In this first-century culture, doing something in someone's name meant accomplishing that task as a representative of that person. In verse 17, Paul is telling the Colossians that they are going out as representatives of Jesus, and they are to accomplish every task as if He was doing it Himself (3:17).

At the end of verses 15, 16, and 17 is a command to give thanks. Thankfulness is the sign of a person who is submitted to the Lord Jesus Christ.

📄 **3:18–4:1**

MODELING CHRIST

In the whole of chapter 3, Paul describes how the Colossians' actions should reflect the new life they have been given in Christ. He now declares that the life of Christ should be modeled in their homes—husbands to wives and fathers to children.

First, the wife is to be subject to her husband (3:18). Some translations declare that wives are to "submit." This word has been the source of much conflict. It means to voluntarily place oneself under someone's authority. It denotes order and authority. It is a voluntary action by the wife, not a forced action by the husband. It is not a position of inferiority, but rather a different role on the same team. The essence of this verse means that a wife finds her identity not apart from her husband, but in conjunction with her husband.

Paul continues his description of the family relationships with two commands to the husbands (3:19)—to love their wives and not be embittered against them. The word *love* here is the self-sacrificing love that causes one to place the needs of others above his or her own. A husband is to give love, and self-sacrificially meet his wife's needs. It is not the role of the husband to dominate his wife and treat her like a slave. He should treat her as more important than himself.

The idea behind the command to not be embittered is that there is no reason to let bitterness boil up to the degree that a husband begins to treat his wife out of that bitterness, rather than the love of Christ. This would refer to a husband who is sharp and rude to his wife.

Take It Home

Implied in Paul's description of the husband and the wife is the concept of teamwork. One of the reasons that God developed marriage was to allow a couple to work together to accomplish that which He has established for them.

A husband's love should serve as a visual representation of God. The common goal is to declare Jesus Christ as redeemer. God has established marriage as a vehicle for this to be accomplished.

Paul continues with instructions for children (3:20). The Greek word translated "obey" combines two very distinct thoughts. It carries the ideas of both *hearing* one's parents and *heeding* their wishes.

The Greek word translated "fathers" (*patters*) in 3:21 could also mean "parents" (Hebrews 11:23), and this may be the meaning here. A different word is used for parents in verse 20, however, so most scholars think Paul here means "fathers" (and most English versions translate it this way). In this case Paul is addressing the one in the family whom God will hold most responsible for what happens in the home.

This instruction is not focusing on the actual duties of raising a child, but rather on the attitude of the parent. The picture painted is that of a father who presumes upon his child's obedience without the appropriate balance between rules and relationship. Paul notes that a father's unappropriate behavior can cause a child to "lose heart" (NASB), or give up.

While still in the arena of relationships, Paul's instruction moves from family relationships to slave and master relationships. This is a relationship of obedience and authority. Typically, this command is linked to employees and employers, but there are other relationships in life that apply. One would be the teacher-student relationship. Another might be the civil law and the citizen. There is a principle in this text that could govern anywhere a person is subject to authority.

In the time of this letter, slavery was a common part of life. A slave was the property of his owner. The master had all the rights, and the slave had none. According to Paul's instruction, even in this situation, the motive of the slave should be wholehearted obedience, the same kind of obedience given to children in verse 20—to listen and to obey.

Paul develops this command by building a contrast between external service and sincerity of heart. The Greek word translated by some as "eyeservice" (NKJV) means to do something only when someone is looking. The Christian slave should work with sincerity of heart. Paul adds another qualifier to the motives of the slaves—fear of the Lord. Every task should be done in light of the reality that God is present (3:22).

Paul then tells the slave how to work—wholeheartedly (3:23). The idea around this word is that all you do derives from the passions of your life, and that everything you have goes into your work.

In a slave-master relationship there are many issues that can get in the way of work. Bitterness, resentment, apathy, lack of respect—all of this can affect the work of the slave. A believing slave must not let those issues get in the way of his service, though. He must understand that obedience is service to God more than service to his master.

Paul continues his thought by explaining to the slave that the true rewards of life come only from God (3:24). The slave, who may never know an earthly family inheritance, is going to get one in heaven—the glories of eternal life. That is why Paul adds that last statement of verse 24—it is God he serves. All of life is to be lived in devotion to Him.

Verse 25 contains the concluding principle for slaves—God will deal without partiality and fairly in the end. Then, whoever does wrong, whether slave or master, they will receive the consequences for that wrong without partiality. This is important to understand in a world that is unfair.

Paul ends this section of instruction with a statement about masters (4:1)—both the master's actions toward the slave and attitude toward God. He is to treat his slave with justice (ethically) and fairness (equality) because that is the way Jesus deals with each of us. Also, the master is not one who holds supreme authority; he, too, is under authority, and must humbly serve his Master, just as the slave has been instructed to do.

COLOSSIANS 4:2–18

IN CONCLUSION

Setting Up the section

In this final section of scripture on being raised up in Christ, Paul draws the Colossians' attention outward—to their responsibility to make Christ known, both by praying for those who are actively involved in sharing the gospel and by living out the life of Christ and sharing the gospel in love.

It is not enough to reflect Christ to one another in the church. We are also to take the message of Christ to the world outside of our community of faith. Paul desires to see the Colossians as active participants in the progress of the gospel through responding to the issues and questions of the world.

📄 4:2–6

WHAT MESSAGE ARE YOU SENDING?

The Colossians must understand that they are fully dependent on Christ for everything. This dependence is seen through a life of continual prayer. Paul's instruction is to be devoted to prayer (4:2)—continually faithful, not lacking in endurance. Paul further describes the believer's prayer life as alert. This is a picture of vigilance and undistracted focus.

Gratitude is a part of prayer because of God's gift of mercy and grace. When someone realizes that it is because of God and His great mercy that he or she can even approach God's throne, thanksgiving is a part of that believer's prayer life.

Paul now turns his attention to a specific prayer request. He asks the Colossians to pray that a door of opportunity would open up so that he could share the Word of Christ. Notice that Paul does not pray that his circumstance will change, or that he will be freed from prison so that he can share more. He simply prays for an open door. What Paul desires in this open door is to speak of the mystery of Christ in clarity and boldness. In this context, the mystery of Christ (4:3–4) is a reference to all of redemptive history centered on Jesus.

The Colossians are to pray continually, but also be aware of their behavior and how it comes across to those outside of the faith (4:5–6). This means their lives should reflect the purity and the holiness of God. When Paul states that they be wise (4:5), the idea is that they should be able to apply the truth of God. In making the most of every opportunity there is a sense of aggression in seizing the opportunities that God places in a believer's path. This requires a balance between zeal and tact. How should they accomplish this? By speaking the truth in love, with graciousness (4:6).

Gracious words are words that are meek, compassionate, and reflective of the mercy and compassion of God. Words that are seasoned with salt add to a conversation that will improve or edify the situation. Neither of these descriptions implies diminishing the truth, but rather communicating it with tenderness and mercy.

WHAT JESUS ARE YOU WORSHIPING?

What Colossians offers the child of God is the fundamental understanding of what it means to be a Christian. With this section, Paul's instruction to the Colossians is complete, and now he desires to give the Colossians some closing greetings and remarks. This is not an instructional part of the letter, but it does contain for us some thoughts worth expounding on as we conclude a study of this epistle.

First, Paul desires to keep the lines of communication open. Even though he is in prison and has not personally seen the Colossians, he desires to ensure them that they are a part of his life, and for them to know about the progress of his ministry. Therefore, he is sending two men, Tychicus and Onesimus (4:7-9). Onesimus is the runaway slave that the New Testament book of Philemon is written on behalf of.

Paul not only keeps the lines of communication open between the Colossians and himself, but also between other believers and the Colossians. In verses 10-14, Paul relays the greetings of six fellow laborers.

The first three men are fellow Jews that are, in essence, Paul's ministry team: Aristarchus, Mark, and Justus (Jesus).

The next man who sends his greeting is Epaphras. He is the one God used to begin the church in Colossae. As a result, he carries a deep burden of prayer for these believers. Notice the content of Epaphras's prayer (4:12)—that the church would stand perfect and be assured in God's will.

Within this context, perfection carries the idea of maturity. To be fully assured carries the idea of being fully confident in the understanding of God's will.

Finally, Paul relays the greetings of Luke and Demas (4:14). Luke was a traveling companion of Paul, and that is why he was able to give such detailed accounts of Paul's ministry to Theophilus in the book of Acts. Demas is another traveling companion.

Paul also wants to keep the lines of communication open between himself and the surrounding churches, so he sends his own greeting and provides instruction for distribution of this letter, as well as the one sent to Laodicea (4:15). This request reflects Paul's desire to keep the churches united.

Paul's words to Archippus are an encouragement to faithfully do what he's been called to do without shrinking back (4:17).

Finally, the fact that Paul personally recorded this greeting is a sign of endearment (4:18). It shows that the Colossians are special to him and that he cares deeply for them. This is not just a form letter, but something that is close to his heart.

The essence of his request for the Colossians to remember his imprisonment is a request for continued prayer. Then his final farewell of grace brings the letter full circle, beginning and ending with the grace of God (1:2; 4:18).

Take It Home

There are three basic instructions in this last chapter.

1) Pray continually: Be dependent on God.

2) Live godly lives: Do not add offense to the gospel.

3) Speak the truth in love: Be ready to respond.

Every believer in this world will have an opportunity to respond to a situation with the truth, and there is a way it is to be done—out of a life that is godly and a mouth that is gracious and prepared to share the truth of Christ to this world.

1 THESSALONIANS

INTRODUCTION TO 1 THESSALONIANS

First Thessalonians is a short letter written to a predominantly Gentile church of new converts. It provides all the basic requirements for holy living (a regular "walk" with God), as well as great insight into the importance and specifics of the anticipated return of Jesus. As such, it is a worthwhile study for believers of all ages.

AUTHOR

Early church authorities agree that Paul is the author of this epistle, and little serious opposition has been raised since. With the possible exception of Galatians (for which the date is debated), this is most likely Paul's first letter among those that are included in scripture.

PURPOSE

The church at Thessalonica was facing persecution, yet it was continuing to grow and had developed a dynamic testimony of faith. Paul's letter was an effort to comfort and motivate the believers there with the truth of the Lord's sure return.

OCCASION

Paul had taken the gospel to Thessalonica, but had to leave abruptly when persecution broke out, for the good of other believers in the city (Acts 17:1–10). It would have been natural to wonder if, after his hasty departure, the new Gentile converts would soon drift back to their old ways. Paul had wanted to return on numerous occasions, and had been frustrated when unable to (2:18). So he was overjoyed when Timothy arrived from Thessalonica with a glowing report of their continued faithfulness (3:6–10). This letter was written in response to that report and in anticipation of a personal visit by Paul (3:11).

THEMES

The primary doctrinal issue of 1 Thessalonians is the second coming of Christ. Jesus' return is mentioned at the end of every chapter of this letter, and it is the focus of the end of the epistle.

In addition, Paul's emphasis on holy living is a call to unity, and he uses the term "brothers and sisters" (*adelphoi*) twenty-eight times in 1 and 2 Thessalonians.

HISTORICAL CONTEXT

Originally called Therma, because of many hot springs in the surrounding area, the city of Thessalonica had been renamed in the 300s BC, in honor of the half-sister of Alexander the Great. It was conquered by Rome in 168 BC, and became capital of the province of Macedonia. Today known as Thessaloniki (or Salonica), it is again the capital of Macedonia and one of the few cities from New Testament times that still exists, with a population of three hundred thousand.

The city's strategic location, with access to a major Roman military highway (the Egnatian Way) and a sheltered harbor, attracted many people. As a result, Thessalonica was a wealthy city, though it had also developed a reputation for evil and licentiousness.

CONTRIBUTION TO THE BIBLE

As an early letter of Paul, this epistle shows that even then he was both emotionally vulnerable and theologically strong—a combination that would continue to make him an outstanding writer and church leader. Specifically, the First Epistle to the Thessalonians contains perhaps the clearest picture of the rapture that is connected with Jesus' second coming (4:15–17).

OUTLINE

1 THESSALONIANS 1:1–10

A FAITH THAT INSPIRES OTHERS

Setting Up the Section

Having heard of the persecution and suffering within the church in Thessalonica, Paul wrote to encourage the believers. His opening in this section is filled with genuine praise. Not only were the Thessalonians enduring difficult times, they were also setting an example that other churches were noticing. Theirs was a faith that was helping others grow stronger.

📖 **1:1**

MORE THAN A STANDARD GREETING

Many Bible readers tend to skip over the personal greetings in the epistles to get to the meat of the letter. The greetings and closings of any letter can be mere formality, but sometimes the words chosen for the salutations and sign-offs reveal love and concern. In addition, much important and practical truth is to be found in the warm greetings of biblical letters.

In this case, the greeting first identifies the writer, Paul (1:1). The great apostle had formerly been known as Saul, but his name shift in the Bible is not explained. There are four main theories about Paul's double name:

1) He had both names from childhood;

2) Perhaps he was short of stature, and Paul ("little") suited him better than Saul ("asked for");

3) He took his second name from Sergius Paulus, an intelligent Roman proconsul whom he had met (Acts 13:4–12); or

4) He chose *Paul* in self-deprecation (1 Corinthians 15:9; Ephesians 3:8).

The first option is most likely. It was common for Jewish males to be given two names at birth. As Paul became the apostle to the Gentiles, he may have simply started using his more Roman-sounding name. Yet we never find the names Saul and Paul used together as is the case in other people, such as Simon Peter.

Paul's greeting also identifies his companions, Silvanus (Silas) and Timothy. *Silas* was probably an Aramaic name, and *Silvanus* a Roman one. He had accompanied Paul on his second missionary journey (Acts 15:40). He was a Jew (Acts 16:20) and a respected church leader (Acts 15:22), who later assisted Peter as well (1 Peter 5:12). Timothy was a younger man, the son of a Jewish Christian mother and a Gentile father (Acts 16:1; 2 Timothy 1:5). Paul may have led Timothy to Christ, and he was a mentor to the younger man (1 Timothy 1:2).

So from Paul's first few words, it becomes evident that he was considerate of others and acknowledged their part in his ministry, that he was a team player, and that he was eager to train and involve others in his work for God.

As for the recipients of his letter, Paul addresses the church (singular) of the Thessalonians (plural). Based on his other letters, we might expect Paul to address "the church at Thessalonica." It appears to be a minor difference, yet his terminology here is a bit more personal and reveals a concern not only for the church, but for each individual of the congregation who was persevering under difficult circumstances.

After acknowledging the *local* sphere of the believers' life—Thessalonica—Paul turns their attention to the *spiritual* sphere of existence. They had an intimate union and spiritual relationship with God the Father and the Lord Jesus Christ (1:1). The linking of both phrases with a single preposition stresses the unity of God the Father and God the Son—Paul's immediate emphasis on the deity of Christ.

Only then does Paul get to his official greeting. *Peace* was the traditional greeting among the Jews, and "grace" (*charis*) sounds like the common Greek greeting *chairein* ("greetings"). Paul not only combines the two, but personalizes them as well. His usage indicates a prayerful concern and desire for his readers to experience what only God can supply. The order is important as well: Without the grace of God, peace is impossible (2 Peter 1:2–4).

📄 **1:2–10**

GOOD REASONS FOR GIVING THANKS

In essentially all of Paul's letters (Galatians being the exception), he begins by giving thanks for his readers. But the Thessalonian believers received some of his most glowing words. Paul says that he and his associates frequently thought of the godly characteristics of the Thessalonians as they prayed for them (1:2–3). Throughout this chapter, the faithfulness of a struggling church is seen from the perspective of mature and dedicated church leaders.

Demystifying 1 Thessalonians

The Greek sentence structure of verses 2–5 is long and somewhat complicated, but the segment contains three participles that draw attention to how Paul and his associates expressed their gratitude to the Lord: (1) making mention; (2) constantly bearing in mind; and (3) knowing they were chosen by God. Applied to the prayers of Paul and his companions, these phrases include the *means* of giving thanks, the *occasion* for giving thanks, and the *cause* for giving thanks.

The qualities of faith, hope, and love (1:3) are frequently grouped together in the New Testament (most familiarly in 1 Corinthians 13:13) as they are here. They are all Christlike characteristics, as well as fruit of the Holy Spirit. The church can work for God but will be effective only as long as it maintains these godly motives. The church in Ephesus was noted for its hard work and perseverance, yet had lost its first love (Revelation 2:1–7). The church in Thessalonica had no such problem.

The Greek word translated "brothers" (1:4) could also mean "brothers and sisters," and in this context would almost certainly mean "fellow Christians." More than a title, it is an affectionate term used to highlight the Thessalonians' new spiritual relationship as members of the family of God. Paul leaves no doubt by immediately referring to them as beloved by God. They were being persecuted by a hostile world, yet remained under God's fatherly love and care.

Paul knew that the Thessalonian believers were loved and chosen by God—a reference to the doctrine of election. But his was not simply a cognitive awareness. Paul, Silas, and Timothy had first taken the gospel to Thessalonica. It was more than a job to Paul. He hadn't just preached a sermon; his message had been delivered with power, with the Holy Spirit, and with deep conviction (1:5). Paul and his associates realized the way they lived their lives was just as important as what they were saying in their sermons. They didn't depend on looks, personalities, eloquence, oratorical skill, or methodology. Their calling was from God, their strength came from Him, and He was the One they remained accountable to.

Still, their reception in Thessalonica hadn't been entirely positive (Acts 17:1–10). The fact that some of the people there had believed and established a church was proof that they were going against the tide of their community. They had welcomed the message, which would have been Paul's verbal presentation of the gospel since the New Testament was not yet in existence (1:6). And they had imitated Paul and the other teachers not in the sense of mimicking actions, but by seeing their lives as an ideal example to be followed.

Critical Observation

The gospel is spread through actions as well as words. Paul followed the example of Christ (1 Corinthians 11:1). The Thessalonians followed Paul's example (1:6). And as a result, people throughout all of Greece (Macedonia and Achaia) saw the example being set by the Thessalonians (1:7).

Macedonia and Achaia (1:7–8) were Roman provinces that comprised what is now Greece. Because of the faithful witness of the Thessalonians, the gospel was heard through the entire land like the peal of a trumpet. The change in the lives of the Thessalonians was clearly evident. Many had been idolaters and some probably continued to battle the pull of their past. Yet they had welcomed God's message by faith and were putting their trust in Jesus.

The gospel had revealed the foolishness of their faith in empty idols and pointed them to the truth of the living God. The Thessalonians did not put off their old life *in order* to be saved; it was their understanding of and belief in the message of the gospel that led to salvation. Their salvation came only because of their willingness to acknowledge what God had already done for them.

Some might have tried to add Christ to their existing pantheon of idols, which would have been, in essence, to reject Him as the way, the truth, and the life. But the Thessalonians understood Paul's teaching, and as a result turned their backs on idols and became living and ongoing examples of faith for their community and their world. They understood that their Lord was God's Son. He was from heaven. He had been raised from the dead. And He would surely rescue them from God's wrath (1:10).

Such a future perspective helped the Thessalonian believers deal with their present difficulties. They may have been experiencing persecution, but that was nothing in contrast to the coming judgment of God. They were assured that they would be saved from the truly horrible times. Paul would have much more to say about the Second Coming and future events in this letter (and in 2 Thessalonians as well). Paul's original writing isn't divided into chapters and verses, of course, but every chapter in this epistle concludes with a reference to the return of Jesus Christ.

Take It Home

After reading Paul's praise for the Thessalonian believers in this section, it's hard not to ask the question, What would the church look like if everyone imitated *my* faith and behavior? Who have been your models to demonstrate what authentic Christian faith looks like in this world? And whose eyes might be on you, looking for an example of what a follower of Jesus looks like?

1 THESSALONIANS 2:1–20

PAUL'S ASSOCIATION WITH THE THESSALONIANS

Setting Up the Section

After a warm and encouraging greeting (1:1), in this section Paul begins to recall his personal experiences in Thessalonica. He has fond memories, and will compare himself to both a loving mother and concerned father. He writes as an evangelist as well as an edifier of believers.

📄 **2:1–6**

FAITHFUL STEWARDS

A believer's personal life speaks powerfully to the nature of his or her ministry in regard to the motives, methods, and means used to accomplish the work of God. Paul had spent time with the Thessalonians. They knew not only what he said, but also who he was. Consequently, Paul refers to their knowledge of his life numerous times in this short letter (1:5; 2:1–2, 5, 11; 4:2).

What does Paul mean by saying his visit with the Thessalonians had not failed (2:1)?

The original word would have been used to speak of an empty jar. So Paul's meaning is that the Thessalonians had not gone away empty-handed when it came to the things that he had proclaimed: God's truth, essentials of Christian character, sincerity of faith, and so on. The Thessalonians had come away with a deep understanding of the things of God, and their lives had been changed as a result.

Their positive response must have meant a lot to Paul and his traveling companions because he had not been without opposition while trying to spread the gospel. He was still receiving criticism from some who wanted to undermine his credibility because they promoted a more legalistic approach to God. So he takes time to recall his original association with the Thessalonians (2:1-2), and then moves immediately to his current relationship with the church there (2:3-5). Because of the strong opposition they had faced, it had been risky for Paul and his companions to share the gospel with the Thessalonians, but God had provided the courage they needed (2:2).

As an apostle of God (2:6), Paul spoke with authority. Others might have misused the position, yet Paul was always a good steward of the weighty authority he had. He never attempted to wield it to make himself look better, to manipulate his message, or to intimidate his listeners. Some of his critics had used those tactics, but Paul knew *he* hadn't. Even more importantly, the Thessalonians could attest to his conscientious use of authority (2:3).

Traveling speakers generally depended on the gifts of their listeners for their daily needs. Occasionally churches raised collections for Paul, but he never expected or demanded such offerings. In fact, he seemed glad to make the point that he had nothing to gain from his ministry other than seeing the gospel of Christ taken to people who needed to hear it.

Sometimes Paul and his associates would pass through less populated towns in order to establish churches in larger cities, knowing that those churches would then reach out to the smaller towns. Yet they didn't evaluate success in terms of size or numbers. What characterized their ministry and made it fruitful was the authoritative and true revelation of God. Being entrusted with the gospel (2:3-5) was all the motivation and reward that Paul needed. And his ministry was conducted with dignity, simplicity, and vulnerability.

2:7-12

MINISTERING AS LOVING PARENTS

In defending his role as a faithful steward of the gospel, Paul denies several specific accusations (2:5). Then he shifts the emphasis from the negative accusations to his actual feelings toward the Thessalonians.

In this section (2:7-12), Paul compares his ministry to both a loving mother (with an emphasis on gentleness and willingness) and a concerned father (focused on instruction backed up by godly example). The mother he describes is a nursing mother, and the care she shows is the same word used of birds covering their eggs with their feathers. There is not only devotion involved in Paul's meaning, but a loving tenderness as well.

Critical Observation

Various aspects of Paul's ministry are detailed throughout this section:

- Ministry in selflessness (2:5–6)
- Ministry with gentleness (2:6–7)
- Ministry with willingness (2:8)
- Ministry without heaviness (2:9)
- Ministry in holiness (2:10)
- Ministry with admonition (2:11)
- Ministry with God's mission (2:12)
- Ministry centered in Bible exposition (2:1–4, 13)

The word Paul uses for this degree of love and affection (2:8) is very strong and rarely used, though it is found in the parental inscriptions on some ancient graves of small children who had died. Paul was serious about his feelings for the Thessalonians, and those feelings led to his willingness to work hard and share his very life with the recently converted Christians (2:9).

The fatherly aspect of ministry is a bit more diverse. A father certainly shares the mother's desire to love, encourage, and comfort his children (2:11), yet he has primary responsibility for seeing that each child learns to live a worthy life—to find his or her place in the world. Parents want to love and nurture their children, but the long-range goal is to see them grow strong and independent.

The call of God is ongoing—present tense rather than past tense (2:12). Paul wanted his spiritual "children" in Thessalonica to be ready and able to respond to God's calling.

📄 2:13–20

THANKSGIVING INSPIRED BY SUFFERING

Paul is emphatic about something contemporary believers tend to take for granted. He makes it clear that what he had preached to the Thessalonians did not originate with him. He presented it as, and they received it as, the Word of God (2:13). God uses human instruments for transmitting His message, but He is the Author. The Thessalonians had heard a lot of words from Paul's mouth, yet had discerned that the message was indeed God's.

The proof that they had encountered God's truth was evident in their response. They began to receive persecution from their own countrymen, and stood firm rather than backing down (2:14). Just as the believers in Jerusalem had been persecuted by fellow Jews, the Thessalonian believers were persecuted by fellow Gentiles. There was a geographic distinction, but a spiritual commonality in the church of God.

Paul's statement in verses 14–16 can sound like religious bigotry until one remembers that Paul was among the very group he is describing. Though he doesn't go into detail here as he does in other places, his conversion had been so sudden and life-changing that the Christian persecutors he had once been partnered with were the same ones who immediately tried to hinder his newfound zeal for Christ.

Demystifying 1 Thessalonians

It seems that the Thessalonians had opponents from all ranks. Paul had experienced trouble with Jews in the area (Acts 17:5–10), yet he acknowledges that the believers there were suffering at the hands of their own countrymen, who would have been Gentiles (2:14).

The Thessalonians should have been comforted to hear that they were not suffering for any legitimate cause, but only as a result of their faithfulness to God. They were sharing in the suffering of Jesus, of Paul, and of other Christians near and far. Paul projects the future for both groups: The ones who hear the gospel will be saved; the ones who continue to oppose God's message will certainly experience His wrath (2:16).

Paul then shifts from the perspective of what the Thessalonians must have been thinking and feeling to his own thoughts and desires (2:17–20). This section reads as though it is written by a parent to a child, which affirms what Paul has already said (2:7, 11). Physical absence from the Thessalonians had been hard on Paul, and they were continually on his mind (2:17).

Paul attributes to Satan his inability to return. Various Greek words are used to designate Satan, some of which are translated "serpent," "slanderer," or "defamer." The word here is found three dozen times in the New Testament, and each time refers to an adversary or opponent. As the enemy of God, Satan opposes all who belong to Him.

Paul ends this section with a rhetorical question (2:19). He is still using the plural pronoun *our*, showing that he isn't trying to take all the credit for delivering the gospel to the Thessalonians. All those who were with him personally, and who had supported him in prayer, were able to share in the joy of seeing the Thessalonians continue to demonstrate the love and grace of Christ. When Jesus returns, the Thessalonian believers will stand among His faithful followers to receive a reward for all their suffering on His behalf.

And just so there is no doubt as to his meaning, Paul answers his own question (2:20), confirming his appreciation and fondness for the believers in Thessalonica.

Take It Home

Paul was the one in the role of spiritual leadership, yet he was more than open about how much the Thessalonians meant to him. His ministry wasn't just a job. He had established some very real and very strong relationships and wanted to keep them going, even during his absence. Can you think of someone (or some group) that you have had an influence over in the past, yet haven't followed up with in a while? If so, take some time to contact the person(s) to express your feelings.

1 THESSALONIANS 3:1–13

CONCERN AND ENCOURAGEMENT

Setting Up the Section

Paul spent the previous section answering a number of accusations leveled against him by people who opposed the gospel and his presentation of it. Now that he has set straight the false insinuations of his opponents, he continues to express personal concern for the Thessalonian believers. As their spiritual parent, he wants to see their faith continue to develop. Two key ideas he stresses in this section are spiritual stability and spiritual growth.

📄 **3:1–8**

THE ASSISTANCE OF TIMOTHY

Paul had a pastoral heart. Not only was he concerned for the evangelism of people in the areas he visited, but he also remained concerned for their ongoing spiritual maturity. Thinking back to his initial encounter with the Thessalonians, he recalls the dilemma he had felt. He and Silas had been the primary targets of persecution (Acts 17:5-10), and felt compelled to leave the city for the good of the believers there. He had repeatedly wanted to return, yet so far had been hindered by Satan (2:18). So in lieu of a personal visit, he did the next best things: He sent a helper to Thessalonica, he prayed earnestly for them, and he sent this letter to encourage, instruct, and warn them.

The helper he sent was Timothy (3:1-3). Paul didn't make decisions impulsively. Rather, he considered all his options and willingly determined what he thought was best (3:1). Timothy's ministry helped put Paul's mind to rest (3:1, 5), and helped provide stability in the persecution-ridden church in Thessalonica (3:2-4).

Still, it was not an easy choice. Timothy was of great value to Paul. The word Paul uses to describe Timothy's leaving (3:1) is the same word someone would use to describe the departure of a loved one who had died. Paul would certainly feel the effects of Timothy's absence, yet his devotion to the Thessalonians was that strong.

Timothy was not only a brother (a fellow believer), but was also Paul's coworker in God's service (3:2). He was active in ministry and a team player. He had been traveling with Paul long enough to know what to do when he arrived in Thessalonica. It would be his job to strengthen and encourage the believers in their faith, even though they had been doing well. The key to spiritual strength and stability is faith, so that was also Timothy's goal (3:2).

Paul mentions his concern for the Thessalonians' faith four times in this section. He wants to ensure that they continue to trust in God's provision and control. Ongoing stability during the ups and downs of life requires faith anchored in the Lord.

Timothy's ministry would be to ensure that the Thessalonians didn't become unsettled (disturbed or shaken) by their trials (3:3). He would remind them that Paul already warned of impending persecution and that such testing of believers is appointed by God (3:3–4). Afflictions are not accidents. Believers are expected to suffer for the sake of Christ when necessary (Philippians 1:29). In addition, sometimes God allows the persecution of His people to demonstrate the evil nature of humankind and the righteousness of His judgment (2:14–16).

Critical Observation

Paul has just written about Satan in his role as an adversary of God's people (2:18). He follows up here by referring to him as "the tempter" (3:5). The title describes Satan's character as well as his strategy. One of the tempter's continual objectives is to negatively affect a believer's faith in the promises and truth of God's Word. He wants believers to doubt God's love. He wants them to depend on works-oriented strategies to handle life rather than placing complete trust in the effective and completed work of Jesus Christ.

When Paul mentions the possibility that his work might be useless (3:5), it is in the sense of being incomplete, or without effect. He knew that work for God is never in vain (1 Corinthians 15:58), but he was also aware of the spiritual opposition believers were up against. Just as Jesus had warned in His parables of Satan's snatching away the Word of God before it could be implanted in someone's heart (Mark 4:14–15), Paul knew his teachings were subject to the influence of the tempter (3:5).

Yet all of the concern and anxiety Paul felt toward the condition of the church in Thessalonica was alleviated by the return of Timothy with an encouraging report (3:6). The word Paul uses here for Timothy's good news is the same that he usually uses in reference to the gospel—this is Paul's only exception. It reflects just what a rejuvenating effect Timothy's report had on Paul.

To hear that the Thessalonians were standing firm was enough to lift Paul's mood even in light of his own personal distress (3:7). It is an example of both Paul's selfless attitude and the kind of influence one person's (or group's) faith can have on someone else.

📖 3:9–13

PAUL'S PRAYER OF THANKSGIVING

Paul had been instrumental in getting the Thessalonian church started, yet he took no credit for it. In fact, he thanked God for the believers' influence on *him*—not the other way around! Paul was a thankful servant, one who always lived with the perspective of God's hand on his life. His heart was filled with gratitude for the work of God in the lives of others.

Paul found words inadequate to express his appreciation for what had happened in the lives of the Thessalonian Christians. His change in mood was dramatic: His concern and distress (3:7) had turned into joy (3:9). This was not superficial euphoria, but heartfelt and sincere joy that could only be experienced in the presence of God.

Praying night and day (3:10) is not a reference to specific times, even though faithful Jews had regular prayer times throughout the day. Nor did Paul mean that he did nothing but pray for days on end. He simply wanted the Thessalonians to know that he prayed for them regularly. His prayer habits illustrate the reality of his faith and his ongoing dependence on God. In addition to consistent prayer, it was prayer in earnest. Paul and his fellow ministers devoted themselves to prayer because they knew God heard and answered.

Paul's prayer for the Thessalonians includes a number of specific desires. First, he wants to see them again, primarily to help them grow and mature in the Lord, completing anything that might still be lacking in their faith (3:10). This is Paul's main objective, and it motivated everything he did. He loved people, yet his driving desire to visit was fueled by his concern for their spiritual growth and stability.

Second, Paul prays that God would remove obstacles that might prevent his return to Thessalonica (3:11). Again, he is referring to the spiritual opposition he had experienced (2:18), so his prayer is for both God the Father and the Lord Jesus to clear the way. There are circumstances where no amount of human desire or effort will accomplish the desired results, and Paul is quick to turn to God's fatherly care to achieve what is best for him.

Third, Paul prays that God will cause the Thessalonian believers to abound in love (3:12). The church was struggling with persecution, and sometimes such circumstances can create a sense of isolation and self-preservation. But if the persecuted believers all unite and continue to place their confidence in God to eventually deliver them, then their love for one another could actually *increase* during those trying times. Knowing what they were going through, Paul's love had increased for them, and he prayed that the same would happen *among* them.

And finally, Paul prays that God would make the Thessalonians strong enough to remain blameless and holy (3:13). He turns their attention from their present sufferings to their future reward.

Demystifying 1 Thessalonians

Believers are declared righteous (holy) at salvation, but this positional sanctification is not what Paul is referring to (3:13). Nor does he mean the perfect condition believers experience after death. Rather, Paul is writing about experiential sanctification, one of the objectives for all spiritually maturing believers. It is an ongoing effort to put on the character of Jesus Christ and become blameless—preparing through faithful service on earth to eventually live in God's perfect eternity.

As believers grow in faith and strengthen their hearts in love, their inner motives and desires improve. They will never be confronted with their sins in heaven because sins are remembered no more (Romans 8:1; Hebrews 10:17), but the quality of their works will be tested (1 Corinthians 3:10–15). The Thessalonians were likely to continue to suffer in the present age, but Paul prays that they would experience only the best that God had to offer in the world to come.

Take It Home

We see from the example of the Thessalonians that an active faith—one lived in the light of the gospel and a personal relationship with God—can inspire loving ministry among others. A stable and growing faith will lead to acts of love. However, it is possible for a person's faith to be real and based on a genuine trust in Christ, yet be temporarily dormant, unfocused, and unfruitful due to failure to continue to grow in the grace and knowledge of Jesus (1 Corinthians 3:3; 2 Peter 1:8–11). How would you evaluate your current level of faith? Are you going strong in spite of all obstacles? Or do you need a bit more clarity and a renewed focus on Jesus?

1 THESSALONIANS 4:1–12

HOLY LIVING

Setting Up the Section

In the previous section, Paul was rejoicing over the arrival of a message from Timothy that affirmed the ongoing faithfulness of the believers in Thessalonica. He had expressed thanksgiving for the church, reviewed his ministry with them, and shown his deep concern for their sufferings. At this point, Paul now begins a series of exhortations regarding appropriate Christian living.

📄 4:1–2

WALKING TO PLEASE GOD

The word translated "finally" (4:1) is a term indicating transition and an alert to the reader that everything to follow is based on what has already been written. Paul had already made it clear that he and the church leaders with him had been earnestly praying for the faith and spiritual growth of the Thessalonians; now he is exhorting them, in keeping with those prayers, to rise to a level of holiness in their daily living. Even though they were doing well, Paul encourages them to improve their consistency even more.

Some people live as if all that is important is salvation and escaping earth to get to heaven. Yet God is deeply concerned with each believer's daily walk—how he or she lives the Christian life. Jesus came not just for the eternal aspect of believers, but also to enable them to live as examples in a dark and sinful world that does not know Him.

Since the church in Thessalonica was predominantly Gentile, Paul's instructions in verses 1-8 are particularly relevant. In contrast to Jewish believers who started their

Christian lives with a good understanding of the law, the Gentiles had come from a culture of gross idolatry that placed little or no restraint on issues of moral character—especially in matters of sex. Slavery had allowed citizens more free time to indulge in decadent living. What Paul is telling the Thessalonians would have been new and groundbreaking information for them.

As he had done in his letter to the Galatians, Paul compares the Christian life to walking. (Some Bible versions translate the word as "living," but "walking" is the more literal translation.)

Critical Observation

Walking is the mode of transportation that moves a person from one sphere to another. It requires taking one step at a time, and while one foot is off the ground with each step, the person is susceptible to being knocked off balance, stumbling, or stepping into trouble.

Walking becomes a visual aid to teach believers how to live. By using the word *walk* (or *live*), Paul puts an emphasis on *actions*, but then he immediately adds that it is to please God (4:1), which demonstrates the importance of *motives*. He first asks for their positive response as a fellow believer, and then urges them, in the name of the Lord Jesus, to respond. He wants their attention, because what he is about to say is very important.

4:3–8

HOLINESS AND SEXUAL PROPRIETY

After a general exhortation (4:1–2), Paul begins to provide specific instructions. He begins with the topic of sexual purity (4:3–8) followed by brotherly love (4:9–10) and orderly living (4:11–12).

By nature, people tend to follow desires that are against the will of God (Ephesians 2:1–3) and can never please Him (Romans 8:8). Paul begins by clarifying that what he is about to say is God's will. The doctrine of sanctification (4:3) has to do with being set apart, consecrated, and dedicated to God. As Paul broaches the topic of sex, he isn't saying it is evil or wrong. Sexual desires are natural and God-given. From the beginning, God created marriage as a sacred union between one man and one woman, and sex is part of that union, serving both as a means of continuing the race and providing pleasure within the marriage. It is only sexual activity outside of God's design that Paul opposes.

Paul's clarifications are very specific: (1) Abstain from immorality (4:3); (2) Learn to control one's body in a holy and honorable way (4:4–5); (3) Don't take advantage of a fellow believer (4:6).

The term translated "sexual immorality" is broad and includes many sexual practices: adultery, premarital and extramarital intercourse, homosexuality, and all other forms of immorality. Many of these would have been practiced openly and even encouraged by many in the Gentile culture. Yet Christians, Paul writes, are to avoid such things.

It isn't just active sexual immorality that is to be avoided, but all passionate lust as well

(4:5). Even then, mere avoidance was not enough. Christians are instructed to maintain control over their bodies in a way that is both holy and honorable. Clearly, one way to avoid sexual impurity is through marriage and a proper understanding of sex as God designed it. Scripture sets marriage apart from the motives, ideas, and values of a world that does not know God.

Paul's reference to one's brother (4:6) is unusual. Essentially every other time he uses the word, he intends it as a synonym for *believer*. In this context, however, he seems to refer to a fellow human being—either male or female. His message is that inappropriate sexual behavior has victims. Adultery on the part of one spouse betrays the other. Premarital sex robs both parties of the gift of virginity at marriage. Prostitution destroys not only lives, but affects entire communities. It may not be as apparent at first, but sexual immorality is just as much a sin as stealing from another person.

And verification of its destructive nature is the fact that God will exact punishment on all such sins (4:6). Sexual promiscuity has its own risks, but even if those involved escape the diseases, broken relationships, and such, they are still accountable to God. Holiness is at the other end of the scale from impurity. God's will for believers is for them to be set apart from the mentality and actions of a secular worldview. Paul never suggests it is easy to leave behind one's involvement in sexual immorality and begin living a holy life for God, but he does promise that believers will have help from the Holy Spirit (4:8).

Demystifying 1 Thessalonians

Greco-Roman ethics were based largely on the principles of self-interest and respect for another's property. The individual was entitled to do what was to his or her advantage (regardless of its effect on others) as long as he or she did not violate another person's property. The people's religion had little, if any, impact on sexual mores. Incest was about the only sexual taboo in their society. So Paul's connection between one's sexual activity and holiness before God was a new concept to many of his readers.

📖 4:9–12

BROTHERLY LOVE AND OTHER BASICS

In contrast to sexual sins, most of which are self-centered and exploitive, Paul directs his readers' attention to brotherly love (4:9–10). Secular society tries to define sexual immorality as "love," but the love that comes from God is genuine and exposes selfish desires for what they are. What Paul calls brotherly love is a deep, affectionate love between friends, which is certainly applicable to marriage partners as well. He doesn't go into detail, because believers who had experienced the love of God and fellowship in the church would already know what he was talking about. This is another instance where the believers already knew what to do, yet Paul exhorts them to do so more (4:10).

Paul's next statements (4:11–12) are a continuation of demonstrating love for one another. He provides some regular, consistent goals: leading a quiet life, minding one's own business, being productive in work, and not being dependent on anyone. The ultimate result would then be the respect of those who aren't believers, and they would be attracted to the kingdom of God.

Paul isn't suggesting Christians should appear boring or disinterested in life. It is quite the opposite. By being quiet Paul means less stressed, not less enthused. Few outsiders would be drawn to an inert and lackluster group promoting joy and abundant life!

A major motivating factor in doing as God instructs is the expectation of Jesus' return. That would be Paul's next topic.

Take It Home

It seems that far too often Christians mostly want to hear *new* truth. Certainly God wants them to continue to grow in the knowledge of His Word, yet sometimes they need motivation to excel more in the truths they *already* know. One goal should be to press on toward a greater and greater appreciation of the truths they are already practicing. Can you think of specific examples in your own life where this goal would be applicable?

1 THESSALONIANS 4:13–5:28

LIVING IN EXPECTATION OF CHRIST'S RETURN

The Comfort of Jesus' Coming	4:13–18
The Challenge of Jesus' Coming	5:1–11
Proper Conduct While Awaiting Jesus' Coming	5:12–28

Setting Up the Section

Paul has already alluded to the return of Jesus several times throughout this letter (1:10; 2:19; 3:13). Here he turns his full attention to what the Thessalonians could expect. They were a church under persecution, and the anticipated return of the One to whom they were being faithful was an ongoing comfort for them. Still, they had a number of questions that Paul answers in this section.

📖 4:13–18

THE COMFORT OF JESUS' COMING

In first-century pagan culture, the Christian concept of resurrection was peculiar and objectionable for many people. Mythology referred to an afterlife, and some Greek philosophers had attempted to teach that pleasant existence would continue after death, but few people in pagan society had real expectation or hope of life after death.

When Paul had first preached about resurrection in Athens, a handful of people had wanted to know more, but many sneered at him (Acts 17:32). It was a goal of the Greeks to shed the body in order to place all one's emphasis on the spirit. They couldn't understand *why* anyone would desire a bodily resurrection, much less *how* resurrection would take place when decomposition and decay was so evident.

The Thessalonian believers had witnessed the lack of hope among their culture, and they had questions. They were expecting the return of Christ at any time, but what about their loved ones who had died since trusting Him? Would their deaths hinder them in any way? Would those who were alive when Jesus returns have an advantage over those who had died?

Paul wants to alleviate the grief of the Thessalonians, but the solution to their grief lay in first removing their ignorance and providing hope (4:13–14). Comfort would follow hope, which would in turn reduce their grief.

Critical Observation

Sleep (4:13) is a common figure of speech for death in scripture, but is applied only to those who are believers because it anticipates an awakening (resurrection). Through faith in Christ, death for the Christian is no longer the threat it was prior to salvation. A sleeper doesn't cease to exist; his or her subconscious is still at work. Similarly, a believer's soul and spirit are active after death until he or she "awakes" to a full bodily resurrection.

Paul diminishes the fear of death by referring to it as sleep, but the reference is only to believers and not to Christ Himself (4:13–14). Jesus had to experience complete separation from God in His atoning work as Savior. Thanks to Him, believers never have to. Because death was very real to Christ, it is no more than sleep to those who have placed their faith in Him.

After assuring the Thessalonians of the reality of resurrection, Paul gives them some further assuring words with which they are supposed to encourage one another (4:18). He says that just as Jesus had died only to rise again and be with God, so would believers. Paul writes that Jesus' return is imminent, and counts himself among those alive and awaiting the moment (4:15).

Paul provides a number of details. Jesus' return won't go unnoticed. It will be accompanied by a shout of command, the voice of an archangel, and the trumpet of God. Those who had died will be resurrected before the believers who are still alive because they are dead in Christ (4:16), just as living believers are in Christ. Though the body is dead, the soul and spirit are still secure in the Lord and kept by the power of God.

As for the believers who are alive, they will be caught up in the air (the word actually means "seized" or "snatched") together with the resurrected dead (4:17). Clouds make an appropriate meeting place for God's people during this event because clouds are frequently associated with the presence and glory of God. Israel was led out of Egypt by a pillar of cloud. Moses received the law in the clouds of Mount Sinai. Jesus ascended into the clouds after His resurrection—and His disciples were told He would return the same way (Acts 1:9–11).

The most promising of Paul's words is that this incredible heavenly gathering will never end. Believers past and present will be with God forever (4:17). This event has come to be known as the rapture.

Demystifying 1 Thessalonians

The word *rapture* is never used in scripture. The term is derived from a Latin word meaning "to catch up." The same word is used by Paul to describe his being caught up into the third heaven (2 Corinthians 12:2–4), and in a (symbolic) reference to Jesus in Revelation 12:5. The mechanics of the transformation of the believers' bodies are never explained, but some kind of change is necessary based on Paul's writings to the Corinthian church (1 Corinthians 15:35–58).

📄 5:1–11

THE CHALLENGE OF JESUS' COMING

The day of the Lord (5:2) is a subject of a great deal of biblical revelation. The phrase is used in the Old Testament about twenty times, along with "the last days" (fourteen times), "in that day" (over one hundred times), Daniel's "seventieth week," and "the time of Jacob's distress." Such references are typically to future things. Paul doesn't expect the topic to be completely new to his readers.

Some of the expectations for the day of the Lord were:

- A time of great judgment and wrath on all the nations and on Israel (Amos 5:18–20; Joel 1:15–2:11)
- The overthrow of God's enemies (Isaiah 2:12–22)
- The purging of the rebels from Israel, resulting in Israel's return to the Lord (Ezekiel 20:33–39)
- After judgment, a time of great blessing as the Lord (Christ) will reign with His people (Zephaniah 3:19–20)

Although much has been written to prepare people for the day of the Lord, it will come suddenly—like a thief in the night or a pregnant woman's labor pains (5:2–3). (According to the pre-tribulation viewpoint of the rapture, all believers would have already met their Savior in the air [4:16–17], so God's sudden and harsh judgment would fall only on those who had purposely rejected Him.)

Throughout this passage, Paul uses analogies of extreme contrast to emphasize the importance of what he is saying: knowledge vs. ignorance (5:1–2), expectancy vs. surprise (5:3), light vs. darkness (5:4–5), sleep vs. alertness (5:6), and soberness vs. drunkenness (5:7–8).

It appears that some of the Thessalonians had heard that Jesus would return soon, and had decided to stop working and just hang around until He took them away with Him. Paul is attempting to motivate them (5:5) to action. They were to remain aware, informed, ready, awake, and sober.

The way Paul phrases his statements in Greek makes a specific point. For example, he isn't stressing "night" as a specific period of time, but rather as a kind of time. In other words, he is referring to the tendency of some people to adapt a nighttime kind of existence, preferring darkness to light. And the spiritual applications then become evident.

Believers should remain spiritually awake. Paul compares essential Christian qualities to a soldier's armor (5:8), as he does in his letters to Rome (Romans 13:12) and Ephesus (Ephesians 6:10–18). The call to sobriety and watchfulness is also part of a soldier's discipline. And in this context, Paul once again groups faith, hope, and love (5:8), as he is prone to do.

In a final dramatic contrast, Paul compares salvation to God's wrath (5:9–11). The fact that God has appointed believers to receive salvation is the basis for there not being a need to fear the day of the Lord and the reason they should live alert and sober. On the day of the Lord, unbelievers will experience the wrath of God as never before, and believers will experience their salvation in a way not yet realized.

There is good reason to believe that Paul's final reference to sleep (5:10) has a different meaning than the sleep of death (4:13). In this different context, he appears to be distinguishing between spiritually mature believers and those who are apathetic or spiritually dull. It explains why he follows with the admonition to encourage and build up one another (5:11). In view of what is certain to happen one day, those who are mature need to reach out to fellow believers who seem to be struggling in their Christian walk.

📖 5:12–28

PROPER CONDUCT WHILE AWAITING JESUS' COMING

As Paul begins to close out his letter, he provides a pithy list of specific guidelines (5:12–22). Church leaders are often admired for the wrong reasons (status, verbal eloquence, physical appearance, etc.), but they *should* be esteemed (loved) because of their work (5:12–13). By showing proper respect, it is easier to learn to live in peace (5:13).

Paul's urging (5:14) is a stronger plea than his previous asking (5:12), as he lists things expected of believers in regard to their dealings with one another (5:14–15). Some of the guidelines seem natural and normal: Help those who are weak, comfort the fainthearted among the congregation, be patient toward everyone.

Following the additional commands, however, can be harder or more uncomfortable. For example, admonishing the undisciplined (5:14) means confronting those who refuse to work. It can be difficult to correct a fellow believer for being too idle, yet such people need admonishment as not only a comment on their conduct, but also as a reminder that such behavior is out of line with the teachings of scripture. It can also be quite difficult not to repay evil for evil (5:15). It is a natural tendency to retaliate for a wrong suffered, no matter what the injury. Believers need reminders that God enables them to exhibit an above-average level of patience—especially with one another.

Next Paul provides a list of instructions for one's personal life (5:16–22). In his first few commands, it's not *what* he says to do that is so challenging, but rather how often he says to do it. He says to be joyful *all the time*. Pray *without ceasing*. In *all* circumstances give thanks. Maintaining a joyful spirit, a prayerful mind, and a thankful attitude are not random goals; they are God's will for believers (5:18). Such things depend on one's focus and faith in God—His person, plan, principles, promises, and purposes set forth in scripture.

So it makes sense that Paul concludes his list with instructions that relate to worship

(5:19–22). The Holy Spirit is frequently likened to fire in scripture (Matthew 3:11; Acts 2:3-4; 2 Timothy 1:6). The warning about quenching the fire of the Spirit (5:19) is clearly a prohibition against hindering the work, ministry, and gifts of the Holy Spirit. And Christians should not disparage any authoritative revelation—neither those that were delivered through the gift of prophecy in the first-century church nor those that have been preserved by the Holy Spirit in scripture (5:20).

False prophets were already beginning to infiltrate the churches as Paul wrote this letter, so he warns his readers to examine everything (5:21). Ever since, the church has had to contend with various doctrines that reject or distort the gospel of Christ. Paul's commands are just as important today as they ever were. Believers should test what they hear against the truths of scripture. The teachings that are true and good should be kept and applied. The others should be rejected, as should every other form of evil (5:22).

If Paul's list of guidelines sounds a bit difficult to master, his closing challenge is even more so. He challenges his readers to be completely holy, or as some versions read, sanctified through and through. This holiness would apply to spirit, soul, and body (5:23). Yet Paul doesn't expect believers to simply start living up to such a standard. Rather, he asks them to allow God to make the change. That way, the high standard is not such a struggle because God provides peace (5:23-24).

Paul knew the power of prayer, and he prayed regularly for the churches he had worked among. It is natural that he would ask for prayer in return (5:25). The holy kiss he endorses (5:26) had been a practice in Jewish synagogues, which may have appropriately carried over into the close fellowship of the Christian church.

This is no ordinary letter Paul was writing; it was God's message to the believers in Thessalonica. So Paul strongly charges that it be read to everyone (5:27). And he ends the letter as he started it, with the recognition of God's grace (1:2; 5:28).

Take It Home

Paul has been making references to the return of Jesus throughout his letter, but he dwells more on the topic in this section. Did he provide any information you didn't already know? Do you have any unanswered questions regarding the day of the Lord? Regardless of what you *don't* know, what things *do* you know that can provide encouragement and hope during difficult times, as they did for the believers in the Thessalonian church?

2 THESSALONIANS

INTRODUCTION TO 2 THESSALONIANS

The second letter to the Thessalonian church is a timely follow-up to 1 Thessalonians, and as such, deals with the same concerns for the believers in Thessalonica. (See the introduction to 1 Thessalonians.) Yet some in the church were not responding to the first epistle, so 2 Thessalonians has a more urgent tone.

AUTHOR

Paul's authorship of 2 Thessalonians has not been as widely accepted as that of 1 Thessalonians. The early church never doubted it, but as skeptics arose in the nineteenth century and began to dispute the divine inspiration of the Bible, 2 Thessalonians was one of the books that was challenged based on vocabulary (a few words not otherwise used by Paul) and the writer's approach to future events (warning signs for the day of the Lord and references to the man of lawlessness that weren't found in 1 Thessalonians). Yet most scholars have been convinced that the similarities between the two letters far outweigh the differences, and support the authorship of Paul.

PURPOSE

As persecution in Thessalonica continued to increase, one of Paul's primary purposes in this letter is to offer additional encouragement and comfort. He offers incentive to persevere while also attempting to correct any potential confusion resulting from a forged letter, using his name but twisting his teachings. And while Paul writes, he adds instructions to discipline those who use their spiritual beliefs as an excuse not to work.

OCCASION

Though believed to be written very soon after 1 Thessalonians, the persecution of the Thessalonian church seems to have intensified since the previous letter (1:4–5). So Paul writes this follow-up epistle from Corinth after Silas and Timothy inform him of the recent developments in Thessalonica.

THEMES

The primary intent of 2 Thessalonians is to refute false rumors and clarify the truth about the expected return of Jesus. But in that context, a second emphasis of the letter is the problem of idleness among certain church members.

HISTORICAL CONTEXT

The historical circumstances for 1 and 2 Thessalonians are so similar that most people believe this epistle was written within six months of the first one. (See the introduction to 1 Thessalonians.)

CONTRIBUTION TO THE BIBLE

The Second Letter to the Thessalonians contains scripture's only reference to the "man of lawlessness," at least, by that title (2:3). And the letter's exhortations to avoid idleness provide valuable guidelines for those who continue to anticipate the coming of Christ.

2 THESSALONIANS 1:1–12

RESPONDING TO PERSECUTION

Setting Up the Section

Paul had written 1 Thessalonians largely to encourage the believers in Thessalonica to remain faithful as they encountered persecution from various sources. But not long after sending the first letter, he heard that the opposition was getting worse, not better. Much of what he says in this opening section is in acknowledgement of what they were facing.

📄 1:1–2

A SLIGHTLY DIFFERENT SALUTATION

Paul's salutation (1:1–2) is essentially the same as the one he uses in 1 Thessalonians, with two small exceptions. First, "God the Father" (1 Thessalonians 1:1) becomes "God our Father" (2 Thessalonians 1:1). And, where he had wished them grace and peace before (1 Thessalonians 1:1), here he adds "from God the Father and the Lord Jesus Christ" (2 Thessalonians 1:2). Both alterations are likely attempts to comfort the persecuted believers by pointing them to the source of all that is worthwhile in their lives.

📄 1:3–4

COMMENDATION IN THE FACE OF PERSECUTION

As is consistent with the grace-oriented thinking of Paul, he begins with an expression of thanks to God for what had miraculously taken place in the hearts and lives of the Thessalonian believers (1:3). Paul and his associates never took for granted the growth and spiritual change in the lives of those they ministered to, nor did they attempt to attribute those things to anything they had done (hard work, methods, plans, etc.). They realized that they were simply instruments of the grace of God, and rejoiced at His work among the various churches.

Paul describes God's work, demonstrated in the love and faith of the Thessalonians, as flourishing (1:3). The word he uses is found only here in the New Testament, and provides an image of the abundant and above-normal output of a fruit-bearing tree. In spite of the increase in persecution the church was experiencing, the believers' love and faith were increasing as well (1:4)—an answer to Paul's previous prayer (1 Thessalonians 3:10, 12).

COMFORT AND PROMISE IN THE FACE OF PERSECUTION

Paul sums up his introduction with two key thoughts (1:5). The first is a statement of fact. He says that the Thessalonians' persecutions and sufferings are clear evidence of righteous judgment that vindicates the work of God in their hearts. Their opponents had rejected the gospel, so the believers' contrasting love and endurance demonstrates their faith in God. Each group would eventually be judged accordingly.

Paul's second comment is a statement of purpose, a call for the believers to endure their sufferings so that they might be considered worthy of sharing in Christ's rule in the kingdom of God. Yes, they are being persecuted, yet their endurance is proof of God's work in their hearts and a guarantee of His promises regarding their future reward in the kingdom. Therefore, they should take comfort.

From there, Paul moves to an explanation of the future righteous judgment of God (1:6–10). Readers of this letter might want to know *why* their suffering and persecutions are evidence of God's future righteous judgment. Because God is absolutely righteous (just), He will do what is right. He will recompense tribulation to those who have persecuted believers (1:6), as well as reward those who remain faithful to Him. He may not take action during a believer's lifetime, but each devoted follower can be assured that God certainly will not ignore or tolerate sin and rebellion. The fact that God will punish the people who troubled the Thessalonians is based on His justice—it is not like human revenge that is based on a sense of indignation or injury.

Critical Observation

Jesus' return is imminent, yet no one knows when it will occur. So in Paul's writing, he sometimes includes himself with the living who will experience transformation rather than death (1 Corinthians 15:51–52; 1 Thessalonians 4:16–17), sometimes with the dead who will experience resurrection (2 Corinthians 4:14), and sometimes in the category of either possibility (2 Corinthians 5:1–8).

In verses 8–10, Paul continues to explain the recompense (judgment) of God, which falls into two categories: affliction and rest. The Greek word used for affliction (1:8–9) suggests a full and complete punishment—a vindication of God. The essence of heaven is being in the presence of God. So although it is difficult for sinful humans to understand, the ultimate punishment is eternal removal from the presence of God (1:9).

It has been noted that 2 Thessalonians 1:9–10 is perhaps Paul's clearest indication of an ongoing eternal punishment for the wicked. The reference to "eternal" *destruction* suggests that Paul does not mean annihilation, but perpetual punishment. Just as believers can look forward to eternal life with God in heaven, those who reject God face an eternal death.

Yet for believers, Paul presents God's judgment as rest (1:7). The word he uses means "a loosening or relaxation" and refers to the kingdom rest that all believers will enjoy after the Lord deals justly with sin and with those who have persecuted His people while ignoring, rejecting, and even mocking His grace and His right to rule.

When will these things take place? On the day the Lord Jesus is revealed from heaven (1:7). The coming of Christ to earth will initiate the recompense, the time of God's "paying back" (1:6)—both for those who afflict others (unbelievers) and the ones afflicted (believers).

Demystifying 2 Thessalonians

Paul's accounts of the return of Jesus differ in his two letters to the Thessalonians. Here Paul portrays a much bolder picture than he had in 1 Thessalonians 4:16–17, with Jesus accompanied by mighty angels and revealed by flaming fire (2 Thessalonians 1:7–8). He provides no timetable because the emphasis should remain on the glory due to Jesus rather than the date. Yet those who hold that 1 Thessalonians 4:16–17 is the rapture of the church believe that Jesus' coming described in 2 Thessalonians 1:6–10 is a separate event, when He will return not only with powerful angels, but with all the saints as well (Revelation 17:14; 19:11–14).

The flaming fire that surrounds Jesus on His return may be a reference to the Shekinah glory of God (Exodus 40:34–38). It may symbolize the judgment of God. Or both may be true.

Another of Paul's comments worth noting is that Jesus will be glorified *in* His people (1:10). That doesn't mean that believers will verbally give Him glory. Rather, Jesus is glorified by their lives and actions rather than mere words.

📖 1:11–12

WORTHY OF GOD'S CALLING

Paul's marvelous description of the return of Christ is intended to provide comfort for the suffering believers in Thessalonica. Yet Paul doesn't want the truth of the Second Coming to only comfort their hearts and minds, but also to impact their hands and feet. Believers are to take hope in the future, yet continue to minister in the here and now. So Paul's prayer (1:11–12) is a call to action.

The Thessalonians would continue to suffer, but they could also continue to live in a manner consistent with their calling. It wasn't too soon for them to begin to glorify Jesus in the way they lived their lives (1:12). And as they glorified Him, He would fulfill the good purposes He had begun in their lives through His grace.

Take It Home

Twice in this section Paul writes about Jesus being glorified in His people (1:10, 12). The first is a reference to the future, but the second is clearly for the church in the present. Think about how believers today tend to glorify Jesus. Do you detect mostly verbal praise, or is Jesus reflected in the entirety of their lives? If an outsider ignored everything you say in church and monitored your behavior during an average week instead, would Jesus be glorified? What might help you glorify Jesus more consistently?

2 THESSALONIANS 2:1–17

HOLDING TO RELIABLE TEACHINGS

Setting Up the Section

The suffering of the Thessalonian church has been mentioned several times so far in 1 and 2 Thessalonians. We know these believers were facing a lot of persecution from outsiders. But in this section, we discover some false teachings that had begun to circulate regarding the return of Christ, creating even more stress on those who were trying to remain faithful. Paul will set the record straight and then encourage the struggling believers to stand firm.

📖 **2:1–5**

QUASHING THE RUMORS

Rumors are always problematic, and in church settings especially so. At this point, contemporary readers discover what the Thessalonian believers would have already known: Word was spreading through the congregation that the return of Jesus had already taken place (2:2). Naturally, there was a significant degree of concern and alarm. To make matters worse, the rumor also suggested Paul was the source of the information.

So, as Paul writes about the coming of Jesus and believers being gathered to Him (2:1), he refers (grammatically) to a single event. The coming of the Lord will *include* the gathering of believers to Him. It is Paul's way of immediately pointing out that the sufferings of the Thessalonians (1:4) are not a sign of Jesus' return. Rather, they would know when He arrives because they would instantaneously be gathered to Him. There would be no confusion or overlooked members of the church in a panic.

Paul doesn't want the Thessalonians to be shaken ("unsettled" [2:2 NIV]) in the meantime—his choice of words alludes to a ship that has been torn away from its moorings, out of control amid the strong winds and waves.

He identifies three sources of false reports (2:2). The first is spirits—probably a reference to claims by means of prophetic utterances. Numerous people had the gift of prophecy, but others could easily pronounce a message supposedly from the Spirit of God. The early church leaders had to carefully examine prophetic pronouncements and accept only what was from God.

A second source of false reports is someone's word. Since Paul distinguishes it from prophetic utterances, this source must refer to mere opinion or gossip, perhaps attributed to Paul and his associates.

And the third deceptive source is a letter purporting to be from Paul. Yet the one that had arrived in Thessalonica was in direct contradiction to what Paul had taught them. He reiterates in verse 15 the importance of the Thessalonian believers' remaining aware of what was being taught.

Then Paul clarifies that they should look for two events to take place prior to the day of the Lord: (1) rebellion, and (2) the revealing of the man of lawlessness (2:3).

The current popular view of Paul's first sign is that a *worldwide* rebellion must take place before the day of the Lord begins. In the original Greek, it is not *a* rebellion, but *the* rebellion. A widespread departure from truth and resistance to God will provide the seed for a great system of revolt that will be headed by a man of lawlessness—a reference to the world's last great world dictator, the Antichrist (beast) of Revelation.

Critical Observation

The book of Revelation never uses the term *antichrist*, although this figure has a number of other titles throughout scripture. Here he is called the man of lawlessness (2:3). In other places he is called the little horn (Daniel 7:8), the prince that shall come (Daniel 9:26), the willful king (Daniel 11:36), and the beast out of the sea (Revelation 13:1–10).

Paul describes this figure as a human being, not an angel or "sin personified," as some people teach. He is a man of lawlessness, standing as the epitome of opposition to the laws of God. Yet as soon as Paul introduces this character, he makes clear his destination: destruction. His certain ruin and doom are the result of his religious activity—not only his opposition to God, but his claim to *be* God (2:4). Everything about this future person reeks of Satan, from whom he will get his authority and power (Revelation 13:4).

This shouldn't have been new information to the Thessalonian believers. Paul had taught them these truths in person not too long ago. There is a slight rebuke in his reminder (2:5). The rumors that were spreading should not have shaken the faith of the Christians there.

THE POWER OF GOD THAT RESTRAINS SIN

Paul's first two proofs that the day of the Lord has not yet arrived are the absence of both the widespread rebellion against God and the man of lawlessness. And here he adds an additional proof: the continuing restraining power of God (2:6–7). The reason the man of lawlessness has not yet made his appearance is because God continues to prevent it. The time is not yet right.

It is true that the power of lawlessness is already at work but is being held in check by a restrainer. The first reference to this restraining force (2:6) is a general term, leading readers throughout the centuries to speculate that Paul might be referring to the power of the Roman Empire, the ethical Jewish influence on the culture, or other possibilities. But Paul follows up with a personal reference in his next sentence (2:7). The one who holds back the power of lawlessness must certainly be God Himself.

When God's restraint is withdrawn, the lawless one will soon be revealed (2:8). The temporary nature and sure end of his rule is made clear by two of Paul's statements. The first is, "whom the Lord will destroy by the breath of his mouth" (2:8 NET; see Isaiah 11:4). Whether the phrase "breath of his mouth" is figurative or literal, it highlights the ease with which Jesus will remove the lawless one and his godless system from the earth. He will not cease to exist, but when removed, he will be thrown alive into the lake of fire (Revelation 19:19–20). Paul's second phrase is, "and wipe out by the manifestation of his arrival" (2:8 NET). The very manifestation and splendor of the Savior's presence when He arrives will immediately render the Antichrist impotent and defeated.

However, even though this figure rules for a short time, his activity and actions will be hideous beyond belief. The source behind his coming and influence will be Satan (2:9–10). With the restrainer removed, there is nothing to hinder the work of the devil.

Demystifying 2 Thessalonians

Paul's short summary of the connection between the man of lawlessness (Antichrist) and the source of his power, Satan (2:9–12), is more fully developed by John in Revelation 13:3–8.

The man of lawlessness will be quite convincing in his deceit. He will perform miracles, signs, and wonders—things that usually authenticate divine power, yet are counterfeit in this instance. The tragic irony is that the people so willing to respond to such deceit are those who found no place in their hearts for God's truth (2:10). Even as they respond to the inauthentic signs and wonders, they are perishing—not because they never heard the genuine gospel, but because they rejected it.

Due to humankind's indifference to the truth, God will not only let the people believe a lie, but He will send a deluding influence to promote it (2:11–12). In rejecting God's revelation of Jesus Christ as Savior and Judge, people choose to delight in wickedness.

📄 2:13–17

DELIVERANCE FOR BELIEVERS

Having assured his readers with several convincing reasons why they are not yet in the day of the Lord, Paul returns to the danger they face in failing to hold to what they know to be true. Only by retaining what Paul has taught them will they continue to find comfort and strength in that truth for fruitful living under their stressful circumstances.

Paul was a knowledgeable and well-rounded teacher. He balanced his teaching on prophecy with a focus on practical Christian living. And he had no sooner dealt with the problem of Satan's lies than he returns to a positive emphasis on God's love, thanksgiving, and prayer (2:13–14).

As Paul does in other places, here he shows that salvation is the result of God's sovereignty *and* the belief of the individual (2:13). It cannot be achieved merely on human effort, yet the work of the Holy Spirit requires a response. When unbelievers respond to God's truth, He saves them; when they reject it, they cannot be saved (2:10).

The Thessalonians had begun to waver in their faith, so Paul reminds them to stand firm (2:15). God-breathed teachings had been handed down to His people and incorporated into apostolic traditions. In turn, Paul has handed those teachings on to the Thessalonian believers. They are true and dependable, and a means for standing firm against all forms of false teaching, as well as the various storms of life.

The reason for Paul's prayer at this point (2:16–17) is threefold. First, believing and holding on to the truth should lead to its practice. Second, only God Himself could effectively generate the level of encouragement and stability needed to practice His truth in the midst of a pagan environment. And third, such a wishful prayer is possible only because of what God had done for humankind in the person of His Son, through His grace.

As a result of God's great love, believers receive two wonderful gifts: eternal comfort and good hope. In the midst of the Thessalonians' struggles, these gifts would keep them looking forward to permanent consolation and everything else God has promised His people. They could hardly have asked for anything that would be more appreciated.

Take It Home

Paul isn't afraid to broach the topic of Bible prophecy. As the Thessalonians are suffering, he is able point to the future with significant understanding and clarity. His comprehension of future things led to a much more grounded outlook of the present. How is your own understanding of future things? While some events, dates, and symbols will certainly continue to be mysteries, many other aspects of the future are spelled out clearly in scripture. Do you think a better understanding would have any effect on your day-to-day Christian walk?

2 THESSALONIANS 3:1–18

REMAINING FAITHFUL...AND ACTIVE

Setting Up the Section

As Paul begins to bring this letter to a close, he emphasizes how his (and his associates') confidence lies not in human plans or promotions, but rather in God Himself. The ultimate success of any ministry depends on the faithfulness of the Lord and His Word, even though He chooses to use frail human instruments to accomplish it.

📖 **3:1–5**

CONFIDENCE IN GOD'S GRACE

As he had done at the end of his previous letter (1 Thessalonians 5:25), Paul again asks the believers for prayer for himself and his associates (3:1). Paul's team had spread the gospel to Thessalonica and then moved on to carry it to new places. Who better than the Thessalonians, who were currently experiencing the work of God among them, to pray for Paul's ongoing ministry elsewhere? Paul writes with apostolic authority to help the Thessalonians deal with their problems, yet readily confesses his own inadequacy and the need for God's enablement.

Rather than being vague and general, Paul helps the Thessalonians know what to pray for. He has two specific requests. First, he wants God's Word to spread quickly. The word he uses is *run*. With an emphasis on the message rather than the messenger, Paul desires to see the gospel proceed quickly and without hindrance. And connected with this first request is his desire that the message would continue to be glorified—that the gospel, and therefore God Himself, would receive due honor, respect, and praise.

Paul's second specific request is prayer for his deliverance from perverse and evil men (3:2). This request is certainly related to the first, but much more personal. Paul already has God's promise of personal safety in Corinth (Acts 18:9–11), where he was writing this letter, so this request shows he doesn't take such promises lightly or think himself beyond need of the prayers of other believers.

Paul makes a sharp contrast between human lack of faith (3:2) and God's faithfulness (3:3). He assures the Thessalonians that they can count on God for spiritual strength and protection at any time, and he is confident they would continue to faithfully follow the truths they had been taught (3:4). It's more than just a good feeling; it is confidence in God. Paul's confidence is not in the physical stamina of the Thessalonians to endure, but in God's ability to sustain them in growth and obedience.

Biblical references to the heart often mean the entire inner person—mind, emotions, and will. Perhaps that is the case here (3:5), although Paul might have intended it simply as a synonym for the personal pronoun (*your hearts* in place of *you*). Either way, he desires for the Thessalonians to be drawn into a deeper and more inclusive love (like God's) and a more willing and committed endurance (like Christ's).

📄 3:6–15

BACK TO WORK

In his previous letter, Paul had challenged the believers to work conscientiously (1 Thessalonians 4:11–12). It isn't until this point that he really makes clear what the problem is: idleness of some of the church members (2 Thessalonians 3:6). Apparently, a number of believers had heard Jesus was returning and had given up providing for themselves, creating a burden on others in the church. Clearly they weren't quick to correct their actions, because Paul has to address the problem again in this letter, even more strongly.

Critical Observation

The media frequently cover movements of people who think they have figured out the secrets and dates of the end of the world. Some are Christian and others aren't. Some come to tragic ends while others appear somewhat comic. Such groups have formed throughout the centuries since Jesus' *first* coming. The group at the church at Thessalonica is among the first to misinterpret and misapply the teachings of God's Word. Paul's correction is included in scripture as a guideline for others to follow.

Paul has nothing to do with promoting the sit-around-and-wait-for-Jesus philosophy, and he orders his readers to have nothing to do with those who refuse to work and who twist the teaching of scripture (3:6). The word used for Paul's instruction is the same as would be used for a military officer barking out commands. He is quite firm on the topic.

Paul isn't asking the Thessalonians to do anything he doesn't do himself. Even while performing his ministry among them he had provided for himself and had not expected handouts (3:7–8). It's not that he doesn't think he has the right to expect help (1 Corinthians 9:3–4, 6), but it is more important to him to set an example for the believers (3:9). Paul models appropriate Christian behavior for the Thessalonians and challenges them to imitate it (3:7). And it is more than a request; he insists on it as a moral necessity. As for those who are unwilling to work, Paul recommends letting them go hungry (3:10).

Demystifying 2 Thessalonians

Perhaps it was more than simple laziness causing the Thessalonians' reluctance to work for a living. The Jewish people took pride in their work and taught all males a trade. The Greeks, however, considered manual labor to be fit only for slaves. Having come from such a culture, possibly pride was a prominent motive for the nonworking Thessalonians.

The cessation of productive work was already creating problems. With too much time on their hands, some of the believers were becoming busybodies (3:11). So Paul reinforces the importance of their getting back to work and of all the believers to continue doing what is right (3:12-13). If the group of busybodies still refuse to work, Paul instructs the other believers to separate themselves—not to excommunicate and write off the offenders, but to temporarily ostracize them from close fellowship until they saw the error of their ways and repented. The sinning members needed firm correction for their own good, yet they were still brothers, and deserved to be treated with love (3:14-15).

3:16-18

A PERSONAL FAREWELL

The Thessalonians' disputes could be settled by the ultimate peacekeeper (3:16). Yet it requires a real commitment to Christ in order to experience peace at all times and in every way.

Until this point in his letter, Paul has been dictating to a secretary. But as was his custom—as readers discover here—he takes the pen and writes a short section in his own handwriting (3:17-18). And as he had done in 1 Thessalonians, he concludes this epistle as he had begun it—with a prayer of grace for all his readers (1:2; 3:18).

Take It Home

The promised return of Jesus had been misunderstood by some of the Thessalonians, creating a group of inactive busybodies. Do you detect any problems in the modern church based on similar misunderstandings of future events? What do you think is the best way to maintain a balance between joyful anticipation of Christ's return and the necessity of going on with one's daily life and commitments?

1 TIMOTHY

INTRODUCTION TO 1 TIMOTHY

First Timothy is a letter from a faith mentor to one of his dearest disciples. It is a look into the first-century relationships that made up the early church, and the issues with which they grappled.

AUTHOR

The author of this letter introduces himself as the apostle Paul. Of all the letters of Paul, the Pastoral epistles (1 Timothy, 2 Timothy, and Titus) are by far the most disputed in terms of authorship. Differences of language, style, and theology have caused many scholars to doubt that Paul was the original author. Some believe that a disciple of Paul wrote these after his death. Others think he may also have used one of his missionary companions to write out these letters (see Romans 16:22 for an example of this), and this scribe left his own stylistic mark. In any case, the differences are not as great as is sometimes supposed, and there are many features of the letter consistent with Paul's language and style. Evangelical scholars continue to assert that these letters came from the apostle's hand.

OCCASION

Paul wrote this letter from Macedonia sometime after being released from his first Roman imprisonment—around AD 63–64. Paul had left his protégé, Timothy, to minister at the church in Ephesus (1:3). At this particular time, the church was plagued by false teachers and dissension. Paul was going to be delayed in returning to Ephesus to be with Timothy and guide him in person, so he wrote this letter to offer guidance on how to choose and strengthen the leader of the church and train them to preserve godliness and reject false teaching.

PURPOSE AND THEMES

First Timothy is one of the three New Testament books identified as the Pastoral epistles, along with 2 Timothy and Titus. Paul wrote this letter, as he did the other two, to assistants who were leading communities of faith. In the letter, he offers them instructions in their role as shepherds. In the first century, this included standing against heresy and teaching sound doctrine. Understandably then, the themes of 1 Timothy are along those lines—church leadership, sound doctrine, faith in practice, and church order.

Though this letter is addressed to Timothy, there are several indications that the full intention was for the letter to be shared with the congregation and even throughout the region.

OPENING WORDS 1:1–20

Greeting 1:1–2
False Teachers 1:3–11
God's Mercy 1:12–20

THE LIFE OF THE CHURCH 2:1–15

Priority on Prayer 2:1–7
Appropriate Worship 2:8–15

CHURCH LEADERS 3:1–16

Instructions for Elders 3:1–7
Instructions for Deacons 3:8–13
Instructions for the Congregation 3:14–16

THE LOCAL CHURCH 4:1–16

The Problem of Fallen Faith 4:1–5
Timothy, the Teacher 4:6–16

INSTRUCTIONS FOR SPECIFIC GROUPS 5:1–6:2

Relationships in the Community 5:1–2
Widows 5:3–16
Elders 5:17–25
Slaves 6:1–2

EXHORTATIONS 6:3–21

Heretics 6:3–10
The Faithful 6:11–16
The Rich 6:17–19
In Conclusion 6:20–21

1 TIMOTHY 1:1–20

OPENING WORDS

Setting Up the Section

The opening of Paul's letter to Timothy reveals it to be both personal and official. It also reveals much of Timothy's task in Ephesus—facing teachers of false doctrine.

📄 **1:1–2**

GREETING

Paul identifies himself by noting the authority with which he writes (1:1). He is an apostle, an envoy, one sent with a specific mission. While all Christians are called to serve God, the first-century use of the term *apostle* referred to a very specific group—those who had accompanied Jesus. While Paul had not been one of the twelve disciples, his conversion experience brought him face-to-face with Jesus (Acts 9:1–9). In Acts 13:2, the Holy Spirit calls Saul and his companion, Barnabas, to the missionary work recorded in the book of Acts. This further legitimizes Paul's claim to be an apostle.

Paul's reference to God as "Savior" is unusual in the New Testament, but occurs repeatedly in the Pastoral epistles (1:1; 2:3; 4:10; Titus 2:10, 13).

Critical Observation

Paul's particular use of the word *Savior* to describe God may have included a specific cultural slant understandable to the readers of his day. At the time, the emperor of Rome was to be not only honored as a leader of state, but worshiped as well. The same term was applied to the emperor. At the time Paul wrote this letter to Timothy, Nero was emperor.

The language that Paul uses to describe the "hope" found in Christ has an element of certainty to it. It communicates a shade of meaning that modern language doesn't always communicate. Rather than hoping something will happen but not being sure it will, the hope Paul refers to is a strong confidence in the source of good things to come.

Paul identifies his recipient as one so dear he is like a son in the faith (1:2). Paul reserves this designation for Timothy and for Titus (Titus 1:4). Timothy had grown up in Lystra, a Galatian city Paul visited on both his first and second missionary journeys. It was on this second journey that Paul requested Timothy to serve with him (Acts 16:1–3). From there they developed the bond that is evident in this letter.

While the greeting is similar to most of Paul's letters, the addition of the word *mercy* is unique to Paul's two letters to Timothy (1:2; 2 Timothy 1:2). Unlike grace and peace, mercy was more of an Old Testament concept referring to God's loving-kindness.

▤ 1:3–11

FALSE TEACHERS

Paul had left Timothy in Ephesus to protect the church there from false doctrine (1:3). The very fact that Paul refers to these as false doctrines reveals that at this point in the first century there was a core of Christian doctrine already widely accepted and agreed upon.

Paul's mention of myths and genealogies probably describes two related problems. Both refer to some type of extrabiblical stories that had become accepted as tradition. They provided fodder for debate, but not truth for growing in faith (1:4–5).

The command that Paul refers to in verse 5 is not one specific command, but rather the sum total of the obligations of the Christian walk. The goal of that sum total is love, which comes from three sources:

1) A pure heart. This refers to someone who engages his or her whole self in doing the work to stay spiritually and morally fit.

2) A good conscience. This is the ability to tell right from wrong and to consistently choose right. It is also the absence of unconfessed sin and underhanded motives.

3) A sincere faith. This type of faith calls one to serve not for personal gain, but in obedience to God's will.

The teachers of the law Paul discusses in verses 6–7 may have been Gentiles or Jews. Whichever they were, though, they failed the test of love outlined in the previous verses. What they were teaching was not tightly connected to the scriptures. Their discussions were meaningless (1:6). While they wanted to be seen as authorities, they did not have a handle on the content and meaning of the law (1:7).

This brings Paul to a discussion of the law. Throughout his New Testament writings, Paul maintains the position that the law does not make people right with God or provide forgiveness of sins. The law only served to point out the sin of humanity so that people could realize their need for God, and thus be forgiven and made clean. That is the proper use Paul refers to in verse 8. The list following verse 8, then, makes up those who refuse to see what the law reveals—their need for God's redemption through Jesus (1:9–11).

It has been noted that the first list describes sins against God and the next list describes sins against others, much like the Ten Commandments (Exodus 20:1–17).

Take It Home

Paul's description of the false teachers can be an inspiration to us to remain faithful to the true message of the gospel. In the modern age of the church, it is still just as easy to get involved in controversies or disputes about issues secondary to the message of the gospel. Part of the job of those who lead us is to pull us back on track.

GOD'S MERCY

In verse 12, Paul moves from the sins of others to his own sinful nature, not with self-condemnation but with gratitude that out of his own sinfulness he could have been called to spread the gospel.

Demystifying 1 Timothy

Paul's history as a Pharisee included a vehement opposition to early Christianity. Acts 8:1 paints a picture of Paul approving the stoning of Stephen, the first New Testament Christian martyr. At the time, Paul believed he was ridding the world of false doctrine, but once he came to faith in Jesus, his ideas about what was true and false changed. In writing Timothy, Paul identifies false doctrine as that which stands against the truth of the gospel.

Paul's gratitude focuses on three areas (1:12):
1) God strengthened him. This is not to say that God added to the strength Paul already had, but rather He was the source of Paul's strength.
2) God found him faithful. Paul was not perfect, but because of God's grace He chose to see Paul as faithful.
3) God appointed him for service. It was not just that Paul received the grace of God, he was also a channel of sharing that grace.

In this next section, Paul sets up an interplay between his own sinfulness and God's grace (1:12–16). He claims himself to be the worst of sinners, calling himself a blasphemer, a persecutor, and "a violent man" (NIV). Certainly scripture supports Paul's claims (Acts 8:1–3; 9:1; 22:4; 26:11). But the purpose of Paul's litany of grievances against himself is to illuminate the patience of God in redeeming Paul's life.

Paul's preamble in verse 15—"This saying is trustworthy and deserves full acceptance" (NET)—is a phrase (or a variation of a phrase) he uses only in his Pastoral Letters (1 and 2 Timothy, Titus). It functions much like the Gospel writers, when they quote Jesus as saying, "Verily" (KJV) or "I tell you the truth" (NIV), in that it highlights an important statement. In this case it highlights Jesus' mission to save sinners—Paul claiming himself the worst of them all.

Verse 17 serves as a kind of spontaneous doxology not uncommon in Paul's writing. There is no known external source for this doxology, so it is reasonable that Paul himself wrote it. It highlights God's nature as eternal (no beginning or ending), immortal and invisible (existing as a spirit), and the one true God.

Verses 18–20 close this chapter with a specific instruction for Timothy. Paul's instruction, or charge, has a military connotation, almost like marching orders. It refers to the job Timothy was sent to Ephesus to do—to teach sound doctrine and quiet the false teachers. Within that context, it brings a higher level of seriousness to Timothy's responsibilities in Ephesus.

Paul's mention of prophecies (1:18) may refer to prophecies that Timothy claimed for his own life or things said about Timothy at his ordination (4:14; 2 Timothy 1:6–7).

A second time, then, Paul uses military language, encouraging his spiritual son to fight the good fight. Verse 19 tells how he will do this—with faith and a good conscience.

The two men singled out by Paul—Hymenaeus and Alexander—had evidently been members of the church. Hymenaeus had claimed the resurrection had already taken place (2 Timothy 2:17–18). Alexander was possibly the coppersmith mentioned in 2 Timothy 4:14. When Paul says he handed these men over to Satan, it means they were removed from the church. This practice, while a part of church discipline, was not simply about punishment. The hope was that the men would see their error and return.

Take It Home

Paul's encouragement to Timothy speaks volumes to the church today. Just as faith and a good conscience were Timothy's tools to fight the good fight, so are they ours today. These two—our beliefs and our practices—go hand in hand. They protect us as armor. They provide us the tools with which to fight the enemy.

1 TIMOTHY 2:1–15

THE LIFE OF THE CHURCH

Priority on Prayer	2:1–7
Appropriate Worship	2:8–15

Setting Up the Section

There has been much conversation in the church since Paul wrote the words in this chapter regarding the behavior of the women in the Ephesian community of faith. When applying this teaching universally to the modern church, it's important to keep in mind that Paul was writing for a specific situation—to help Timothy know how to deal with the false teachers assailing the community. It may not be safe to assume that Paul would have given these exact same instructions had Timothy been facing a different situation.

In both chapters 2 and 3, Paul describes the kinds of people who should be leaders in the church. He is not listing the responsibilities of those leaders so much as describing the kind of people they should be.

2:1–7

PRIORITY ON PRAYER

Since Paul does not make more than one point in this section, his "first of all" (2:1) should probably be taken as a statement of priority rather than a structural outline. He is instructing Timothy about prayer.

The different elements of prayer included here are not intended to be a list of all things related to prayer, but a reminder of the scope of prayer—requests, advocacy, thanksgiving. It is noteworthy that Paul includes thanksgiving, as he emphasizes in many of his letters, which is an element of prayer that can be so easily overlooked.

Timothy is urged to pray and give thanks for everyone, but especially for those in authority. Some have noted that those in authority may have included the false teachers Paul was warning Timothy against. These prayers likely involved prayer for the salvation of those in authority (2:3–4). Such an outcome certainly would enable believers to practice godliness without as much fear of persecution.

Both of the descriptions Paul uses—"godliness and dignity" (2:2 NET)—refer to the Christian life lived in community. Godly living is faith in practice. Dignity has to do with the earnestness with which someone walks out his or her spiritual journey. It is these kinds of examples that help others come to the knowledge of the truth—the good news of the gospel (2:4).

When Paul writes that God wants everyone to be saved, he isn't implying that everyone will be, though some have interpreted this passage that way. Taken with the rest of scripture, it is obvious that some reject Christ and face judgment. Nevertheless, God desires that all would come to know Him.

Critical Observation

Paul's encouragement that Timothy pray for his authorities takes on new meaning in light of the fact that Nero was ruling at the time, and persecution of Christians was on the rise. After Nero blamed the Christians for the fire that destroyed much of Rome, the persecution only became more severe. Nevertheless, throughout Paul's teaching, Christians were encouraged to support rather than rail against the government (Romans 13:1–7; 1 Peter 2:13–17).

Verses 5–6 function as a creed or perhaps an early Christian confession. Whether this is an external creed that Paul is quoting or his own creation, it is an affirmation of three important truths:

1) Monotheism—one God to be worshiped by all. While today this concept is familiar and foundational to the three great monotheistic religions (Christianity, Judaism, and Islam), in the first century the worship of many gods (polytheism) was the norm. Only Judaism (and Christianity that arose from it) claimed that there was only one true God.

2) Jesus' unique role as the one mediator between God and humanity. Part of the heresies of the first century involved the role of angels, which some saw as mediators between God and His creation. This is clearly refuted here.

3) Jesus' act of redemption, revealing God's purpose. The price Jesus paid was enough to ransom everyone, if they choose to receive it. This connects with Paul's statement in verse 4, that God wants all people to be saved, thus He did what was necessary at the right time, through the work of Jesus (2:6).

Paul reiterates his appointment as a herald (someone who announces important news), an apostle (one who is commissioned for a specific purpose), and a teacher (2:7). (These three claims are repeated in 2 Timothy 1:11 in the same order). He claims that he was not self-appointed, but that he was commissioned to minister to the Gentiles. Paul's life bore out this calling. He traveled to Gentile lands and spread the gospel to those who did not have the Jewish foundation of Christianity, yet who were equally in need of redemption.

Why would Paul have needed to emphasize the truth of his words as he does in verse 7? Keep in mind that while this letter was written for Timothy, it was intended to be shared among the believers in Ephesus and perhaps even farther. In the face of the false teachers who had undermined Paul's authority and teaching, this emphasis is entirely appropriate.

📖 **2:8–15**

APPROPRIATE WORSHIP

Paul returns to the notion of prayer that he first introduced at the opening of this chapter. Given Paul's claim of authority in verse 7, these next instructions carry more weight than merely a preference. Paul expects his listeners to act on them.

While contemporary prayer is often accompanied by bowed heads and closed eyes, the first-century posture for Jews and early Christians was often with face and hands looking upward toward heaven. Thus, lifting one's hands in prayer indicated a calling out to God. The fact that the hands were described as holy suggests purity of conduct, which would result in relating to each other without anger or disputes (2:8).

Just as the men receive instructions to pray with holy hands, the women are instructed to adorn themselves with good works rather than elaborate clothing and jewelry (2:9; also see 1 Peter 3:3–5 for similar instructions from the apostle Peter). Neither the wardrobe nor the speech of the women of the Ephesian church was to draw undue attention to themselves (2:9–10). These instructions may have been making reference to the temple prostitutes in Ephesus, but certainly were highlighting the struggle for these women of faith not to blend into the cultural mores that would highlight a woman's body but not her heart and soul. Paul's instructions here are not so much about specific hairstyles or fashion statements, but about the general principle that should guide a believing woman's demeanor and appearance. What is she drawing attention to and for what purpose?

Paul considers the women's faith, evidenced by good works, to be an appropriate adornment. Rather than being attractive through merely outer enhancements, these women of the Ephesian church should be attractive because of how they live and how they portray God's good work in their lives (2:10).

The instruction regarding women being silent in church is likely a specific remedy to the situation Timothy was facing in Ephesus. While it was customary that only men lead prayer in Jewish worship, it is somewhat unusual that Paul specifies only the men to pray. Elsewhere, 1 Corinthians 11:5 for instance, Paul gives guidelines for women both praying and prophesying, so the directive across the board is not for women to always keep silent. In the case of the Corinthians, though, Paul did give specific instructions—the women were to have their heads covered to reflect the authority under which they did their praying and prophesying. It is likely that each of these instructions were geared toward their particular situations rather than laying claim to universal regulations.

Paul is not supporting inequality among men and women, but contending that they have different roles. Both the created order (2:13) and a woman's susceptibility (2:14) suggest that men occupy the role of leadership.

Paul's comments regarding childbearing should be taken within context. While he says that a woman will be saved through childbearing, this doesn't mean that a women's salvation is contingent on bearing children. No other New Testament passages support that. Paul probably had in mind the preservation of a woman's significance when she practices her unique roles—in this case, the role of childbearing.

Some have offered the possibility that the women of this church were being particularly drawn in to the false teaching that was plaguing the whole congregation. While we cannot know this for sure, it does fit well with Paul's comments about the deception of Eve and his protective guidelines for women's participation in leadership roles.

The characteristics to which Paul calls the women of the church—faith, love, holiness, self-control—are no different than the standards he calls all Christians to. These are the distinctives that set these Christian women apart from their cultural counterparts outside of the faith in a way that no amount of alternate dress or hairstyle could.

Take It Home

While Paul's instructions regarding women in the church have given him a discriminatory reputation among some people, it is important to see the reason he is calling for order in the church and what that order is supposed to accomplish. This particular church was facing an attack on its doctrine. It was important for these believers to establish an order for their worship and their communication to preserve the truth and protect themselves from those who didn't speak the truth. If this body of believers allowed themselves to fall into chaos, they would only be prey for any new, louder doctrine that came along. Paul's call for order in the relationships and practices of the body are important to contemporary churches just as they were in the first century.

1 TIMOTHY 3:1-16

CHURCH LEADERS

Setting Up the Section

First Timothy is considered one of the Pastoral epistles (along with 2 Timothy and Titus) because Paul was *pastoring* his protégé in the organization and character of the church and the principles of its leadership. It would make sense then, that Paul would discuss the kind of people that Timothy would choose to lead the church with him. The instructions here are not exhaustive lists, but they offer a glimpse into the kind of mature person that can effectively rise to leadership in the local church.

📄 **3:1–7**

INSTRUCTIONS FOR ELDERS

Having set some groundwork for conduct in the church, Paul turns to the characteristics of the church's leadership. He refers to another trustworthy saying (1:15; 4:9; 2 Timothy 2:11; Titus 3:8)—aspiring to lead a congregation is noble work (3:1). In this passage, the word translated "aspires" (NET) means to set your heart on something.

The title *elder*, or *overseer*, is a term that applies to anyone who has an oversight function in the church (3:1). Its original use was not specific to the church; the term referred to anyone in a supervisory position. In Paul's letters, the overseer is most often also the teacher.

Paul lists several qualifications for the overseer in verses 2–3:

- Above reproach. This is an opening summary of the character of the overseer. It speaks to a reputation that contains no flaw that could be grounds for accusations.

- Husband of one wife. While some interpret this to mean the overseer must be married, it is more likely that it is a description of his faithfulness to the vows he has made.

- Temperate and self-controlled. He shows good judgment, living a life of balance and moderation.

- Respectable. His behavior should be appropriate to each situation.

- Hospitable. To the first-century Middle Eastern culture, hospitality, even to strangers, was highly valued.

- An able teacher. He should have knowledge of the scriptures and be able to communicate that knowledge.

- Not drunk or violent. There are obvious reasons that an overseer is not to be an immoderate drinker—it would stand in the way of many of the characteristics already listed. But also, this may appear in the list as a reaction to the false teachers that were troubling the church at Ephesus.

- Gentle, not argumentative. He should not easily be threatened or insecure, which often makes someone quick to disagree. He should also be free from harshness.
- Free from the love of money. The overseer mustn't be addicted to wine or money. He must be trustworthy to handle the finances of the church.

The next characteristics Paul lists relate to family life. Again, this is not to say that in order to be a church leader the overseer must have children, but that his management style at home (which will inform his style in the church) should be compassionate, effective leadership (3:4–5). Note that the children of the overseer aren't merely to obey, but are to obey *out of respect*. This distinction reflects on the manner in which the overseer manages his children.

Paul's admonition that the overseer not be a novice Christian is quite understandable (3:6). The word translated "conceited" or "proud" could also mean "deluded," "blinded," or "foolish" (the word originally meant "wrapped in smoke"). Because of the new faith and the quick leadership, a novice Christian may get a distorted view of himself.

The reference to the devil points to the pride that is attributed to Satan's fall. The devil is again mentioned in verse 7, in which Paul recommends that the overseer have a good reputation, even to those outside the community of faith. While we don't have any further information on exactly what Paul means by the devil's trap—whether or not it actually means a trap laid by Satan—we can feel sure that an overseer with a poor reputation in his city or region would be more of a hindrance than a help to the gospel message. That would be the kind of trap the devil would lay.

📄 **3:8–13**

INSTRUCTIONS FOR DEACONS

Paul now turns to the role of deacons. *Deacon* means "one who serves," and this appears to have been a role associated with day-to-day ministry tasks, rather than leadership or teaching. Though the seven helpers chosen in Acts 6:1–6 to distribute food to poor widows in the Jerusalem church are never explicitly called deacons, they are often viewed as the model for this service ministry in the church.

Critical Observation

Keep in mind that Paul is not setting out to define the leadership roles within the church. He is describing the kinds of service and leadership that are already being provided. He is instructing Timothy to be wise about the kinds of people who are allowed to take on these responsibilities.

Paul lists eight characteristics for deacons, many of which overlap with the list for elders in 1 Timothy 3:2–7:
1) Worthy of respect (3:8). While this is not the same term used for the overseers, it still holds the idea of a person who is serious about what he does, and who carries himself honorably.

2) Not hypocritical (3:8). This is the idea of sincerity, though sometimes it is translated "double-tongued" (NASB) or "two-faced" (NET). It is not simply that their words match their actions, but even more, that their words are the same no matter the audience. They don't say one thing to please one set of ears, then change their story for another audience.

3) Not drinking too much wine (3:8). Sobriety would be necessary for someone of the character and responsibility described by Paul here.

4) Not greedy for money (3:8). It is not that a deacon shouldn't have money, but that he shouldn't be greedy for it, addicted to it, or always anxious for more of it.

5) Holding the mystery of the faith with a clear conscience (3:9). The mystery of the faith is simply the gospel. A deacon should be deeply rooted in the Christian faith and in the lifestyle that best acknowledges and shares that faith. While this should be true of any Christian, it is something that should be proven in the life of someone before they are named a deacon.

6) Blameless (3:10). The kind of testing mentioned here is not an official test that a person must pass to be a deacon. Rather, it is the test of a person who has been observed within the community and seen to model these traits.

7) Husband of one wife (3:12). Just as with the overseers (3:2), this requirement doesn't mean that a deacon *must* be married. Instead, it speaks to his faithful character within his relationships.

8) Managing children and their households competently (3:12). Again, this is not to say that a deacon *must* have children, but that the way he manages his home and his family relationships must be taken into account in determining his ability to lead within the church.

Demystifying 1 Timothy

In the midst of the characteristics for deacons, Paul inserts a short list of four qualities for wives (3:11). Actually the word translated as "wives" could also simply mean "women." Since Paul does not include a list of requirements for elders' wives, this list may have applied to female deacons.

1) **Worthy of respect.** These are serious women. The word Paul uses here is the same that is used for the men.

2) **Not slanderers.** They should not be prone to gossip.

3) **Self-controlled.** These women should be moderate in their lifestyle, just as the overseers should be.

4) **Faithful in everything.** This characteristic is particularly important in a servant role. Dependability in the little things would make all the difference to those whom these women serve.

Though the role of deacon is servant-oriented, Paul makes it clear in verse 13 that God honors the contribution of the deacons.

3:14–16

INSTRUCTIONS FOR THE CONGREGATION

Paul has plans to visit Ephesus in the near future, but gives instructions for the believers' conduct in case his trip is delayed. God's household is the church, though this doesn't refer to a church building but to the Christians who collectively make up the body of Christ. Paul's description of the church as the pillar and support of truth carries the idea of the church as the custodian of God's truth (3:14–15).

Verse 16 contains what is probably a part of an early hymn or confession of the church. Though made up of three couplets, each phrase reveals a part of the mystery of the gospel. This mystery was revealed in Jesus' life, work, and sacrifice:

1) Revealed in a body
2) Justified in the Spirit
3) Seen by angels
4) Preached among the Gentiles
5) Believed on in the world
6) Taken up in glory

While there are differing ideas among commentators as to what each line of the hymn or confession refers to, it is agreed that this first-century writing walks through the life of Christ from His incarnation in Bethlehem to His ascension back into heaven. By including this confession of faith in his letter to Timothy, Paul offers him and his congregation a wonderful tool to moor them to the truth of the gospel in the midst of the false truths they were facing.

1 TIMOTHY 4:1–16

THE LOCAL CHURCH

The Problem of Fallen Faith   4:1–5
Timothy, the Teacher   4:6–16

Setting Up the Section

Chapter 4 picks up right where the last chapter leaves off. Paul takes the logical next step from the responsibility and role of the church to the obstacles that prevent this fellowship from being all that God had called it to be. This section includes both warnings against false teachers and instructions for Timothy in his leadership role.

4:1–5

THE PROBLEM OF FALLEN FAITH

Paul anticipated a future apostasy, a time of people falling away from their faith (4:1; 2 Timothy 3:1). Though he does not list the specific ways the Spirit gave warning of this event, a number of sayings by Jesus and the apostles could be cited (for example Mark 13:22).

The later times Paul makes reference to are the centuries between Christ's resurrection and His eventual return to set up His kingdom (4:1).

Paul clearly attributes this falling away to the work of Satan and his armies, rather than teachers who simply misunderstand the truth. In verse 2, he identifies the teachers as hypocritical liars characterized by a seared conscience. This is the image of a conscience that is deadened to feeling. They no longer sense the spirit or the voice of God.

The false teachers wrongly believed that certain appetites of the body—sexual and even dietary—were evil. Paul counters that God created both appetites to be sated with thanksgiving when they are received prayerfully and practiced biblically (1 Corinthians 10:26; 1 Timothy 4:3–5). The conclusion these troublesome teachers reach—that the physical world is inherently evil, and the more one denies him- or herself, the more spiritual he or she will be—seems to have a semblance of the truth, but is actually a perversion of the reality of the kingdom.

Paul says that nothing God created is to be rejected (4:4). The word translated "rejected" means to be "thrown away," or "regarded as forbidden." Certainly there are some things that should be abstained from, because such things have proved themselves harmful. There is even more of a case for not abusing or overusing God's gifts—being a glutton with food, for instance. These moderations, though, were not the point of the false teachers. Instead, they were calling shameful what God calls good gifts.

Verse 5 declares all these gifts of God to be sanctified by God. Paul's use of the phrase "word of God" is probably a reference to the Creation, when God called all that He created good. If God created the gifts of marriage and food as good things, then our best response is gratitude, not a sanctimonious abstinence that we imagine makes us more spiritual because of our restraint.

📄 **4:6–16**

TIMOTHY, THE TEACHER

One often thinks of spiritual leaders as those who teach what *not* to do, but here Paul tells Timothy that he should point out the truths of this epistle, and specifically the admonition he has just given (4:1–5)—that God's gifts are good and are to be enjoyed by His children. In doing this, Timothy will nourish himself as well as his congregation on the gospel of Jesus (truths of the faith) and Paul's good teaching.

Paul refers to the false teaching that Timothy must refute as myths and wives' tales (1:4; 4:7). He then gives Timothy the admonition that captures the message of this entire letter: training for godliness. This training is highlighted by a contrast between physical and spiritual training (4:8). Physical training yields temporary benefits, and the spiritual training yields eternal benefits. The function of this word picture is to not only contrast spiritual and physical training, but also the silliness of the false teaching versus the seriousness with which Timothy should take his own spiritual development.

The trustworthy saying in 4:9 (see also 1:15; 3:1; 2 Timothy 2:11; Titus 3:8) may refer back to verse 8, which functions more as a proverb in this context. The contemporary structure of scripture with verse and chapter breaks was not part of Paul's original letter. In this case, he may well have simply reversed the order of his pet phrase for highlighting an important truth.

The hard work described at the opening of verse 10 refers to the daily spiritual exercise required of training in godliness, but notice that the Christian's hope is not in that struggle but in the living God. This is a theme throughout this letter as Paul sets straight the false hope of the teachers who would have the Ephesian Christians believe that they can trust in their own struggle to make themselves holy.

The living God (3:15; 4:10) is worthy of the Christian's hope because He is Savior of all. Salvation is available to everyone because Jesus was a ransom for all (2:6). However, it is obvious that although God is the potential Savior of everyone and desires for everyone to be saved (2:4), only some will exercise the saving faith necessary to experience God as Savior. This is why Paul adds, "especially of those who believe."

Critical Observation

Paul's insistence on salvation being available to all is yet another strike at the false teachers in Ephesus. The spirituality that they proposed had an elitist quality to it, a special knowledge. But Paul reminds Timothy that our hope is in God, who offers His hope to all, not based on rules, but based on the work of Christ.

Verse 11 begins an even more direct instruction from Paul to his protégé. Paul tells Timothy to command, a concept that presupposed authority. This has led many to think that perhaps Timothy was not as outspoken as Paul and needed a reminder that he must take a stand as he leads the Ephesian church into the truths Paul has written.

While Paul does refer to Timothy's youth (4:12), that may communicate a different concept than it would today. Some suppose that Timothy could have been as old as forty when he was leading this congregation. By setting an example in speech, conduct, love, faith, and purity, Timothy will earn any credibility he may lack due to his age. Notice that the first two (speech and conduct) pertain to Timothy's external example, while the last three (love, faith, and purity) have more to do with his internal attitudes that will bear themselves out in his behavior.

From the opening of verse 13, it is obvious that Paul had plans to visit Ephesus and see Timothy's ministry firsthand. Since the scriptures were not reprinted and bound en masse in the first century as they are now, part of Timothy's ministry was the public reading of scripture. Beyond reading the actual text, he also taught doctrine and exhorted his listeners to not only hear and understand what they heard, but act on it as well.

The gift that Timothy received through a prophetic message and the custom of the elders laying their hands on him (1:18; 4:14) probably pertains to his ability, as well as his opportunity, to teach the Word of God.

Timothy was to give attention to, not neglect, this part of his ministry. Paul promises that God will use Timothy's perseverance in sound doctrine to save him, and Timothy's proclamation of that doctrine to save those who hear the message (4:15–16).

1 TIMOTHY 5:1–6:2

INSTRUCTIONS FOR SPECIFIC GROUPS

Setting Up the Section

The rest of Paul's first letter to Timothy includes very specific instructions for dealing with a variety of groups within the church. Using his gift of exhortation in varying contexts, Timothy was to exhort older men respectfully as fathers, younger men relationally as brothers, older women tenderly as mothers, and younger women with dignity as sisters. The majority of these instructions relate to widows and the church's care for them.

📄 **5:1–2**

RELATIONSHIPS IN THE COMMUNITY

Verses 1 and 2 serve as a transition between Paul's guidance in the previous chapter regarding Timothy's leadership and the specific instructions that follow regarding widows, elders, and slaves. Since Paul had already framed the church as a household, it makes sense that he would offer guiding principles within the parameters of family relationships.

Critical Observation

The purity that Paul emphasizes in verse 2 involves respect and protectiveness. It is the same quality mentioned in 4:12. There is evidence in Paul's second letter to Timothy that some sexual impropriety may have been taking place in the Ephesian church (2 Timothy 3:6–7). If so, Paul could be offering these guidelines to protect the church and its leaders from these kinds of dangers.

WIDOWS

Considering the historical context of the first century—the low status of women, the importance of the husband in the family inheritance, the obstacles for widows to make money—a widow was often unable to support herself. If a widow had no family to support her, Paul suggests that the church should fill in the gap. On the other hand, if the widow had children or extended family, then the family should carry the primary responsibility. When Paul mentions that a widow's family's caring for her pleases God, he is referring to the fifth of the Ten Commandments (Exodus 20:12; Deuteronomy 5:16), which commands us to honor our father and mother (5:3-4).

To clarify which widows are truly in need of the church's support, Paul offers these parameters—the widow that is left entirely alone, yet continues to live out her faith (5:5). His reference to the widow who seeks pleasure may refer to widows who resort to prostitution to support themselves (5:6).

In the general culture of this day, even outside of the Christian community, there was an acceptance that children were to shoulder the burden of caring for their parents. Paul's exhortation here protects the church community from the shame of being less responsible for its own than the pagan worshipers around them (5:7-8). Those who deny assistance to their aging parents and grandparents are disgraceful not only to their families, but also to their faith.

To prevent women from taking advantage of the church, Paul requires widows to be sixty years old and (formerly) the wife of one husband before including them on the official support list. They should also model good works, including child-rearing, hospitality, servanthood, and benevolence (5:9-10).

The requirement that they have had only one husband does not communicate that it is a shame for a widow to remarry. It may be simply a practical truth that a widow who had only one husband is less likely to have extended family support than a woman who has had two or more marriages (5:9).

The good works mentioned in verse 10 would not only have prepared the widow for service, they would have built her reputation. She is to be known for these good works.

It seems harsh that younger widows should be excluded from ongoing church assistance (5:11), but this refusal on Paul's part isn't based on a lack of mercy. It may be that the vows required of an older widow who is cared for by the church included a vow not to remarry, thus Paul's reference to their first, or former, pledge (5:12). By requiring younger widows to remain in circulation, these guidelines offer them another life with marriage and family.

The "sensual desires" (5:11 NIV), or "passions" (NET), are not necessarily evil, and perhaps could even be defined broadly enough to include the simple desire to have more children. But these passions were potential markers of a woman who was not ready for a life of chastity and celibacy. This woman is still in the process of building her life, thus entertains the possibility of remarriage and not merely serving the church. She may not be as single-minded as her older counterpart.

Paul also points out that assisting these women would allow them too much idle time for unhealthy gossip and socializing (5:13). The word picture he paints is one of destructive behavior both for the women involved and for the community of faith. This is not due to their age or their gender, but to the free time that entices almost anyone to fall into unhealthy behavior patterns. Instead, younger women should fill their lives with children and homes to manage. This will allow them to avoid the excessive idle time that the enemy could leverage (5:14). This seems an obvious reference to Satan, but may also refer to those who would tear down the burgeoning Christian church.

The reference to those who had already turned toward Satan (5:15) may not mean a complete departure from the church so much as someone who had entered into the behaviors that Paul describes in the previous verses: sensual desires, idleness, gossip, and so on.

Critical Observation

There has been some discussion about whether this list that Paul refers to was a kind of order of service that widows joined (5:9). Certainly this would shed some light on the judgment that would fall on a younger woman who backed out of a pledge of service to the church in favor of remarriage (5:11–12). Unfortunately, we don't have enough information to know the details for sure.

In short, the plan Paul presents for the church is that the Christian families take care of any widows in their extended family. Then those widows who have no one will be cared for by the church (5:16). Paul has sometimes been regarded as a person who has a limited view of the roles of women, but in light of this specific situation in Ephesus, he provides a generous amount of information dealing with the care of women in the church.

📄 5:17–25

ELDERS

In contemporary churches, the term *elder* has become specifically defined to certain leadership roles and functions. Keep in mind that at the time Paul wrote to Timothy, these roles were not so fully defined. All of the older men were to be revered. Even more reverence was offered for those who rose in leadership.

When Paul instructs Timothy regarding honor for the elders, this likely means both respect and financial remuneration. In other words, he is to allocate an ample honorarium for those elders who distinguish themselves—particularly in the area of preaching and teaching. The phrase "double honor" (NIV) is not a reference to twice the money, but to the double honor of respect as well as financial compensation (5:17).

To justify such remuneration, Paul quotes two scriptures (5:18). Deuteronomy 25:4 teaches the principle that the laborer should not be denied compensation for his effort. It draws from the illustration of an ox that is harnessed to a large millstone. The animal walks around in a circle accomplishing two things: (1) He is trampling the grain, separating the kernels, and (2) he is turning the mill stone that makes the flour. This animal should be allowed to eat from the grain it is threshing, rather than be muzzled so that it offers work but receives nothing in return. In the same way, those that work in the church should receive payment for their efforts.

The second citation is a direct quote from Jesus' teaching in Luke 10:7 (also Matthew 10:10): "The worker deserves his pay" (NET). The New Testament scriptures as we know them today were still in process when Paul was writing this. Paul may have encountered this teaching of Jesus in written form or oral history still being passed around among Christian communities.

Paul writes that an accusation against an elder is to be verified (5:19). This demand for two to three witnesses reflects the Jewish law. In the Old Testament, two to three witnesses were offered before a person was required to answer a charge (Deuteronomy 17:6; 19:15).

If the accusation stands, then the elder should be rebuked (5:19–20). This rebuke might take place before the whole congregation, but it also could be referred to as a public rebuke even if it took place simply before the other elders. Either way, Paul charges Timothy with the responsibility for taking seriously the doctrine of the church and the leadership of the church.

Demystifying 1 Timothy

It is entirely possible that the false teachers referred to in this letter were elders that fell from the faith. Considering this possibility sheds new light on Paul's words to Timothy regarding elders and regarding the amount of corroboration required to discipline these older men when they faced these kinds of allegations.

Paul's charge in verse 21 is made in the sight of God, Christ Jesus, and the angels. All three included in this short list are attributed with the role of judgment in the Bible (Matthew 25:31–46; 2 Peter 2:4; Revelation 20:1). The "elect angels" probably refers to those angels who did not fall with Satan. The fact that Paul specifically frames his request this way, regarding Timothy not playing favorites, communicates how serious the request was.

Also, Timothy should refrain from appointing leaders hastily. The laying on of the hands (5:22) was often a ritual that went with appointment to office. (Some churches today still include this kind of ritual when they ordain deacons and other church leaders.) Paul had already given some guidelines in choosing leadership in 3:1–13. If Timothy followed these guidelines carefully, these preventive measures could keep him from having to later be forced into a situation where he must avail himself of Paul's advice regarding elders who must be rebuked.

Timothy is also warned about appointing or accommodating sinning leaders. This may relate back to the teaching in 3:6 about not inviting a novice too quickly into leadership. If Timothy allowed someone into leadership who was then revealed to be unfit, then Timothy had a role to play in that person being given authority he was not ready to use righteously.

Paul's words here to Timothy to keep himself pure (5:22) seem to imply that once a leader has been appointed, those who appointed him are partially responsible for how well he carries out the responsibilities of his office. This may or may not have been the intent. Certainly, though, it was essential for Timothy to first keep himself pure so that he could then enable purity in the leadership of his church.

Critical Observation

Paul's concern for Timothy extends to his health, which could be improved with a little wine rather than the water of the day, which could often be contaminated. The fermentation process of wine made it cleaner to drink. While this directive to Timothy does appear abruptly, this kind of parenthetical phrase is often the way of a letter to a dear friend (5:23).

This is not a text that should be misinterpreted as open permission for the use of alcohol, nor does it prohibit its use. Paul has already warned that leaders shouldn't be given to drunkenness (3:3), but in the first century wine was a cultural reality.

While this verse should not be applied as a blanket statement on alcohol use or abuse, it does give us an insight into the everyday concerns of these men, much like our own, and the compassion on Paul's part for Timothy's well-being as a person as well as a spiritual leader.

Verses 24 and 25 pick up where verse 22 leaves off—choosing qualified leaders. The process is difficult, as 5:24–25 reveal, because everyone sins, though some are more conspicuous than others. The judgment Paul refers to can be applied either to the judgment of God or the judgment Timothy and the other church leaders must use when deciding who will serve the church in a leadership position.

Inherent in Paul's words is the idea that what appears on the surface of individuals may not reveal all you need to know in giving them responsibility—that's why it takes time to know people and to know whether they are suited for leadership. The good works of individuals may take time to see, just as their sins may take time to become obvious. This supports the advice Paul has already given Timothy not to choose leaders hastily.

📄 6:1–2

SLAVES

Slaves—noncitizens who served Roman citizens—were common in the Roman Empire of the first century. Slavery in the Roman Empire, though certainly a degrading institution, was very different than slavery in the American South most readers are familiar with. It was not based on race. Many slaves were drawn from the ranks of prisoners of war. Others sold themselves into slavery for financial reasons. Working as a slave in a wealthy household was considered better than living in poverty and destitution. Slaves could achieve very high social status, even serving as managers of large estates. They were often paid and could even purchase their own freedom. Some owned slaves of their own. Imagine the complexity of masters and servants both being a part of the church at Ephesus. While in their households they operated from very different statuses, within the community of faith they were to be considered equal. In fact, a slave could be serving as a leader in a congregation, but his master may join the community as a new convert. In that scenario, the slave might have some leadership over the master, at least as far as the church family is concerned. It is not surprising then, that Paul offers insights regarding these relationships.

Paul often offers biblical counsel for Christian slaves (Ephesians 6:5–8; Colossians 3:22–24; Titus 2:9–10). He instructs these slaves to grant their masters full respect. The same word that is translated "respect" here (6:1) appears as the recognition given to widows (5:3) and the honor that should be given to elders (5:17).

Even if, within the faith community, a slave serves shoulder-to-shoulder with his master, within their working environment it would be the slave's responsibility to grant the respect due and the owner's responsibility to grant the mercy that comes with his position of authority (6:2).

You may notice that in some versions the closing phrase of verse 2 is pulled away from the text. In those versions, this phrase functions more as an introduction to the next section regarding false teachers. Whether it applies to the preceding section or the section to come, it certainly applies to all of Paul's instructions and is one of the themes of Paul's letters to Timothy.

Take It Home

The principles Paul offers to Timothy regarding church leaders are helpful today. It takes time to know the character of the people who serve. Too often we rely on similarities in speech or thought, similar pet peeves, or past experiences. But these characteristics are superficial and can be cultural. We must live and serve with someone for a time to truly understand his or her faith journey.

1 TIMOTHY 6:3-21

EXHORTATIONS

Setting Up the Section

This final section of Paul's first letter to Timothy functions much as the closing to many letters. Rather than being a section all on one theme, it is a smattering of information: additional information on false teachers, teachings about wealth, personal notes, and a closing doxology.

📄 **6:3–10**

HERETICS

The last sentence of verse 2 may pertain more to the following verses than to the specific instructions for slaves offered in verses 1 and 2. Either way, Paul certainly wants Timothy to teach his congregation all the truths included in this letter.

Paul describes the destructiveness of those who do not agree with sound doctrine and godly teaching. The word translated "agree" has the connotation of attachment. It's not that the false teachers simply disagreed with the truth; they were detached from the teachings *about* Jesus, and thus, the teachings of Jesus (6:3).

Regarding the instruction mentioned in verse 3, the word translated "sound" has the idea of health attached to it. The truth or doctrine about Jesus is life-giving truth. It is when that truth is twisted that it becomes destructive. The words "godly teaching" (NIV) refer to the practical instruction and application that is based on the sound doctrine. If the doctrine is in error, then the life lived will be in error.

Paul's description of these false teachers—arrogant, ignorant, craving conflict—paints the picture of someone very unlike what Paul has encouraged Timothy to be as a leader. In the Greek text, these words suggest someone who is almost diseased with his penchant for dispute and dissension (6:4–5).

The reference to material wealth may imply that the teachers charged high fees, or that they simply used ministry to acquire wealth (6:5). We aren't given enough background information here to know the particulars, but we can be sure that this attitude is different from that described by Paul of a godly leader in the church (3:3, 8). The clear word picture that is painted here of those with selfish motives who stir up dissension provides a powerful backdrop for Paul's next teaching on contentment (6:6–8).

In verse 6, instead of a means to financial gain, godliness leads to contentment. Paul uses the same words that he uses in verse 5, but with a twist. Instead of the material wealth on which the false teachers had focused their ministries, godliness brings its own kind of wealth (6:6).

Paul's proverb-like truth in verse 7 is a theme that also appears in Old Testament scriptures such as Job 1:21 and Ecclesiastes 5:15.

Take It Home

In 1 Timothy 6:8, Paul sets the most basic parameters of contentment: the essentials of food and clothing. This speaks to our contemporary cultural bent of wanting more and more and more. Throughout the Bible, this theme is expressed in a variety of ways. God gives us good gifts according to His will. Finding contentment in those gifts is a result of godly understanding.

According to Paul, those who pursue wealth (instead of godliness) will find themselves in a trap that leads to ruin and destruction. It is love of money (6:10), not money itself, that is the root of evil. Lusting after money, that element of greed, is the root. It results in wandering from the faith and in many self-inflicted pains. The idea here is a person impaled on something who continues to force himself against the object, thus increasing his injuries.

It seems apparent that Paul is not talking in theory about people falling away from the faith because of greed. There may have been those in the congregation at Ephesus with whom he or Timothy had firsthand experience (6:9-10).

Paul's warnings about the love of money should not be interpreted as the idea that Christians should disregard financial issues. It is more of a warning against greed than money management. Certainly there are plenty of New Testament scriptures that encourage good money management.

📄 **6:11-16**

THE FAITHFUL

Typical of Paul's use of contrasts, he instructs Timothy to both flee and to pursue certain things (6:11; 2 Timothy 2:22).

The exhortation to flee probably applies to more than simply the immediately preceding verses on financial greed. It probably refers back to all the issues listed since verse 3 of this chapter.

The list of pursuits is similar to Paul's list of the fruit of the Spirit in his letter to the Galatians (Galatians 5:22-23), and his list of qualifications for church elders earlier in this letter (3:1-3). The list here in 6:11 is not intended to be an exhaustive list, but gives examples:

- Righteousness and godliness. This use of righteousness does not refer to the righteousness that God gives us by faith, but to the righteousness that we offer back through our obedience. Godliness adds to the right actions the right motives, not simply doing the right actions, but desiring to be made like God.
- Faith and love. In Paul's writings, these two can almost stand alone as the prerequisite to all the rest. They involve the ability both to trust someone with your heart and to offer your heart back to him or her.

- Endurance and gentleness. This is the ability to persevere through difficulty and touch with a light hand. From what we know from Paul's letters, Timothy already appears to be somewhat timid. This mention of gentleness may be an affirmation of what Timothy already is.

The word translated "fight" (6:12) has military connotations, but also conveys the image of a contest, perhaps like the Olympics. It carries the idea of an ongoing struggle to win the prize—in this case, eternal life. This third reference to Timothy's good confession may refer to commissioning for ministry, but it also may refer to his baptism in the faith (1:18; 4:14).

Timothy's confession reminds Paul of Jesus' confession before Pontius Pilate. It was before Pilate that Jesus confessed Himself as the Christ (Matthew 27:11). It was before witnesses that Timothy confessed Jesus as the Christ.

Demystifying 1 Timothy

Pontius Pilate was the Roman appointed prefect of Judea (AD 26–36). After examining Jesus both publicly and privately, he reluctantly had Jesus flogged and ultimately crucified. His full name only occurs in the writings of Luke and Paul (Luke 3:1; Acts 4:27; 1 Timothy 6:13).

Paul now cites God and Jesus as the witnesses to his exhortation to Timothy to keep his command. "Command" (6:14 NIV) here is in the singular to include all of Paul's instructions collectively (see also 1 Corinthians 14:37), perhaps including Paul's whole history all the way back to Timothy's commission at his baptism. And Timothy is to keep this command flawlessly until Christ appears, a reference to Jesus' eventual return (6:14). While in some New Testament writings (even Paul's earlier writings) Jesus' return is spoken of in more immediate terms, this particular language is a reference to the distant future. At this writing, Paul is nearing the end of his life and perhaps is acknowledging that he may die before Jesus returns.

Verses 15 and 16 may be part of a first-century Christian hymn or faith confession. It has a Jewish flavor in its style and may be reminiscent of the worship in the Jewish synagogues or local teaching centers. Paul's lofty description of God paints the picture of an authority with whom there is no peer in sight (6:15). He is the immortal, thus eternal. His unapproachable light is His glory through which we cannot see Him, though certainly we can come to know Him. God is not unapproachable—the life and work of Jesus made that point—but God's glory and essence are unapproachable for humanity. He is worthy of honor and the recognition of His power (6:16).

📄 6:17–19

THE RICH

Paul now picks back up on his discussion on wealth from verses 6–10. This is typical for Paul's writing, inserting almost a parenthetical topic in the midst of another. In this case, he inserts an exhortation to Timothy in the midst of an ongoing topic of material goods. This second installment of the discussion on wealth focuses not on those who hope to get wealth (as did 6:3–10), but on those who already have it. Since an underlying theme throughout this letter has been the false teachers, it may be that they were wealthy men and this last word from Paul relates to them.

Those who are rich must fix their hope on God (4:10; 5:5) rather than wealth, which is uncertain. Notice that Paul's words do not make a judgment simply on those who are wealthy. Instead he gives guidelines for rich people to maintain God's perspective on life. They are not to be arrogant because they have wealth, nor are they to depend on their wealth to keep them safe (6:17).

Critical Observation

Paul's statement that God has given all things for us to enjoy is an important one (6:17). Asceticism purported that the more spiritual a person was, the more pleasures of life he or she would abstain from. But with the idea that God gives us all things to enjoy, the spiritual path would also be marked by receiving those gifts and even taking pleasure in them, but within God's will.

Instead the wealthy are to match their amount of wealth with their amount of good deeds. Also, they are to be generous, ready to give at all times. And finally, their attitude must be one of willingness to share what they have (6:18). Each of these things requires a denial of self. It is only natural instinct for a person who has much to protect what he or she has. Yet Paul writes that those who have must maintain their dependence on God and share their resources.

Verse 19 is reminiscent of Jesus' Sermon on the Mount about laying up treasures in heaven rather than merely storing up wealth on earth (Matthew 6:19–21). It is in this way that we live real life. Again, Paul's teaching is reminiscent of Jesus' own words; He came to provide the fullest life to humanity (John 10:10).

📄 **6:20–21**

IN CONCLUSION

Paul closes both of his letters to Timothy with the similar instructions about guarding his ministry. When Paul writes of what has been entrusted to Timothy's care, the idea is almost like a deposit made into a bank. It is deposited there in order to be kept safe and to sometimes even earn interest. In the same way, Timothy's ministry in Ephesus was given to his care. He is to keep it safe and to allow it to return on the investment.

This idea of avoiding false knowledge and empty chatter is Paul's last blow to the false teachers plaguing the Ephesian congregation (6:20; 2 Timothy 1:14; 2:16). Paul is probably referring to the early Gnostics here. This was an esoteric movement, not full-blown until the second century. They believed themselves to be protectors of secret knowledge. But whether Paul was specifically referring to that particular burgeoning movement or not, these false teachers clearly claimed some sort of special insight that set them apart from the mainstream church. The same is true of cults and false religious movements today.

Paul mentions those who wandered from the faith because of these false teachers (6:21). The word translated "wandered" (NIV) carries the idea of someone who misses the mark. It is not the idea of someone who has left the faith never to return, but rather someone who gets sidetracked and detours, missing the point of the truth.

Paul leaves Timothy with the same closing greeting in both of his letters: "Grace be with you" (6:21; 2 Timothy 4:22). The *you* in this case is plural. Since the expectation was that this letter would be read to the congregation and even shared among congregations, Paul's farewell reflects that reality.

Take It Home

Paul's first-century letter to Timothy about the matters of the community of faith has much to offer us today. Discerning between the truth and the almost-truth is essential to the life of the church. Choosing leaders who have something to offer and can sustain that investment is something we still strive for. Understanding the balance between having good gifts from God to enjoy and using those gifts to invest in His kingdom is a balance we struggle to maintain. May we read Paul's words and all aspire to live the life that is truly life (6:19), being faithful in our doctrine and our behavior. Paul's first letter to Timothy reminds us how to do so.

2 TIMOTHY

INTRODUCTION TO 2 TIMOTHY

AUTHOR

Of all the letters of Paul, the Pastoral Epistles (1 Timothy, 2 Timothy, and Titus) are by far the most disputed in terms of authorship. Differences of language, style, and theology have caused many scholars to doubt that Paul was the original author. Some believe that a disciple of Paul wrote these after his death. Others think he may also have used one of his missionary companions to write out these letters (see Romans 16:22 for an example of this), and this scribe left his own stylistic mark. In any case, the differences are not as great as is sometimes supposed, and there are many features of the letter consistent with Paul's language and style. Evangelical scholars continue to assert that these letters came from the apostle's hand.

PURPOSE

Paul wrote this letter to Timothy, someone who came to faith through Paul's ministry, then worked as a colleague, and finally took on a leadership role at the church in Ephesus. The instructions in this letter serve to give Timothy guidance in leading the church, which included battling with false teachers.

OCCASION

When Paul wrote this letter, he was in prison in Rome and had been deserted by most of his colleagues. He was also aware that his life was reaching its end and may have had some sense of passing the torch of leadership on.

Timothy was in Ephesus, troubled by corrupted doctrine that was affecting his congregation. Paul reached out to Timothy through this letter to offer guidance and to connect and communicate as old friends will do.

THEMES

The themes of 2 Timothy center on the need for boldness in leadership and the need for faithfulness in the Christian walk. Additional themes are instruction in church leadership and how to identify false doctrine and do away with the needless controversy it creates.

CONTRIBUTION TO THE BIBLE

Along with 1 Timothy and Titus, 2 Timothy offers a real-life look at the church, its conflicts, and its leadership in the first century. It offers some key insights regarding scripture itself (3:16–17).

2 TIMOTHY 1:1–18

GREETINGS AND SALUTATIONS

Setting Up the Section

Paul opens this letter, as he does many of his other letters, with a salutation and personal greetings. This letter is a peek not only into first-century Christianity, but a personal window into the relationships that made up the church—both those that involved valued solidarity and those that involved obstacles and conflicts.

📄 **1:1–7**

THE GOSPEL IS WORTHY OF CONFIDENCE

The author identifies himself as the apostle Paul (1:1). *Apostle* means "one who is sent." This is a title of authority. While all Christians are called to serve God, the first-century use of this term referred to a very specific group—those who had accompanied Jesus. While Paul had not been one of the twelve disciples, his conversion experience brought him face-to-face with Jesus (Acts 9:1–9).

The fact that Paul notes he is an apostle *by God's will* means he is responding to a call rather than simply choosing a vocation of his own volition. This reality gives authority to his words and a greater responsibility on the part of his readers to listen and apply his instructions.

The affectionate title, "dearly loved child" (1:2 HCSB), not only conveys Paul's instrumental influence in Timothy's spiritual life but also affords Timothy credibility in the Ephesian church, where he was probably still serving the Lord (1 Timothy 1:3). Certainly it communicates the depth of the relationship between Paul and his protégé.

The threefold greeting of "grace, mercy, and peace" is unique to Paul's two letters to Timothy (1:2). Grace and peace are included in many of Paul's greetings, but here the word *mercy* is added.

In this thanksgiving section of his letter, Paul's mentions his ancestors. This may be in part a foreshadowing of the words he will write in the next few verses about Timothy's family, but it also serves to build a bridge between Paul's past experience in Judaism and his current faith in Jesus (1:3). Paul had certainly served God with as much zeal as a Jewish Pharisee as he did as a Christian missionary. Believing in Jesus did not cause him to reject his religious roots. While his strategy certainly changed with his understanding, it was all connected; he served the same God.

His mention of a clear conscience communicates a sense of no regrets (1:3; Romans 1:9). Someone who didn't understand the grace of God as Paul did could have become mired in the reality that he or she had once vehemently worked against the faith he or she now evangelized. But Paul's clear conscience was that he had served God wholeheartedly at each point in his understanding.

Paul's mention of Timothy's tears (1:4) is probably a reference to the last time they were together—possibly when Paul was taken to prison in Rome. While this may seem an out-of-place reference considering the Western culture in which men are often pressured against expressing strong sentimental emotion, the first-century Judean culture held a different bias.

Paul's longing to see his son in the faith is a portal allowing us to see some of Paul's own loneliness in prison. As he will reveal later in this letter, he has been abandoned by most of his colleagues (1:15; 4:10, 16).

Paul's next words affirm Timothy's faith and the source of his early Christian teaching—his grandmother Lois and mother Eunice (1:5).

Demystifying 2 Timothy

Paul and Barnabas visited Timothy's hometown of Lystra (in Galatia) on their first missionary journey. It is likely where Paul first met Timothy and his family. When Paul visited Lystra again on his second missionary journey, he was so impressed with Timothy's faith that he took him along as a missionary companion. Timothy was one of his closest and most trusted associates from that point onward.

Timothy was the child of a mixed marriage. His mother was Jewish, and his father was a Greek (Acts 16:1). When Paul says that Timothy's faith "first lived in" his grandmother Lois and his mother Eunice (1:5), he may be referring to their Jewish faith, which gave Timothy a solid foundation for receiving the message about Jesus, the Jewish Messiah. Or it may mean that Lois and Eunice first believed Paul's gospel, and then passed that faith on to Timothy. (Acts 16:1 refers to Timothy's mother as "a Jewish woman who was a believer," meaning she was a Jewish Christian.) In either case, Timothy had a solid religious upbringing that centered on God's Word.

Paul calls Timothy's faith sincere; in other words, not hypocritical (1 Timothy 1:5; 2 Timothy 1:5). This kind of sincere faith would have stood in great contrast to those who had not stood by Paul in his most difficult days (1:15; 4:10, 16).

Finally, Paul reminds Timothy of what God has done in his life. The gift of God that Timothy is to keep ablaze is not specified, though it is more than simply his natural gifts and abilities (1 Timothy 4:14; 2 Timothy 1:6). This gift is related to the ministry and calling of the Holy Spirit in Timothy's life.

In encouraging Timothy to *fan the flame*, Paul is not indicating that Timothy had fallen from the faith and needed restoring. Instead, he is affirming something Timothy has already received and is using. It was Timothy's responsibility to be a steward of that gift, to keep it blazing.

Paul's use of the word *spirit* in verse 7 (spirit of timidity. . .spirit of power) probably does not mean the Holy Spirit. Instead, it refers to a gift God's Spirit offers those in whom He dwells. The Holy Spirit inside of Timothy enables Timothy to live with a spirit of power and love and the absence of fear. Taking verses 6 and 7 together, this may be Paul's way of encouraging Timothy to move beyond his own timidity and lead in a bolder fashion.

📄 1:8–12

THE GOSPEL IS WORTHY OF PROCLAMATION

Three times in this chapter Paul warns Timothy against being ashamed—all in the context of suffering or persecution (1:8, 12, 16). These warnings do not mean that Paul felt that Timothy was already ashamed. Instead they are meant to have more of a bolstering effect.

Paul also invites Timothy to join his suffering (1:8; 2:3). In Paul's thinking, when a believer is not ashamed, he proclaims the gospel, resulting in suffering and persecution (3:12). This kind of suffering—that which proceeds from sharing the gospel—is the "holy life" (1:9 NIV) God has called us to live. Paul often reminds his readers that it is the gospel, not good works, that saves the believer. His reference to God's purpose highlights the sovereignty and intentionality of God.

Because of God's grace, which is available in Jesus, Christians anticipate the eternal life that the gospel promises rather than fearing death (1:9). The word translated "appearing" in verse 10 is the noun form of the verb used in 1 Timothy 3:16, which says that Christ "appeared in a body" (NIV). It's also the term Paul uses to refer to the return of Jesus, or His appearing. The gospel of Jesus, in its entirety, brings all these things to light.

Critical Observation

Some translations set 2 Timothy 1:9–10 apart as a poetic chorus, perhaps an early Christian confession. The truths included here fit so well within Paul's text, though, that some have concluded that even if it is a part of hymn text, Paul may have written the hymn or confession himself.

In the face of his own persecution, Paul embraced his role as a spokesperson for the message of grace, the gospel, and he denies being ashamed of it (1 Timothy 2:7; 2 Timothy 1:11–12). The basis of Paul's boldness, however, is not personality or even character—it is God Himself. Paul's relationship with God, in whom he believes, is the key to his ability to stand in the middle of difficult circumstances without being destroyed by them.

Paul's mention of that which he has committed or entrusted to God (1:12) is actually a financial concept, like a deposit at a bank. It paints the picture of someone giving his or her valuables to a friend to hold in safekeeping.

The language at the end of verse 12 has been interpreted in different ways. Either God is able to guard what He has entrusted to Paul (the gospel), or God is able to guard what Paul has entrusted to God. In either case, God is able to do what needs to be done in both the spread of the gospel and in the lives of those who spread it. The day Paul refers to at the end of verse 12 is the second coming of Jesus.

THE GOSPEL IS WORTHY OF PROTECTION

Verse 13 opens with Paul's reference to what Timothy has heard from him. That would encompass all of the teaching shared between this mentor and his protégé, not simply what has been written in this particular letter thus far.

Aware that the threat of persecution may entice fearful Timothy to compromise his message, Paul writes that he should hold on to the "pattern of sound teaching" (NIV). In 1 Timothy 1:16, the same Greek word that is translated "pattern" here, is translated "example." Both concepts work.

The word that is here translated "sound" can also mean "healthy," as in "sound mind," "sound judgment," and "sound investment."

The "deposit" (NIV) that Timothy is charged with protecting in verse 14 is a concept that comes from the same word translated in verse 12 as what has been entrusted to God. In verse 12, though, God is keeping the deposit safe. In verse 14, Timothy is placed in charge of that duty with the help of the Holy Spirit.

As Paul closes out this section of his letter, he galvanizes his warning to Timothy by naming individuals who used to follow Christ but have turned aside along with those in Asia, presumably due to persecution (1:15). We don't have any further information about this incident in Asia or about Phygelus and Hermogenes, but we are safe to assume that Timothy knew the situation. From this text it seems obvious that these men were ringleaders in opposition against Paul.

In contrast to Phygelus and Hermogenes, Onesiphorus is mentioned as a positive example for Timothy. While Onesiphorus is mentioned only here in the Bible, other historical literature refers to him as one of Paul's converts. He was unaffected by any stigma attached to Paul's imprisonment or fear of the consequences that associating with Paul might bring (1:8, 12). He ministered to Paul in Rome and Ephesus (1:17-18). Since only his household is mentioned here and in 4:19, many conclude that Onesiphorus may have already died for his faith.

Demystifying 2 Timothy

If Onesiphorus was already martyred, why did Paul pray for him? This passage is not a proof text for praying for those who are already dead. Paul's reference to "that day" (1:18) is to the final judgment before Christ that everyone—those living and dead—will face. The focus of Paul's statement is on Onesiphorus's behavior while he was living. In light of the way Onesiphorus has lived his life, Paul hopes for mercy to come to his family and mercy to come to him at the final judgment.

In verse 17 Paul refers to Onesiphorus's efforts in searching for him in Rome. The difficult search may have had to do with the lack of support offered by others whom Paul has mentioned. Perhaps they were afraid to offer any information that would associate them with Paul, thus Onesiphorus couldn't get enough information. Or it may have simply been that navigating the Roman penal system was a difficulty (1:17).

Take It Home

Paul and Timothy's journey in faith is one of intertwining relationships and interpersonal investment. Their stories and all the players in them—Lois, Eunice, Phygelus, Hermogenes, Onesiphorus—remind us of the power of community in faith. The support that we offer each other, or fail to offer, has ramifications beyond each individual situation. That's because we are a body—in fact, the body of Christ. How we live and move together sends a message to the world around us.

2 TIMOTHY 2:1–26

PERSEVERANCE

The Gospel Is Worthy of Hardships Endured　　　　　　　　2:1–13
The Gospel Is Worthy of Faithfulness　　　　　　　　　　2:14–26

Setting Up the Section

Rather than focus on the doctrines that have been tainted by false teachings, which is a topic that makes up much of the Pastoral Letters, chapter 2 opens with a warm exhortation from Paul to Timothy regarding Christian service.

📖 2:1–13

THE GOSPEL IS WORTHY OF HARDSHIPS ENDURED

At the close of chapter 1, Paul urges Timothy to follow the example of Onesiphorus's faithfulness. The use of "therefore" (NASB), or "so" (NET), suggests that these next thoughts from Paul are a continuation from the previous section (2:1).

Paul's encouragement for Timothy to be strong is not simply an exhortation for Timothy to gather his own self-will and bravado. The fact that Timothy is to be strong in *the grace of Jesus* tempers self-will with the enabling of the indwelling Spirit. Timothy's strength will find its source in grace.

Paul had entrusted the message to Timothy (1:14) and now commands Timothy to entrust it to others who would faithfully protect and proclaim it. The witnesses Paul mentions (2:2) could refer to the elders at Timothy's ordination and baptism (1 Timothy 4:14), but in this case it more likely refers to all those who had heard Paul's teaching along with Timothy. Rather than one specific truth, it encompasses all of the truth that Timothy has been exposed to under Paul's teaching. It is the full scope of that truth that Timothy is now bound to release to listening ears and hearts.

Paul's use of the word *entrust* (2:2) places Timothy in the role of a guardian over this message of the gospel. This is part of Timothy's discipleship under Paul. While some have perceived this particular statement of Paul's to be a kind of apostolic succession (one apostle conferring his special position to someone else), a more likely description is one mentor's encouragement that his disciple go and do something with all he has been taught.

Critical Observation

Paul employs three metaphors for the Christian life (soldier, athlete, and farmer) to help Timothy understand and apply his responsibilities:

- The soldier. Suffering is as common to the Christian as it is to the soldier. In order to please a commanding officer, both the soldier and the Christian will abandon the conveniences of civilian life for the sake of a higher calling. They will endure (2:3–4).

- The athlete. By breaking the rules, a Christian can disqualify himself for effective ministry— thus leaving his contest incomplete—like an athlete can disqualify himself from a race (2:5).

- The farmer. Finally, the hard work of faithfulness to Christ will be rewarded just as the hard work of the farmer is rewarded in the harvest (2:6).

Each of these metaphors is worthy of reflection on its own merit as Paul suggests (2:7), but together they also point to a common truth—the importance of enduring to the end.

In verse 8, Paul defines the gospel by highlighting Jesus' resurrection (He is Lord) and lineage (He is King). These two descriptions also highlight both Jesus' deity (by His resurrection) and His humanity (by His lineage). This may have been an indirect hit from Paul to the false teachers who were troubling Timothy's church. While there is much we do not know about the specific heresies being bandied about, it seems clear that they were based on a misunderstanding of who Jesus was.

The most important message of verses 8 and 9 is not the reference to Paul's imprisonment, but to the fact that God's message cannot be hindered by the schemes or misfortunes of anyone.

Paul clarifies his own role in God's sovereign plan as an instrument to bring the elect to Christ and thus to eternal life (2:10). The "elect" here refers to those who had not yet placed their faith in Jesus.

Paul introduces his next thought with a reference to its trustworthiness (2:11). This kind of setup can also be found in 1 Timothy 1:15; 3:1; 4:9 and Titus 3:8. In some versions of the Bible, the verses that Paul introduces as trustworthy—verses 11–13—are set apart as a poetic chorus, perhaps a hymn of the day of an early Christian confession. It is made up of three couplets: The first contrasts death and life; the second contrasts endurance and rewards; the third highlights total commitment. As a whole, this poem communicates that God will reward both martyrdom and endurance. Although God's faithfulness supersedes our unfaithfulness, He will reject those who reject Him.

📄 2:14–26

THE GOSPEL IS WORTHY OF FAITHFULNESS

Not only is Timothy to remember Paul's teaching (2:8), but he is also to remind others (2:14) of it. Fighting or debating over terminology is useless. The phrase "before God" (NIV) increases the seriousness of the warning.

Second Timothy 2:15 is a key verse. Some scholars have connected Paul's thoughts here to Jesus' parable of the talents (Matthew 25:14–28). The idea of the words *correctly handling*, regarding the word of truth, carries with it the idea of cutting straight. Instead of quarreling over terminology, the Christian should do his or her best to correctly teach God's Word. This carries more than the idea of being studious; here it's the idea of a person who has a great zeal for his or her ethical responsibilities.

The "godless chatter" (2:16 NIV) and the follow-up comparison to gangrene (2:17) is a direct hit on Paul's part against the heresies of the day. In the first century, gangrene was considered fatal, so Paul's use of it here paints an apt description of the spiritual malady of false doctrine (2:17).

Timothy probably knew Hymenaeus and Philetus, whom Paul names as examples of those who "wandered away from the truth" (2:18 NIV). According to 1 Timothy 1:20, Hymenaeus was excommunicated from the church because of his heresy. Knowing this makes the illustration of gangrene even more apropos. Often gangrenous limbs have to be amputated in order for the body to remain healthy.

Demystifying 2 Timothy

The specific nature of the resurrection that these two men misrepresented is unclear, though it was not regarding Jesus' resurrection (2:18). Perhaps they were teaching that the resurrection we are promised in Christ is a spiritual concept rather than an actual event to anticipate. This could have been a by-product of the melding of Christian concepts with the Greek philosophy that all physical things were innately evil. Therefore, a physical resurrection was not to be desired. Whatever the exact nature of their teaching was, it caused many to lose hope.

Paul counters with the notion that God's foundation will stand firm and that "the Lord knows those who are his" (2:19 NIV). The building metaphor seems to be one of Paul's favorites. In this case the foundation refers to the church, which has received God's seal, or mark of ownership. The first inscription that Paul quotes is from Numbers 16:5. Its context for this statement is a rebellion led by a man named Korah. It occurred during the time that the Israelites were on their journey to the promised land (Numbers 16:1–5). The second inscription is not a direct quote from the Old Testament, yet it carries the same theme: that God knows the difference between those who are truly His and those who claim another truth.

In verses 20–21, Paul shifts focus to the proper kind of conduct that flows from the gospel. In his illustration, two categories of objects are described: ordinary wooden and pottery bowls (or utensils), and gold and silver bowls (or utensils). Both of these types of articles would be used in a house, but with different functions. The gold and silver would be used for honorable uses, such as at a banquet table, while the wood and pottery for dishonorable functions, such as carrying garbage. There are two main interpretations. Paul may be referring to the dishonorable actions of the false teachers, which demonstrate their true nature as dishonorable objects. Or he may be calling Christians to purify themselves so that God will use them for greater and more noble tasks (see verse 21). It is possible that both ideas are present.

Next, Paul instructs Timothy to flee from youthful passions, including the desire to win arguments by quarreling (2:22). Since Paul and Timothy knew each other well, Paul could fashion his advice specifically for his young friend. The passions mentioned here are not merely sexual, but include all the extremes of youth. As Paul often does, he contrasts what Timothy should *flee from* with what he should *pursue*: righteousness, faith, love, and peace.

After all of this discussion about controversy and empty debate, Paul closes this section with a final admonition to Timothy against quarreling, in this case a reference to drawn-out verbal bouts. Paul's reference to the Lord's servant points to Timothy, specifically in his role as church leader. Timothy was not to give in to quarrelling. Instead, he was to focus on the truth and the walk that God required of him (2:23–24).

Paul goes on to say that gentleness characterizes the Lord's servant and may lower the defenses of opponents. The tone here is not one of retribution, but of actions committed with the hope of the return of those who have fallen from faith. God alone grants the repentance (Romans 2:4) necessary to escape the devil's trap (2:25–26).

The idea of bringing those fallen back to their senses is that of sobering up after being deluded. The phrase that in English refers to the devil taking these fallen ones captive carries with it the idea of someone taken alive. It is actually the same phrase Jesus used when he told Peter he would catch men instead of fish (Luke 5:10). The difference, of course, is that Jesus intended to make His catches in order to save, and the devil laid his traps in order to destroy. Paul wanted Timothy to be wise in dealing with those caught by both.

Take It Home

Quarreling over words is a topic that comes up several times in Paul's letters to Timothy, and it seems obvious that Paul hopes the believers in Ephesus will not waste their time and energy disagreeing over words and thus be distracted from living the life God has called them to.

In contemporary culture, with denominational differences in doctrine and lifestyle, there are many opportunities to disagree. Paul's words remind us, still, to choose what is important, and to live the life Jesus modeled for us, focusing on the gospel message rather than quarrelling about details.

2 TIMOTHY 3:1–17

THE LAST DAYS

Setting Up the Section

This next section of Paul's letter casts a shadow. There are difficult days ahead, and Paul predicts that the uphill battle against sin will only get steeper over time.

📄 3:1–9

THE GOSPEL IS WORTHY OF ACKNOWLEDGEMENT

Paul opens this section with a call to pay attention—"Mark this" (3:1 NIV). The words "terrible times" (NIV) also mean "hard to bear, dangerous."

The last days referred to in verse 1 specifically represent the time immediately preceding Jesus' return. But in a broader sense, the last days actually encompass the whole era between Jesus' ascension back into heaven until His second coming.

The vice list that follows in verse 2 includes eighteen indictments. Perhaps the first one listed, "lovers of self" (NASB), governs the rest of the list (especially with "boastful," "proud," and "conceited" following 3:2–4). In company with more offensive sins, Paul includes being disobedient to parents (3:2) and slanderous behavior (3:3)—a sober reminder of the wickedness of every sin, even those we may consider less offensive.

There isn't an obvious structure to this list, though a theme could be those who substitute personal pleasure for God (3:4).

Paul sums up the list with a reference to false godliness (3:5). This form of godliness exhibits none of the potential regeneration attributed to faith in Jesus. It was more than faulty or empty religious ritual. It was a turning away from things of the Spirit. Timothy was to turn himself away from people who practice this form of godliness without power.

In verses 6–7, Paul offers more information about the people described in the preceding verses. They would worm their way into positions from which they could deceive susceptible women. The words translated "worm their way" (3:6 NIV) took away any idea that this deception had benign motives. Instead, it was intended to trick and to destroy.

The fate of the women described here is not a statement about females in general, but rather about these specific women who were being easily swayed by false philosophies. They were spiritually immature and ignorant of the truth.

Jannes and Jambres (3:8) are not names you will find in the Old Testament. They were the traditional names given to the Egyptian magicians who contested Moses before Pharaoh (Exodus 7:11, 22) and became symbols of those who oppose the truth. Just as those magicians were exposed in their trickery, those who stand against the truth in Ephesus will be exposed (3:9).

Demystifying 2 Timothy

Exodus 7–9 records Moses' encounter with the Egyptian Pharaoh and his magicians that Paul references in 2 Timothy 3. God had instructed Moses to perform certain miraculous signs to convince Pharaoh that he'd been sent by God. At first, the magicians in Pharaoh's court performed similar signs, but eventually they were unable to accomplish what Moses could accomplish by the power of God's Spirit (Exodus 7–9, specifically, 8:18–19).

📄 **3:10–17**

THE GOSPEL IS WORTHY OF STANDING AGAINST OPPOSITION

Paul offers Timothy a list of positive traits (3:10) from his own life that contrast with the list of vices in verses 2–5. The fact that Paul practiced the first seven traits in this list—teaching, lifestyle, purpose, faith, patience, love, and endurance—may have invited the persecutions and sufferings that he experienced (3:11). Paul had been persecuted in Antioch, Iconium, and Lystra (Acts 13–14), but this resistance didn't prevent him from returning later to encourage believers in those cities. In fact, it was during his return visit to the city of Lystra that Paul found Timothy (Acts 16:1–3).

Paul follows up these thoughts about his own persecution with verses that paint a picture of a world in which evil people increase, and Christians face persecution (3:12–13). This persecution may or may not come in the physical form, but certainly even Jesus Himself prepared His followers to suffer in His name. The word translated "impostors" can also mean "wizards." This may be a reference back to Jannes and Jambres, the magicians mentioned in verse 8.

With persecution on the rise, Paul instructs Timothy to weather such turbulent times by continuing in what he had believed since childhood, presumably under the influence of his mother and grandmother (1:5; 3:14–15). The mention of the holy scriptures here refers to the Old Testament. While some of the stories of Jesus had been gathered by the time Paul wrote this letter, the New Testament was not yet complete in the form it is today.

Paul provides two indispensable characteristics of scripture:

1) It is inspired by God—God breathed it out.
2) It is profitable to prepare godly people for every good work.

This preparation for every good work happens in four ways: teaching, rebuking, correcting, and training. The first two—teaching and rebuking—are related more to doctrine. The second two—correcting and training—are related more to practice. If all scripture originated with God, who cannot lie (Hebrews 6:18), then it is true.

Critical Observation

Inspiration refers to the supernatural process whereby God influenced people to record scripture. The Christian church reveres the Old and New Testaments (collectively, the Bible) as inspired by God (specifically, through the Holy Spirit) and as authoritative in Christian living. The process of inspiration is further explained in 2 Peter 1:20–21.

2 TIMOTHY 4:1–22

IN CONCLUSION

Setting Up the Section

This final chapter begins with a solemn charge to young Timothy "in the presence of God and of Christ Jesus, who will judge the living and the dead" (4:1 NIV). The opening introduction adds urgency to all that follows. These final words come from a man who has spent time on both sides of Jesus—persecuting Him and proclaiming Him. Writing from prison, Paul shares his mission with Timothy.

📄 4:1–8

THE GOSPEL IS WORTHY OF ENDURANCE

It is likely that Paul wrote to Timothy with the knowledge that he was facing the reality of his imminent death. His reference to Christ's judging the living and the dead is probably a quote from a baptism or confessional creed (4:1).

Paul offers Timothy a charge of five commands (4:2):

1) Preach the Word. There is an underlying urgency to the language of this command, almost in the sense of responding to a crisis.

2) Be prepared. The idea of in and out of season means to be prepared whether you have an obvious opportunity or not; it is to always be ready.

3) Correct. Show the right way life is to be lived.

4) Rebuke. While closely related to correction, the idea of rebuke has a bit more of a confrontational element to it.

5) Encourage. Going a step beyond correction and rebuke, encouraging those in the community adds a positive element of going alongside others as they need it.

Critical Observation

Timothy's five charges should be executed with patience and careful instruction. This speaks to both the manner in which Timothy goes about his ministry—reflecting the patience of God—and the sound doctrine upon which his ministry is to be based. Since doctrinal decay usually precedes moral decay, the rejection of sound doctrine will likely precede the difficult times of immorality Paul warns of in 3:1–5.

"Insatiable curiosity" (4:3 NET) is a phrase that describes those who no longer want the simple truth or sound doctrine (4:3–4). Instead, they want novelty and entertainment. While Paul has already described the false teachers who harassed Timothy's church, here he is turning the tables and highlighting the audience that is attracted to those false teachers. Understanding that audience, though, it makes sense that the teachers who are willing to satisfy that itch for novelty build their popularity by substituting fantastic myths for the truth. The language in verses 3 and 4 is reminiscent of Paul's initial warning to Timothy in 1 Timothy 1:4 about "myths and endless genealogies" (NIV).

In verse 5, Paul takes a right turn and shines the light on Timothy again. He uses these admonitions:

1) Timothy should avoid the kind of nonsense described in verses 3 and 4. Paul's admonition that Timothy *keep his head* means that Timothy should live a sober, morally alert life, staying within legal, moral, and ethical bounds (4:5).

2) Timothy should anticipate and endure hardship, like Paul himself (2:3, 9). In the coming years, Timothy will endure imprisonment as Paul did (Hebrews 13:23).

3) Timothy should do the work of an evangelist—proclaiming the gospel. This is not a formal term or office, as we might describe an evangelist today. Timothy's call as an evangelist is the same call given to all Christians.

4) Timothy should fulfill his ministry, allowing nothing to deter him. This summarizes Paul's final exhortation to Timothy, covering the whole scope of ministry.

Paul then shifts the spotlight from Timothy to himself, describing himself as a *drink offering* (Philippians 2:17; 2 Timothy 4:6). This is language that signifies a sacrifice. Typically a drink offering takes the form of wine being poured out on an altar, a powerful image considering the blood shed by martyrs for their faith.

Paul's death was imminent, thus the mention of his departure (4:6). In this case, though, the word that Paul uses to describe his departure has an almost triumphant quality. Rather than signifying his leaving, it more so signifies the loosening of something that has been bound.

In verse 7, Paul's clear conscience from 2 Timothy 1:3 is evident as he reflects upon the faithful completion of his ministry. There is a sense of finality to the wording, and another example of Paul's use of metaphors. *Fighting the fight* and *finishing the race* are obvious metaphors. But even *keeping the faith* has the connotation of an athlete's promise to keep the rules of the game and a soldier's promise of fidelity to the cause.

In the next verse as well, the *crown of righteousness* is reminiscent of the Olympic wreaths worn by the winners of the contests. Jesus will award the crown on the Day of Judgment, and not just to Paul, but to all believers who persevere. Regarding Jesus' *appearing*, the word that is translated "longed for" in the NIV is a strong verb (the verb form of *agape*) that carries the idea of a deep longing, stronger than mere desire toward something.

📄 **4:9–22**

THE GOSPEL IS WORTHY OF PARTICIPATION

As Paul draws this letter to a close, he sends greetings and exchanges information on mutual friends. Although Paul twice beckons Timothy to come quickly (4:9, 21), it is not known whether Timothy arrived prior to Paul's execution.

Demas, according to Colossians 4:14, was a close associate of Paul's. The wording here gives the impression that Demas actually deserted Paul on a personal level. Some have supposed he had taken a different, perhaps easier, assignment. Others have supposed he was afraid of suffering Paul's same fate if he associated with him too long. When Paul writes that Demas loved the world, he uses the same verb as in verse 8 (*agapao*)—meaning a deep longing or affection (4:10).

We don't have any further information about Crescens, and with the information given here, we can't be sure whether Crescens and Titus left Paul on good or bad terms. However, it doesn't seem from the text that Paul is associating their leaving with what he has said about Demas. Under whatever conditions they left, only one associate remained—Luke (4:10–11). Since Luke was a physician, he may have remained specifically to care for Paul's physical needs.

Perhaps it was while mentioning those who had left him that Paul was reminded of Mark, who had rejoined Paul's ministry (4:11).

Demystifying 2 Timothy

In verse 11, Paul mentions two Gospel writers with whom he had extensive experience—Luke and Mark. Mark's story is rather touching. Also called John Mark, he had accompanied Paul and Barnabas (Mark's cousin) on their first missionary journey (Acts 12:25). But along the way, Mark left them (Acts 13:13), presumably due to persecution or difficulties, and Paul refused to allow Mark to rejoin them on a subsequent trip (Acts 15:37–39). Paul's disagreement with Barnabas over this decision caused such conflict between them that they parted ways. Understanding this backdrop makes Paul's invitation here, to bring Mark because of his usefulness to Paul's ministry, an indicator that some growth and reconciliation had taken place.

Tychicus, who is mentioned in verse 12, may have hand delivered this letter to Timothy in Ephesus. In fact, it might have been Paul's intention for Tychicus to relieve Timothy so that Timothy could visit him.

Next Paul makes a practical request of Timothy. He requests his cloak and reading—or perhaps writing—materials (4:13). The materials Paul requested may have included parts of the Old Testament or even unfinished drafts of some of his letters.

Take It Home

While we often look to the scriptures for truth and doctrine, it is verses like these that remind us of the human story surrounding the words we read—the real people grappling with life-threatening realities and daily inconveniences. They had friendships that warmed them and hardships that wore them down. Letters like 2 Timothy offer a unique insight into these kinds of everyday realities.

And letters like these allow us to evaluate our own relationships within the body of Christ. Do we stand by our brothers and sisters in their difficulties? Do we shy away when they may need us most? Are we structured as a group in such a way that it allows us to tend to each other's lives as needed? Each friend and colleague that Paul gives Timothy a status on is an example to us—for positive or negative—of how to be the body of Christ.

Paul's comments and warning to Timothy about Alexander the metalworker (4:14–15) may refer to the same person he says was handed over to Satan in 1 Timothy 1:20, but we can't be sure. Paul quotes Psalm 62:12 in saying that God will repay Alexander for standing against him (4:14).

Paul seems to hold Alexander's actions in a different regard than those who merely didn't rise to his support (4:16). Alexander, after all, stood *against* Paul. His was not simply an absence of support. Here, Paul wishes for God's forgiveness of those who deserted him (4:16).

The first defense that Paul mentions is probably the preliminary investigation that would have preceded his formal trial (4:16). His reference to the Gentiles hearing his message (4:17) may simply be a metaphor, since Rome was the center of the Gentile world. In the same way, his rescue from the lion's mouth may also be simply a word picture of escaping great danger (Psalm 22:21; Daniel 6:20) rather than a symbol of Nero or Satan or an allusion to the amphitheatre in which Christians were killed by hungry lions as some have supposed.

Perhaps most important in Paul's description of his first defense is the way the Lord stood at his side, offering strength. This support stands in stark contrast to the lack of support Paul received from his fellow Christians.

In closing, Paul sends his greetings to a few of Timothy's fellow residents in Ephesus—Priscilla, Aquila, and the family of Onesiphorus (4:19).

Demystifying 2 Timothy

Priscilla and Aquila were Paul's friends and ministry colleagues. The couple is always mentioned together in the Bible (Acts 18:2, 18, 26; Romans 16:3–4; 1 Corinthians 16:19; 2 Timothy 4:19), and most often Priscilla's name is mentioned first. Paul first met them in Corinth and stayed with them for a year and a half, learning from their wisdom. They also influenced other first-century church leaders, like Apollos (Acts 18:24–26).

Paul also informs Timothy of the whereabouts of a few more mutual friends, as he has already done in 4:10–12. In this case the news is of Erastus, who is probably the Erastus mentioned in Acts 19:22, and Trophimus, another mutual friend and companion.

Next, Paul sends greetings to Timothy from a few co-laborers in Rome—Eubulus, Pudens, Linus, Claudia, and all the brothers (4:21). Whether or not they were imprisoned with Paul is unclear. The New Testament gives us no other information on them.

Finally, as Paul opens the letter with grace (1:2), so also he closes this letter with the wish that Timothy would be accompanied by the grace of God and His Spirit (4:22).

TITUS

INTRODUCTION TO TITUS

The book of Titus and 1 and 2 Timothy comprise Paul's Pastoral Epistles—not an entirely accurate name for the three letters. Titus and Timothy were not pastors, at least not by the modern definition. Still, both Timothy and Titus were Paul's associates who did a lot of legwork for him, and his letters to them about the expectations of church leaders is a valuable guideline for spiritual leadership.

AUTHOR

Of all the letters of Paul, the Pastoral Epistles are by far the most disputed in terms of authorship. Differences of language, style, and theology have caused many (more liberal) scholars to doubt that Paul was the original author. Some believe that a disciple of Paul wrote these after Paul's death. Yet the differences in style, vocabulary, and theology are not as great as is often supposed, and they can be satisfactorily accounted for by the different themes and by the fact that these letters were written later in Paul's life. Paul may also have used one of his missionary companions to write out these letters (see Romans 16:22 for an example of this), and this scribe left his own stylistic mark. Because of the many Pauline themes and personal touches, evangelical scholars continue to assert that these letters came from the apostle's hand.

PURPOSE

Titus is not mentioned in Acts, as are many of Paul's other associates, but his name appears in various epistles. Paul's ministry had initiated Titus's conversion to Christianity, and the Gentile convert soon had taken on the responsibility of traveling and ministering with Paul, and at other times on his own. This was one of the latter cases, and Paul had left Titus in Crete while the apostle was elsewhere (perhaps Corinth). Paul desired to stay in touch with his protégé and offers him some practical advice for overseeing a church.

OCCASION

Crete is an island in the Mediterranean, about 150 miles long and anywhere from seven to thirty miles wide. In Greek mythology, it is the birthplace of Zeus, and the Cretans claimed that his tomb was on their island as well. The citizens of Crete had a reputation that was less than stellar (1:12).

Titus, a young minister, had been entrusted to oversee the believers there. Paul was writing to both encourage him and give him some practical instructions regarding church leadership (qualifications of elders, basic teachings, dealing with problems, etc.). A proper understanding of the gospel of Christ was especially needed in the hedonistic and idolatrous culture of Crete.

THEMES

Six times in this short letter Paul makes a reference to "good works"—not as a requirement for God's forgiveness and redemption, but in response to God's free gift of salvation. And he regularly connects such proper behavior with sound doctrine.

Paul also directs the reader's attention to "our Savior," a phrase that appears six times in three distinct couplets. Each couplet has a distinct reference to both God and Jesus (1:3-4; 2:10; 3:4, 6).

CONTRIBUTION TO THE BIBLE

Along with 1 Timothy, Titus is a primary source for clearly stated requirements for church overseers (1:5-9). In addition, Paul's concise description of salvation (2:11-14) is a doctrinal delight in its detail as well as its simplicity.

OUTLINE

TITUS 1:1–16

A CALL FOR AUTHENTIC BELIEFS AND LEADERSHIP

Service and Grace	1:1–4
Expectations of Leaders	1:5–16

Setting Up the Section

After Paul had introduced the gospel to such a broad geographic area, it was neces-sary for him to delegate authority in following up with young and growing churches. To this end, he had placed Titus in Crete—a challenging mission field for anyone. Clearly, the church would need good and strong leadership. So Paul opens his letter to Titus with criteria for church elders and authorizes him to deal with some difficult problems already arising among the believers.

📖 **1:1–4**

SERVICE AND GRACE

The openings in Paul's letters are all very similar. Paul usually begins by identifying himself as a servant of Christ. But in Titus, he calls himself a servant of God (1:1). This single exception is not too surprising when looking at the writings of Paul as a whole. He frequently gives credit to more than one Person of the Trinity in a single passage, viewing the three as one God at work among humankind. A servant of Christ is certainly a servant of God.

Paul's other self-designation, "an apostle of Jesus Christ" (1:1), is more usual. An apostle is appointed by God to minister. Paul's words to Titus, then, are more than per-sonal opinion. They are from God.

Critical Observation

Paul's elaborate greeting, combined with the description of his apostleship, seems quite formal for a personal letter. This has led some to believe that Paul intended the letter not just for Titus, but for the entire church on the island of Crete where Titus was ministering. If so, then Paul was imparting his authority to Titus.

Paul would soon emphasize the connection between sound doctrine and good behavior in this short letter (1:9; 2:1), and he opens with the importance of not only faith, but also knowledge of God's truth (1:2). His notation that God does not lie (1:2) also presages a later observation that Titus was ministering among people prone to lying (1:12).

Paul refers to Titus as his "true son" (1:4 NIV), as he had done with Timothy (1 Timothy 1:2). It is likely that Paul had been instrumental in the conversion of both individuals to Christianity and felt like a spiritual father to them. It is also likely that Paul had established a teaching relationship and served as a mentor to the younger men who were beginning to hold important spiritual positions.

EXPECTATIONS OF LEADERS

Crete is an island of more than three thousand square miles in the Mediterranean Sea. Paul's ministry there (1:5) is not recorded in Acts. Paul's visit was apparently shorter than he wished, so he left Titus there with significant work to do: answer questions, smooth out problems, appoint elders, and so forth. And along with the assignment, Paul gave Titus the authority to act.

The elders could help with the work that needed to be done—as long as they met certain qualifications. Paul lists over a dozen requirements for the position of elder. (Paul uses the words *elder* and *overseer* [bishop] synonymously. See Titus 1:5, 7). Although not identical to the list he had given Timothy (1 Timothy 3:1–10), Paul's list to Titus (1:6–9) contains many of the same prerequisites for elders (husband of one wife, faithful children, not addicted to wine, not a bully, not greedy, hospitable, sensible, and self-controlled).

Demystifying Titus

Paul's standards for elders are high, but not unreasonable. *Blameless* (1:6–7) doesn't mean sinless, but is more along the lines of being above reproach or accusation for anything. "Having one wife" (1:6) is a frequently debated phrase with three primary interpretations: (1) Paul is prohibiting polygamy; (2) Paul is forbidding divorce; or (3) Paul is addressing the problem of unfaithfulness and promiscuity.

The behavior of an elder is an important aspect of his or her life, including how the person interacts with a spouse, family, fellow church members, and outsiders. Both public and private lives are under constant scrutiny. Yet the expectations don't end there. An elder must also know scripture and hold firmly to its teachings, being able to refute heresy and teach sound doctrine (1:9).

The need for competent and spiritually mature elders was essential because of the threats presented to the believers at Crete. They faced the same problems as other churches, yet those who opposed the truth seemed to be in full force in Crete. There were many who had not only deceived themselves, but were spreading heresy to others (1:10–11).

Their false teachings were only empty words that had no real value. Yet the results were devastating for those who believed the lies instead of God's truth. Many such teachers were only out to make money, yet were devastating entire households in the process.

Paul challenges Titus and the elders to have two voices: one to call God's sheep and another to drive away wolves. They were to silence the false teachers (1:11) by refusing them opportunities to speak in the church—and rebuking them emphatically (1:13). They were also to preempt the false teachers by proclaiming the genuine gospel that *would* have lasting value for their hearers.

A clear indication of some of the false teaching is revealed in Paul's references to the "circumcision group" (1:10 NIV) and Jewish myths (1:14). Other churches had been confronted by groups of vocal Jewish believers requesting (or demanding) that all Christians conform to Jewish laws, customs, and traditions. Especially strong was their insistence that believers be circumcised. But Crete was the wrong place for them to lobby for their beliefs. Titus was an uncircumcised Gentile believer (Galatians 2:1–5) who was ministering with the full endorsement and empowerment of the apostle Paul. He was living proof that an authentic conversion did not require circumcision.

Paul quotes the poet Epimenides (1:12), who had lived in Crete in the sixth century BC. Even though the people of Crete were well aware of their culture's ethical and spiritual shortcomings, Paul knew the power of the Holy Spirit to transform lives. He maintains just as high a spiritual standard in Crete as anywhere else. Yet in order for the believers to persevere and overcome, they had to resist the influence of the false teachers and hold fast to the truth of the gospel.

Paul clarifies that the way to please God is not through strict and restrictive obedience to a set of laws, but rather by experiencing the forgiveness of God and choosing a life of purity as a result. Many of the groups attempting to sway the early church had an ascetic approach to their adherence to the law, thinking God would be satisfied, if not pleased, by their self-imposed miseries. Paul, in contrast, reflects the teachings of Jesus (Matthew 15:10–11, 18–20; Luke 11:39–41).

The mind and conscience work as a filter. If God has cleansed the inner person, then all thoughts and actions are pure. If not, then it is useless to attempt to maintain a "good" life because nothing is pure (1:15).

Paul's mention of those who "claim to know God" (1:16 NIV) may be a reference to nonbelievers, or those who wrongly assumed their good works were sufficient for salvation. Or perhaps Paul had in mind those who had undergone a genuine spiritual conversion but were beginning to respond to the false teachings of the Jewish legalists. By attempting to add any requirement for salvation other than faith in response to the grace of God, a person ceases to know (understand) God.

Paul will stress the importance of doing good works many times in this short letter (1:16; 2:7, 14; 3:1, 8, 14). Yet attempting to require anything for salvation other than what God has already done is, in essence, denying God (1:16). People who do so may act from sincerity, zealous fervor, or other well-intentioned motives, yet their actions are detestable to God. Until the mind and conscience are yielded to God, no amount of effort will compensate.

Take It Home

Review Paul's list of qualifications for church leadership (1:6–9). Which of those standards do you feel is your strong point? Which do you need to work on? You may not be an official church leader, yet any kind of ministry (to children, neighbors, extended family, etc.) would certainly benefit by a more consistent application of these standards.

TITUS 2:1–15

A CALL FOR AUTHENTIC BEHAVIOR

Setting Up the Section

After giving Titus a list of requirements for church leaders (1:6–9), Paul now provides guidelines for different groups within the church. As he does, he also provides some personal encouragement for Titus in the challenging position he held.

📄 **2:1–3**

INSTRUCTIONS FOR OLDER BELIEVERS

Paul's writings frequently associate biblical truth with appropriate behavior. He has just pointed out that those who don't fully understand the truth about salvation are incapable of producing any pure actions (1:15). Then, as he instructs Titus to teach only sound doctrine (2:1), Paul begins to enumerate how such truth should be reflected in various groups within the church.

He first addresses older men (2:1). Although he doesn't explicitly say so, it is inferred that a positive example set by older men will model genuine faith for younger men, providing the younger men more than mere verbal instructions. (The following instructions for older women to set good examples for younger ones would certainly apply to the other gender as well.)

Being temperate (2:2) has a specific application to the consumption of alcohol, but could also mean to be self-disciplined and reasonable in a broader sense. The other expectations are self-explanatory: worthy of respect, self-controlled, and sound in faith, love, and endurance. Clearly this is not an exhaustive list of dos and don'ts, yet this short list of general commands addresses a wide spectrum of life situations.

Paul's instructions for older women (2:3) are similar. Titus is instructed to leave the teaching of younger women to the older ones (2:4–5)—a much richer investment of idle time than gossip or excessive drinking. Apparently, slander and drunkenness among older women were among the problems that added to Crete's poor reputation (1:12). But those in the church are called to a higher purpose.

Critical Observation

In other places, Paul provides instructions to women concerning church settings (1 Corinthians 14:33–35; 1 Timothy 2). Here, however, he addresses the importance of their role in the home (Titus 2:4–5). The influence of the false teachers in Crete had not just affected the church, but had also ruined entire households (1:11). The need for accurate teaching of scripture and demonstration of godly living was just as great in the home as it was in the church.

📄 2:4–8

INSTRUCTIONS FOR YOUNGER BELIEVERS

Paul's instructions to Titus regarding younger women in the household wasn't surprising for the times and culture. A woman's opportunities were limited during the first century. Yet even within the home, the relationship between doctrine and behavior was important. Paul knew others were watching. The way that young mothers related to husbands and children would influence the way other people perceived the Christian faith. Just as church elders were evaluated based partially on the proper rearing of children (1:6), so, too, were Christian mothers expected to live out their faith at home, where others would detect a difference in their lifestyles and could find no reason to malign the gospel (2:4–5). Then, after their children had grown and moved on to adult lives, the women were called to serve as spiritual mentors to those who were just beginning marriages and families.

Paul's admonition to young men includes only one item (2:6), yet he was not attempting to provide an exhaustive list. This was, after all, a letter to Titus, who would explain and expound on Paul's words as he related them to the believers at Crete. Self-control is certainly an appropriate challenge for most young men, and it encompasses many other positive qualities.

It is at this point that Paul moves from general guidelines for *all* young men to specific ones for Titus, who would have been included in this segment of the church. Titus couldn't just *teach* the gospel; he also had to *model* it (2:7–8). He would certainly face opposition, but he could put his critics to shame by living a spotless life as he ministered to others.

📄 2:9–10

INSTRUCTIONS FOR SLAVES

Paul includes instructions for believing slaves in a number of his writings (Ephesians 6:5–8; Colossians 3:22–24; 1 Timothy 6:1–2). He expected the influence of the gospel to be evident even in the institution of slavery.

Slaves were noncitizens who served Roman citizens, and they were common in the Roman Empire during the first century. (Perhaps as many as half of those in the Roman ⟨...⟩ were slaves.) Many lived as members of the household in which they served. They were usually paid and occasionally had the opportunity to earn their freedom. Paul tells them to behave in a godly way toward their masters so that the gospel would be attractive (2:9–10).

Demystifying Titus

Many people question why Paul (or scripture in general) seems to condone slavery. But the question itself exposes a misconception. The Bible never endorses slavery, yet since slavery was so widespread in the ancient world, scripture addresses the issue. Slaves were held to certain standards, but so were slave owners. And in most places where the truths of scripture were introduced and implemented, the acceptance of slavery began to decline. Furthermore, the gospel does address the even worse problem of *spiritual* slavery, and how through Christ's sacrificial death all people are able to break the chains of sin and experience freedom and forgiveness. In this regard, there is no distinction between male and female, Jew and Gentile, slave and free person (Galatians 3:28).

📄 2:11–15

INSTRUCTIONS FOR TITUS

At this point, Paul shifts back from outer behavior to "sound doctrine" (2:1). Although the importance of appropriate behavior and good works is emphasized throughout his letter to Titus, Paul makes it clear that God's grace is the foundation for such behavior (2:11).

To make the intangible concept of grace a bit more understandable, Paul defines it as the appearance of Jesus on earth (2:11). Jesus' incarnation was the event that all believers can look back to and see the undeserved gift of God—a Savior who came because He loved them and not because they loved Him. God's only Son was sacrificed on their behalf. Christ's death was the ultimate act of grace, and salvation is by grace alone, through faith (2:14).

As people respond to that act of grace and become believers, their focus turns from past to present. They find the strength to resist the sins and temptations that surround them. On a more positive note, they also choose to live lives that are self-controlled, upright, and godly (2:12). Paul's choice of words reflects a proper relationship with oneself, with others, and with God.

Then Paul moves from a perspective on the present to the future. Believers can choose to go against the moral tide of society not only because of the first appearance of Christ, but also because they eagerly anticipate His second appearance (2:13). Jesus' first coming was a historical reality; His second coming is a blessed hope that should affect all aspects of present-day life.

These doctrinal truths were to be the text of Titus's messages to the people in Crete (2:15). Paul empowered him to encourage and to rebuke as necessary. A young pastor in a culture of self-described liars, evil brutes, and lazy gluttons (1:12) might naturally feel overwhelmed. But Paul reminds his young associate not to be unsettled by his situation. And he will provide more guidelines in his next section.

Take It Home

Choose one of Paul's categories that applies to you—young men, older men, young women, older women, or slaves (substitute "employees" for "slaves" in today's culture). Review Paul's instructions and determine how your behavior compares to the high standards he sets.

TITUS 3:1–15

A CALL FOR AUTHENTIC RELATIONSHIPS

Setting Up the Section

Paul had written this letter to encourage Titus (chapter 1) and provide instructions for various groups within the church (chapter 2). In conclusion, he provides a few more guidelines for the entire church—reminders of how the believers should behave in response to their salvation. Afterward, he signs off as he usually does, with a few personal comments and greetings.

📖 **3:1–2**

PROPER RESPECT FOR ALL PEOPLE

It has been suggested that the primary teaching job of a pastor is to remind the congregation of what scripture says, not necessarily to impart new information. Believers know what they *should* do, but tend to stray when their minds wander or when their spiritual senses grow dull. So Paul instructs Titus to remind the Christians in Crete how to act.

He lists seven specific qualities expected of Christians: (1) to be subject to rulers and authorities; (2) to be obedient; (3) to be ready to do every good work; (4) to slander no one; (5) to be peaceable; (6) to be gentle; and (7) to show complete courtesy to all people. Paul emphasizes good works three times in this chapter alone (3:1, 8, 14). His feelings about submission to others—even secular authorities—have been expressed in other letters (Romans 13:1–5; 1 Timothy 2:1–2).

📖 **3:3–7**

THE DIFFERENCE CHRIST CAN MAKE

Paul contrasts the seven Christian qualities with seven characteristics that had been ~~nt~~ prior to the believers' awareness of Jesus: (1) foolishness, (2) disobedience, (3) ~~deceived~~ by pleasures, (4) enslavement, (5) malice, (6) envy, and (7) both being ~~hating others.~~

Critical Observation

Paul frequently deals with sin directly and frankly. Yet he doesn't come across as arrogant, legalistic, or condemning. Although his upbringing had been considerably different from most of those who grew up in the hedonistic, secular culture of Crete, he makes no distinction (3:3). He includes himself in those influenced by sin: foolish, disobedient, deceived, enslaved, and so forth.

The juxtaposition of these two lists serves to highlight God's grace in salvation, compelling the reader to respond in grateful obedience. God's kindness, love, and mercy (3:4–5) are all aspects of His grace. Redemption is no small gift of God; it transforms all areas of life. It is not accomplished by works of righteousness (3:5), but rather by the work of the triune God—the Father (3:4), the Spirit (3:5), and the Son (3:6).

Believers are to do good works for others in response to the marvelous and unique good work God has done for them. His act of love took place while people were still disobedient, foolish, and hateful. They were enemies of God, but thanks to Jesus' sacrifice on their behalf, they came to be considered God's friends (Romans 5:10; John 15:13–16).

Salvation is through "the washing of rebirth and renewal" (or "regeneration"), by the Holy Spirit (3:5 NIV). The Spirit is instrumental not only in the conversion experience, but also throughout the transformation from foolish and sinful behavior (3:3) to a life of obedience and godliness (3:1–2). And beyond that, the end result for a believer is eternal life as an heir of God (3:7).

Demystifying Titus

Some people tend to emphasize the importance of water baptism in regard to salvation and use this passage to promote that belief. Yet it is unlikely that Paul is referring to water, much less to baptism, as integral to salvation. He is in the midst of making the point that salvation has nothing to do with human works (3:5). The "washing" here is spiritual. It is the Holy Spirit who is "poured out" on believers (3:6).

The work of the Spirit is not a matter of improving and tweaking the old person until he or she is a child of God. Rather, salvation involves a birth from above, resulting in a new creation (2 Corinthians 5:17). This gift of the Holy Spirit is generous (3:6), and His work is directly connected with the will of God the Father and the authority of Christ (Acts 2:33). Those who place their faith in Christ receive the Spirit. Those who don't do not receive the Spirit.

PEOPLE TO AVOID

Paul isn't just expressing his opinions. He instructs Titus to *stress* these teachings—to insist on them (3:8). They are not only excellent and profitable for anyone who heeds them, they are also trustworthy. Even after salvation, those who want to experience the abundant life that God offers must be careful to devote themselves to doing good. God makes all things possible, but believers must be disciplined and willing.

It is easy to get caught up in various forms of foolishness and nonproductive activity. Paul mentions a few potential problems to Titus. Those in the Greek culture were prone to intellectual debate. While there is nothing wrong with verbal interaction per se, it could become problematic when applied to scripture. It is relatively easy to speculate on theological or philosophical what-ifs while ignoring the clear and straightforward truths of God's revealed Word. Even today, it is easy to *talk about* the contents of the Bible rather than *teach* them.

The Jewish culture could also get off track when it came to teaching scripture. Throughout the centuries, rabbis had added myths and legends to the inspired scriptures, frequently based on the same characters. Genealogies of key figures were sometimes doctored to make Jewish heroes appear more impressive. Other teachers could nitpick for hours about, for example, what was or was not appropriate on the Sabbath.

These were the kinds of things Titus was to insist be avoided. A primary purpose of scripture is to inspire believers to act on what they know to be true. Intellectual pursuits have their place, but they are not to replace loving actions among those in the church as well as toward those outside.

Titus is given a mandate to put an end to such time-wasting controversies and the authority to deal with anyone who would not respond. Those who were being divisive were to receive two clear warnings. If they still did not heed the authority of the church, they were to be cut off from fellowship (3:9–10). There will frequently be those attempting to influence the church who are not of God and are unwilling to receive instruction or correction. Church leaders must be willing to deal with such people directly and quickly. It isn't the leader or the church that condemns the troublemaker; it is the person himself (3:11).

FAREWELLS AND FINAL ARRANGEMENTS

Paul's plans in verse 12 reveal a couple of things. First, he was free to travel, so his writing was taking place prior to his second Roman imprisonment. And second, Nicopolis, a city on the western coast of Greece, wasn't exactly an ideal place to spend the winter. However, it *was* a spot where numerous travelers from various places found themselves forced to stay due to the storm season on the Mediterranean. This fact suggests that Paul intentionally went where groups of people were so he could minister even while **t** ⁀g was restricted.

 ⁀d worked with Tychicus (3:12) and spoke highly of him on numerous occasions ⁀hesians 6:21; Colossians 4:7). Nothing more is said of Artemas in the Bible.

Apparently, Paul was sending one of these men to Crete to minister for a while, allowing Titus to take a break and meet him in Nicopolis.

Before leaving, however, Paul requests Titus's help for Apollos and Zenas, who were traveling through the area. Scripture identifies Apollos (3:13) as a spiritually discerning and devoted church leader (Acts 18:24–28; 1 Corinthians 1:12; 3:5), but this is the Bible's only mention of Zenas. His title of "lawyer" might have meant one of two things: If a Jewish reference, it would mean Zenas was trained in the law and had been a rabbi. If a Gentile reference, it would suggest that he was a person of high standing in Rome who had converted to Christianity.

Although the culture of Crete had a propensity for laziness (1:12), Paul challenges the believers to provide for their daily necessities (3:14). This devotion to doing good could then be spread to people like Apollos and Zenas, who were doing God's work full-time and could benefit from the help of fellow Christians.

In closing, Paul does not identify who is with him, yet he sends everyone's greetings and prays for grace for Titus and all those with him (3:15).

Take It Home

In closing this section, Paul twice names pairs of ministers (3:12–13) where one was a prominent and proven leader and the other a relative unknown. This suggests a mentor-protégé relationship during spiritual training. Have you ever benefited from the wisdom and attention of a spiritual mentor? If so, have you passed along that wisdom to a younger Christian who is seeking maturity? Spend a few minutes identifying people who might help you continue to grow spiritually as well as those who might appreciate your help in their own spiritual journey.

PHILEMON

INTRODUCTION TO PHILEMON

Of the thirteen epistles traditionally attributed to Paul in scripture, his letter to Philemon is the most personal. Most were written to entire churches. The three Pastoral Epistles (1 and 2 Timothy and Titus) were to individuals, but had church-wide applications. Philemon, too, contains public greetings and was intended to be read publicly. Philemon's situation was very specific, yet Paul's advice, as usual, contains wisdom appropriate for all believers.

AUTHOR

Paul identifies himself as the author (verses 1, 9, 19), and there is nothing in the letter theologically or grammatically to suggest otherwise.

PURPOSE

Paul had come upon a runaway slave named Onesimus and had convinced him to return to his owner, Philemon. This letter is Paul's appeal to Philemon to forgive the slave and accept him back into the household.

OCCASION

It appears that Paul was in prison as he wrote (verses 1, 9), which would probably have been during his two-year house arrest in Rome (Acts 28:16, 30). As usual, Paul made the most of his time, ministering through the mail when he couldn't travel in person.

THEMES

The theme of Philemon is forgiveness, not as a great theological concept but as a necessity of an effective Christian life. Whether or not Philemon wanted to forgive the offense of Onesimus as his slave, he was obligated to do so as a Christian brother.

HISTORICAL CONTEXT

Paul's imprisonment and trial (AD 61–63) were during the rule of Nero before he had become such a nemesis to the Christian movement. The letter to Philemon was likely delivered at the same time as the letter to the Colossians (Colossians 4:7–9) and near the time of Ephesians (Ephesians 6:21).

CONTRIBUTION TO THE BIBLE

The short letter to Philemon is important in its view on first-century slavery. Some ask why Paul (or other biblical writers) didn't come right out and condemn the practice. Yet if Philemon heeded Paul's appeal, both slave and master would find themselves equal as servants of Christ. The new relationship would certainly undermine the institution of slavery.

Setting Up the Section

Paul uses a great deal of tact in this epistle, so the facts of the matter are revealed slowly. But a slave named Onesimus has run away from his master, Philemon, apparently after stealing from him. In God's providence, Onesimus meets Paul, who facilitates his conversion to Christianity and sends him back to Philemon with this letter.

📄 1–3

A PUBLIC GREETING

In most of Paul's salutations he identifies himself as an apostle of Christ. In this instance, however, such an opening would have been too strong. He is asking a favor rather than attempting to impose his position to coerce Philemon's decision, so he identifies himself as "a prisoner of Christ Jesus" (verse 1). He appears to be a prisoner of the Emperor Nero, but he was in chains because of his faithfulness in speaking for Jesus. The fact that Paul adds Timothy to the salutation (even though he writes as an individual throughout most of the letter) also softens the tone of the opening.

Paul will soon be asking a specific favor of a specific person, yet he begins with a greeting that includes the entire church (verses 2–3). The specific appeal is to Philemon, but the importance of forgiveness and acceptance of others is applicable to all believers.

Many people suppose, with good reason, that Apphia is Philemon's wife, and Archippus his son. The fact that Philemon owned at least one slave and had a home large enough to host the church (verse 2), with a guest room to spare (verse 22), indicates that he was probably wealthy.

📄 4–22

INTERCESSION FOR A REPENTANT SLAVE

You in verse 3 (and later in verse 23, as well as *your* in verse 25) is plural. But for the bulk of the letter (verses 4–22), Paul uses the singular pronoun. His appeal is directly to Philemon. As he first shares his feelings, Paul is being tactful, but he isn't being flattering or untruthful. He is truly thankful for Philemon and encouraged by him (verses 4, 7).

Philemon had a track record of encouraging believers. He had refreshed the hearts (verse 7) of many people already; and Paul will soon ask him to refresh *his* heart by granting his request (verse 20).

Critical Observation

There is no evidence of churches as we know them today, where believers leave their homes to gather in a public building, until the third century. Until then, Christians met in homes of devoted believers like Philemon.

Paul chose not to demand the desired response from Philemon, although he felt he had the right to do so (verse 8). He prefers to appeal to Philemon in love. It isn't until this point in the letter (verse 10) that he even mentions Onesimus by name. The slave had apparently become a Christian after conversing with Paul, based on Paul's reference to him as his son (verse 10).

Demystifying Philemon

Paul uses a play on words in verse 11. The name Onesimus means "useful." So Paul is essentially saying, somewhat tongue in cheek, that Philemon's "useful" servant had temporarily become useless, but was now ready to live up to his name.

Paul genuinely liked Onesimus. He would have liked to recruit him as an assistant, much the way he had with Timothy and Titus (verses 12–14). But it was a matter of law, as well as moral obligation, for Paul to return Onesimus to Philemon. Onesimus had already broken faith with Philemon, and possibly had stolen from him as well. Had Paul kept Onesimus rather than sending him back, it would have amounted to yet another theft from Philemon. The slave needed to seek forgiveness from his master and offer restitution.

Yet Paul wanted Philemon to see Onesimus with new eyes. It had been wrong for him to run away, but the experience had led to his conversion, which created an interesting new development. Onesimus had left Colossae as the property of Philemon, but he was returning as a beloved brother (verses 15–16). On a spiritual level, Onesimus and Philemon were now equals. On a human level, they would need to come to an agreement about how they would continue to interact.

Paul did all he could on Onesimus's behalf. He promises to personally pay any unsettled debts to Philemon, and he asks Philemon to receive Onesimus as if he were Paul himself (verses 17–19). The fact that Paul wrote this letter personally (verse 19) would have made his promise legally binding.

It is a bit frustrating to never discover how Philemon responded to Paul's request. Did he punish Onesimus, as was his right to do? Did he take him back as a slave? Did he free him? No one knows. Yet clues abound to suggest that Philemon might have responded as Paul desired.

It would appear that Paul had been instrumental in not only Onesimus's decision to become a Christian, but in Philemon's as well (verse 19). If so, it must have been quite difficult for Philemon to refuse Paul's request. In the first place, the slave and the slave owner had both found salvation in Christ in response to the truth taught by the same preacher. In addition, Paul was offering to do for Onesimus what Jesus had done for them all: pay a debt He didn't owe in order to provide forgiveness and freedom for someone who had done nothing to deserve it.

Paul also expresses confidence that Philemon would grant his request and even go beyond that (verses 20-21). Aside from taking back his fugitive slave, what more could Philemon do other than set him free? And finally, Paul writes that he will soon be making a visit (verse 22). The expectation of soon seeing the apostle in person might have been additional motivation for Philemon to settle the matter. But regardless of Philemon's ultimate decision, Paul's writing in this short letter provides a vastly different view of the worth of a slave than would have been found in the culture of the Roman Empire.

📄 23–25

COWORKERS AND CONCERN

The people with Paul were essentially the same that he mentions at the close of Colossians (Colossians 4:10-14). And his short benediction (Philemon 25) ends this letter, the final of his thirteen letters as arranged in modern Bibles, in very much the same way he concludes all the others—with a prayer for the grace of the Lord Jesus Christ.

Take It Home

It may be difficult for those in the Western world to relate to slavery, yet many people have unresolved relationship issues. Can you think of a rift you have had with someone that could be mended simply by extending your forgiveness? If so, what is preventing you from taking such a step?

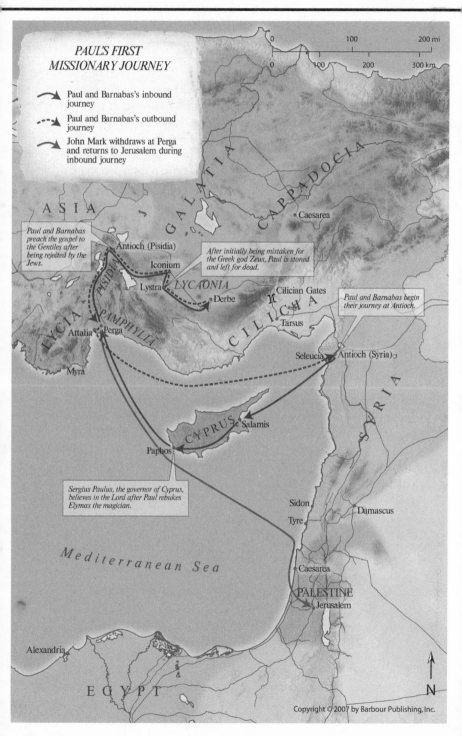

PAUL'S FIRST MISSIONARY JOURNEY

Paul and Barnabas's inbound journey

Paul and Barnabas's outbound journey

John Mark withdraws at Perga and returns to Jerusalem during inbound journey

Paul and Barnabas preach the gospel to the Gentiles after being rejected by the Jews.

After initially being mistaken for the Greek god Zeus, Paul is stoned and left for dead.

Paul and Barnabas begin their journey at Antioch.

Sergius Paulus, the governor of Cyprus, believes in the Lord after Paul rebukes Elymas the magician.

ASIA
GALATIA
CAPPADOCIA
Caesarea
Antioch (Pisidia)
Iconium
PISIDIA
Lystra
LYCAONIA
Derbe
Cilician Gates
LYCIA
PAMPHYLIA
Attalia
Perga
CILICIA
Tarsus
Myra
Seleucia
Antioch (Syria)
SYRIA
CYPRUS
Salamis
Paphos
Sidon
Damascus
Tyre
Mediterranean Sea
Caesarea
PALESTINE
Jerusalem
Alexandria
EGYPT

N

Copyright © 2007 by Barbour Publishing, Inc.

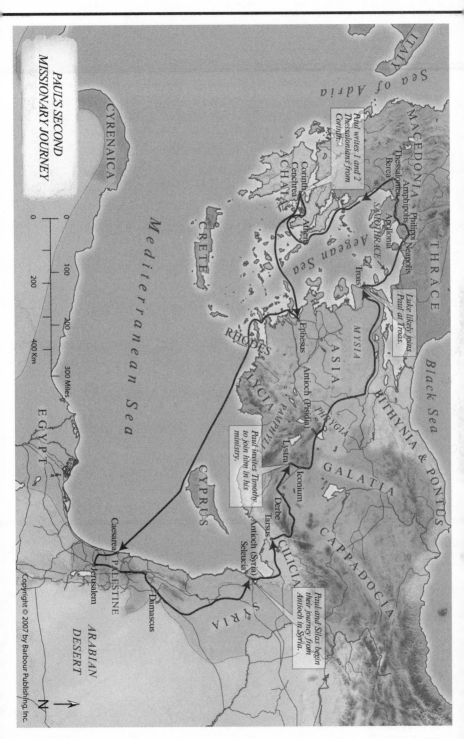

PAUL'S SECOND
MISSIONARY JOURNEY

Paul writes 1 and 2
Thessalonians from
Corinth.

Luke likely joins
Paul at Troas.

Paul invites Timothy
to join him in his
ministry.

Paul and Silas begin
their journey from
Antioch in Syria.

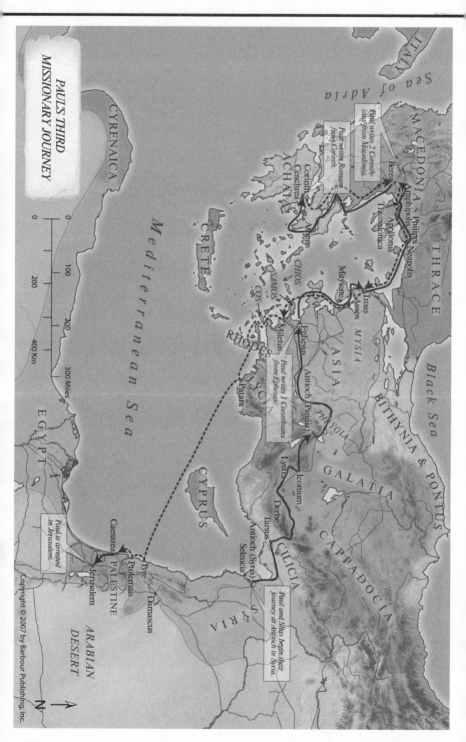

PAUL'S THIRD MISSIONARY JOURNEY

Paul writes 2 Corinthians from Macedonia.

Paul writes Romans from Corinth.

Paul writes 1 Corinthians from Ephesus.

Paul is arrested in Jerusalem.

Paul and Silas begin their journey at Antioch in Syria.

CYRENAICA

Mediterranean Sea

CRETE

RHODES

CYPRUS

EGYPT

Sea of Adria

MACEDONIA

THRACE

Black Sea

BITHYNIA & PONTUS

Berea
Philippi
Apollonia
Amphipolis
Neapolis
Thessalonica

ACHAIA

Corinth
Cenchrea
Miletus

CHIOS

Mitylene
Troas
Assos

MYSIA

SAMOS
COS

Miletus
Ephesus

ASIA

Antioch (Pisidia)

PHRYGIA

GALATIA

CAPPADOCIA

LYCIA
Patara

Lystra
Iconium
Derbe
Tarsus

CILICIA

Antioch (Syria)
Seleucia

Caesarea
Ptolemais
Tyre
Damascus

PALESTINE
Jerusalem

SYRIA

ARABIAN DESERT

0   100   200   300 Miles
0   200   400 Km

N

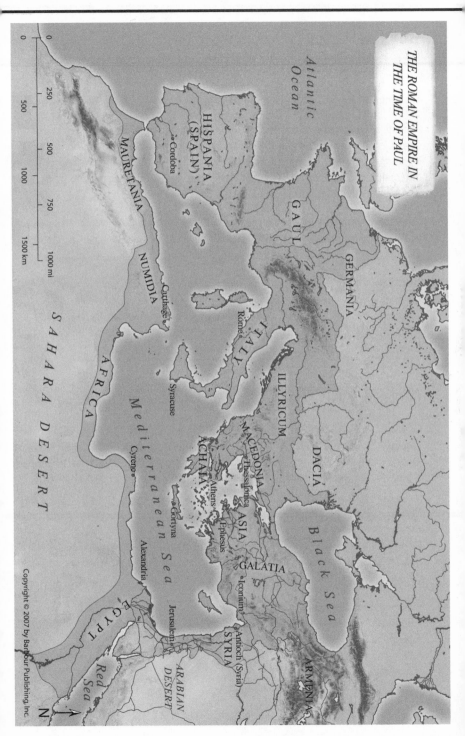

THE ROMAN EMPIRE IN
THE TIME OF PAUL

Atlantic
Ocean

HISPANIA
(SPAIN)

Cordoba

GAUL

GERMANIA

MAURETANIA

NUMIDIA

Carthage

AFRICA

SAHARA DESERT

Rome

ITALY

Syracuse

Mediterranean Sea

Cyrene

ILLYRICUM

MACEDONIA

Thessalonica

ACHAIA

Athens

Gortyna

Ephesus

ASIA

GALATIA

Iconium

Alexandria

EGYPT

Jerusalem

Antioch (Syria)

SYRIA

DACIA

Black Sea

ARMENIA

ARABIAN
DESERT

Red Sea

N

Copyright © 2007 by Barbour Publishing, Inc.

0   250   500   1000   1500 km
0   250   500   750   1000 mi

223

CONTRIBUTING EDITORS:

Dr. Robert Rayburn holds a Master of Divinity degree from Covenant Theological Seminary and a doctorate in New Testament from the University of Aberdeen, Scotland. His commentary on Hebrews was published in the *Evangelical Commentary of the Bible*.

The late *J. Hampton Keathley III, ThM* was a 1966 graduate of Dallas Theological Seminary and a former pastor of 28 years. Hampton wrote many articles and on occasion taught New Testament Greek at Moody Bible Institute, Northwest Extension for External Studies in Spokane, Washington. In August 2002 he succumbed to lung cancer and went home to be with the Lord.

Dr. Stephen Leston is pastor of Kishwaukee Bible Church in DeKalb , Illinois. He is passionate about training people for ministry and has served as a pastor at Grace Church of DuPage (Warrenville, Illinois) and Petersburg Bible Church (Petersburg, Arkansas).

Jeff Miller holds a ThM degree from Dallas Theological Seminary and has been in ministry for nearly ten years. Jeff is coauthor of the *Zondervan Dictionary of the Bible and Theology Words*, enjoys writing articles for magazines and journals, and has written *Hazards of Being a Man* (Baker Books). He is currently working on a Greek-English dictionary (forthcoming with Kregal Publications). Jeff lives in Texas with his wife Jenny and two daughters.

CONSULTING EDITOR:

Dr. Mark Strauss is a professor at Bethel Seminary's San Diego Campus. He is the author of *Distorting Scripture? The Challenge of Bible Translation and Gender Accuracy*; *The Essential Bible Companion*; and *Four Portraits, One Jesus: An Introduction to Jesus and the Gospels*. He is presently revising the commentary on Mark's Gospel for Expositor's Bible Commentary.

WITH SPECIAL THANKS TO BIBLE.ORG

Bible.org is a nonprofit 501(c)(3) Christian ministry headquartered in Dallas, Texas. In the last decade, Bible.org has grown to serve millions of individuals around the world and provides thousands of trustworthy resources for Bible study including the new NET BIBLE® translation.

Bible.org offers thousands of free resources for:
• Spiritual formation and discipleship
• Men's ministry
• Women's ministry
• Pastoral helps
• Small group curriculum and much more. . .

Bible.org can be accessed through www.bible.org.